INHALE FEAR, BREATHE ANGER

DIXIECRATS, T.E.A.PARTY, AND CHANGING POLITICAL PARADIGMS

Douglas Courtney

DEDICATION

To my wife Rhonda, who puts up with all this nonsense and even encourages me to keep trying. And to all my political friends, Republicans, Democrats, and those with no official party, that constantly argues, discuss, and participate in the Democracy and Republic we call the United States of America. It is their passionate arguments that drove my curiosity to understand.

TABLE OF CONTENTS

The Journey Begins   Page   1

Dixiecrats, do they really exist or are they a fantasy of
the Reagan Campaign?   Page   5

So Dixiecrats Exist, What of it?   Page   16

How Do Dixiecrats Affect Us Today?   Page   22

T.E.A Party, do we really have to go there?   Page   30

Who is the TEA Party?   Page   36

So what is wrong, if anything, with TEA Party
ideology?   Page   42

Are TEA Partiers racist and other musings.   Page   59

Republicans. Really? Yes, Really.   Page   65

Republican ideology. Is it comprehensible?   Page   73

Democrats. Finally!   Page   91

Democrat Ideology. Honestly, there is a reason to the
rhyme.   Page 106

Changing Paradigms. What is a paradigm and why is it
changing now?   Page 115

The Democratic Paradigm. Or What are those crazies
really up to?   Page 122

Do Republicans have a paradigm or are they controlled by God!   Page 133

People are Inhaling Fear and Breathing Anger, Paradigms are changing. So what?   Page 151

So why not have a Tweener and First Boomer paradigm?   Page 161

So what is so great about Second Boomer paradigms?   Page 167

So where does this leave us? What now?   Page 179

Guiding Economic Theory. The Argument Over How Our Money is Spent.   Page 183

Graduated Taxes and the Laffer Curve   Page 193

The Sum of All Events   Page 208

THE JOURNEY BEGINS

I am a liberal. Let there be no doubt about that. As defined by my more conservative friends, (yes, I have some), I am a liberal. I believe in Unions, I am pro-choice and I not only believe in public education, I believe that teachers are underpaid, overworked and should not bear the burden of balancing state budgets instead of highly paid hedge fund managers. I am also fervently in favor of the second amendment, to the horror of my liberal friends and associates, even though I don't own a gun and never fired one. I believe strongly in property rights and whenever we can cut an outdated, malfunctioning bureaucratic department in any state, local, or federal government we should do it and now. I think government is too big and still doesn't do enough to help its citizens. Basically I am an American.

I have watched the political landscape for more than forty years, found it fascinating and continued to watch and participate in the United States political process. My father was an ardent Republican, businessman and teacher. We had political discussions at the dinner table since I could remember and he would argue any point. A great night was sitting and watching the election results on television in November with a bucket of popcorn, a coke and my Dad by my side. I have run for office in local, county and state races, (never elected), and passionately worked for election of my candidates for President. I live in Florida and suffered through not only the vote fiasco of 2000, but the subsequent disaster of having one of the Bush brothers my governor and one in the Presidency at the same time! In effect I study and work in politics. I put my money, effort, and time where my mouth is and I don't defer to anyone when it comes to politics or my vote. I am no novice.

With this background I could not help but notice the transition of politics to its present point. I watched the Vietnam process and for a time participated in the opposition to those protests. I then changed position and worked to end the fiasco. The change may have had something to do with reaching the draft age and receiving my number, 235, but I would like to think it had more to do with fighting a stinking war with no end in sight for outdated policies that never really mattered. Even in those turbulent times, with the killings at Kent State included, and the Presidency of Richard Nixon that ended in shame and disgrace, I would have to say the current political climate is worse.

That isn't to say that there wasn't discordant feelings and acrimonious debate in the 60's, 70's, 80's, and 90's, there was, but this is worse. We fought each other, accused each other of dire and terrible deeds done to the country and its people back in that day. Reagan was a God. Reagan was the anti-Christ. Jimmy Carter was an idiot. Jimmy Carter was a man of peace. Tip O'Neil held back the Republican horde. O'Neil was a communist and a socialist. It all depended on what side of the debate you were on, but still it was better. As much as we fought, gave political favors to our friends, argued for war, argued against war, lived through the Soviet Union and the nuclear threat, we did what we did for the United States. Now we do it for our Party, using the United States as a mask for our real personal intentions, a disgrace to our political process and to ourselves. We seek power for power's sake and we seek power for financial gain. We seek political position for ourselves first and then our Party, our country rarely, if ever, is considered.

Now we have a country that finds it citizens making decisions in fear. We don't seem to know who to trust and we are angry. Political strategists and pundits are taking advantage of this fear and pushing their agendas, making money, building fear even further and distrust even stronger. Out of this the people are striking back, most notable currently are the Dixiecrats and the TEA Partiers. What does this say about the United States and its political process? What happens when two influential political organizations are borne out of fear and preach anger? What do we do now?

These questions created a need for understanding, not only out of concern for my country, but to understand how to defeat them in the political contests, (hey, I am a liberal). Am I angry too? Have I succumbed to this fear that is being cultivated? Or is there something else afoot, something that I have not noticed before? With questions in hand it became time for learning and hopefully understanding. And maybe find a way to bring the concern back to how the United States can move forward instead of its political parties and those selfish individuals that inhabit them and profit from the current climate.

To learn meant that my strongly held beliefs might be at risk. It really is convenient to believe that all TEA Partiers are ignorant, bigoted, cotton tops from my fathers and grandfathers generations. Maybe they won't be. They could be concerned sensible patriots. Then again, maybe I will prove it. Cool!

I would also have to look at the Dixiecrats. The conservative Democrats held solely responsible for the Democratic Party not successfully returning Democratic candidates to office, especially in Florida. Who are these guys, these malcontents, these traitors? Don't they know that they are hurting the country? Or are they really doing what needs to be done? Doing what I am preaching. Are Dixiecrats the only sane voters, voting their convictions instead of their party? These are conundrums that must be faced. Understand and risk losing your comfortable assumptions or continue blindly along in ignorance.

My belief in the United States requires understanding. I must move forward and risk my assumptions. What can we do to turn back the tide of greed and restore the belief in the United States as first in line? What can we do to set the Party back to the end of the line, if it ever was? Maybe understanding will give us the key, a way to resolve the problem. One thing is sure. We cannot solve anything when we inhale fear and exhale anger. Nothing is resolved in fear. Countries fall, even the noblest and greatest, when the face of fear controls its citizens. We must find our courage and learn the answers and take back our country from those timid souls that hover in the shadows feeding their greed and avarice on our fear and anger. We must be Americans.

So I begin this study by learning about Dixiecrats and the TEA Party. I try to understand who they are and what they are. What is their place in the national discussion? Are they the cause of this polarization, a symptom of it, or are they the defenders of the democracy we knew? I follow this with research on the political development of Republicans and Democrats to understand how these parties became such a focal point of politics instead of enablers of the democratic system. After this study will be an examination of the current paradigms of politics in the United States and the place of political parties within these paradigms. Hopefully a result will present itself and those will be discussed.

I doubt many will agree. Many may want my head on a platter. But the exploration will continue with a real desire to move our country forward and away from these polarizing politics. But then again, I am a liberal, what do I know?

DIXIECRATS, DO THEY REALLY EXIST OR ARE THEY A FANTASY OF THE REAGAN CAMPAIGN?

When I was sitting in my father's house watching the results of the Reagan/Carter campaign I was rooting for Reagan. Hey, the country was in misery. Interest rates topped 21%. (I bet some of these retirees would like to get that rate now!). Carter represented more of the same. He was a pragmatist. He promised nothing but more of the same and a lot of hard work to keep it that way, at least that is how I remember it.

Reagan promised a new America, a new dawn. He gave hope like we never knew. We didn't know how we were going to get there, but by God we were Americans and we could do anything. This is the first time I heard the term Dixiecrats in any form that made me remember it. We had to have the Dixiecrats to wrest this country from its misery. I didn't know who they were, but I was for 'em. Later conversations discovered they were Democrats in the south that would vote for Republicans. Not knowing everything about them, I believed, as did many in my circle, that this was a nickname for this group, invented by Republicans, so they would vote Republican without shame. Time passed and so did my support of this group; they became traitors to the cause. But who were they?

I found out that Dixiecrats were a real organization with real members, at least at one time. It all goes back to the 1948 elections. Well probably back to the Civil War, (or the war of Northern Aggression. I am in Florida you know. Hey, it was aggression, but that is another book.), if we want to be truthful.

If you remember, and some of you may be old enough to remember, the others need to remember their history books, it was agreed by most that the North won that conflict. Others are not so sure the war is over, (Don't laugh, some don't). Now many would believe that after having a Republican President, the first one mind you, waging war on the South and kicking their butt, most of the white voters in the South would be Democrat. You would also expect that most of the blacks, former slaves, those that could vote, would be Republican. Well you would be right. No self respecting Southern white man would vote for a Republican. (No ladies, this is not a typo, you did not have the right to vote yet. Black males voted before white or black women and that IS another book.) This can easily be shown in the registration statistics from 1865 until 1870.

If one looks at a relief map of the Unites States from 1860, a map that shows the number and general placements of slaves in the South, you can get a correlation about the results between election returns in the South and the registered voters. Basically, blacks voted Republican and whites voted Democrat. Now that is totally backwards from today's vote statistics. What happened? We'll explain it in later chapters, back to Dixiecrats.

White Southern men, and later women, could be reliably expected to vote Democratic for almost exactly 100 years after the Civil War. It was called the "Solid South Vote" and it was a powerful voting bloc, particularly within the Democratic Party, and often controlled the destiny of the Democratic Party. To illustrate the power let's look at the electoral votes in the three elections following the Civil War.

In 1868 to become President of the United States it took 148 electoral votes to win the Presidency. The Solid South had 109 electoral votes that year, or 74% of the needed votes to win. This was without Texas, Virginia, and Missouri as they had not been restored or "redeemed" back into the Union. In 1872, after the 1870 Census and the counting of former slaves as full citizens, it took 177 electoral votes to win the Presidency. The Solid South Vote was 132 of those electoral votes and yes Texas, Virginia, and Mississippi were finally redeemed enough to have their votes counted. Finally in 1876 it took 185 votes to be elected President, (we added a state or two between the elections.), the Solid South still had 132 of the needed votes or 72% of the votes needed to win. Basically if you wanted to be President you only needed the Solid South vote and a couple of more of the other states.

This is nothing as compared to the U.S. Senate. In 1868 the Solid South controlled 28 of the 74 Senate seats or 38% of the Senate votes. This was before the ratification of the Seventeenth Amendment in 1913, which made Senators directly elected by the people. Until the 17th Amendment the state legislatures elected the Senators. Considering that the state legislatures returned to local control after 1876, you could be almost assured that the Solid South vote would place a Democratic Senator in Washington. In fact in the two elections of 1874 and 1876, at the end of reconstruction, the Democratic Party gained 12 seats in the US Senate and moved to 35 Senators from a low of 12 in 1868. The Solid South vote was making itself heard.

To say that the Solid South Vote was racist was not an understatement. The black issue was always a part of the Solid South Vote platform. There was a reason the whites feared the blacks and it wasn't just skin color. Most people's education in the North gives a description of slavery only belonging on large plantations. The impression a lot of elementary, middle and high schoolers get is that slavery was a part of the south, but sort of isolated. Not too many slaves as it were. A matter of fact we are told the South was an agrarian society which gives the impression that it was sparsely populated. Well, the south had a population of 11 million in 1860, 7 million were not slaves, (doesn't mean they were white, mind you) and 4 million were slaves. That's right four MILLION slaves as of the 1860 census. Yep, they counted them, recall your Constitution listed them as three fifths a person so they had to be counted. That means about 1 slave for almost every 2 non-slaves.

If you were one of those that weren't slaves and then had those that were slaves walking your streets at that number, well you could see the issues that could come up. Some serious payback was bound to be fostering in some of those former slaves minds to the horror of the good ole boys and girls. Also what you thought was once nothing more than property, a thing to be used, was now considered your equal and someone that had to be heard. Add to this Southern mind warp the indignities suffered, and perceived indignities suffered, by the white men and women during reconstruction and "redemption" of the South drove a permanent wedge between them, blacks, and the Republican Party that was in charge of reconstruction.

To give a glimpse of how bad it was for Southern whites, in 1867 martial law was declared in 10 of the states that had been a part of the Confederation of States. Federal troops were stationed in each state and particularly in the State Capitals. New elections almost assured that Republican candidates would be elected to State Legislatures and local governments. Voters, (white men) that had been elected officials before or during the war, were denied the right to run for office because of their associations with the Confederacy. Basically northern carpetbaggers and opportunists were taking over the states and telling the locals what to do.

To give even better background, in 1870 the first black man was elected to the United States Senate. Hiram Revels was his name, and he was elected from Mississippi. He served all of one year. But his history is what is interesting. Hiram was born a freedman in Fayetteville, North Carolina. He only moved to Mississippi after the war, during the reconstruction movement. He was elected to that post after a brief stint in the Mississippi Senate. The Solid South was not amused and events like these reinforced their desire to be associated with and vote for the Democratic Party. But back to the formation of the Solid South vote.

Right after the War of Northern Aggression, Republicans made great inroads in the Federal Legislature. Blacks also made great inroads in politics and public service. This golden period lasted until the Southern Votes got organized about 1872. The Southern gentleman was not an ignorant man. He knew how to organize and play politics. The elections of 1872 saw the Southern Vote beginning its way back to prominence under these gentlemen's tutelage. The presidential election of 1876 saw the Solid South reclaim their power and influence entirely. During this election Rutherford Hayes, Republican , was behind Samuel Tilden, Democrat, in electoral votes. Tilden had failed by one vote to win enough electoral votes to claim the Presidency. Hayes was behind by 19 votes and it looked like the Democrats might get one early. But, the Southern States had two slates of electors, Democrat and Republican, both claiming authority to vote. As this had never happened before, Congress in its inestimable wisdom, had a committee of fifteen made to determine the outcome. This committee was made up of 8 Republicans and 7 Democrats, and lo and behold the Republican favoring slate won by a vote of, you guessed it, 8 to 7. Hayes got all of the 19 votes he needed and just passed the Democratic Tilden and won.

The Southern Vote that was to become the Solid South protested and refused to accept the result throwing the election into disarray right up to the week Hayes was to be inaugurated. In an effort to calm the waters and close the chapter the Hayes group made a deal with the Southern Vote, referred to as the compromise of 1877. The compromise removed the troops from the last of the states and cities that they were ensconced and ended the hated reconstruction. The Southern Vote agreed, getting the hated North out of the South was more important than supporting Democrats for president. Hayes became president, instead of Democratic Tilden, and the South was free to reform itself.

Very shortly after that Jim Crow laws became the law of the land in the South. Black voter intimidation, poll taxes and all manner of treatment and threats were implemented by the Southern white vote to control the black and preserve white power. At the same instance of the compromise, the Southern Vote found out how powerful their lobby was with Republicans and within the Democratic Party, a fact that was exploited politically for almost 100 years.

Because of the their historical perceptions of blacks through their use in slavery, the War of Northern Aggression, and the reconstruction period, the Solid Southern Vote was racist and they pushed racist policies on the Democratic Party. The Democratic Party itself did not condone racism, but was strongly influenced by the Solid South vote and party platforms reflected it. Oddly enough, some in the US consider this movement a direct reflection of the Republican Party today. (Hey, I am still a liberal and these Democrats tell me things!).

Well where does all this leave us? Prior to the Civil War you almost had to be a Democrat to get to be President. After the Civil War, Republicans were about the only party winning Presidential elections. Grover Cleveland won in 1884 to break the string, and again in 1892, but a Democrat didn't win again until 1912 and he was a doozy. As for blacks in the U.S. Congress, they went from a high of 17 Representatives and Senators to zero, shortly after the 1877 compromise. They didn't get another representative for 30 years, so much for reconstruction and reforming the South, or North for that matter.

In 1912 Woodrow Wilson was elected President because of the Southern Vote, and while President Wilson may have been many wonderful things he was extremely racist. (Now I bet that statement made a few of you fellow liberals wake up.) He was a member of and relied on the votes of the Solid South to get elected. He was the first Southern Democrat to get elected since the War of Northern Aggression, (OK Civil War for you northerners. Sheesh, what we will do to sell books). Now considering that the first President of the United States was from the South and from Virginia, this was a major event. But let's not get too wistful here, it took an internal party struggle on the Republican side to get it to happen, but hey, it did.

Don't think Wilson was racist? Well, here are some quotes attributed to him. "Segregation is not a humiliation but a benefit, and ought to be recognized by you gentlemen", as spoken to Mr. Monroe Trotter in 1914 during a meeting with Wilson on his segregation policies. How about this one? "Off by themselves with only a white supervisor, blacks would not be forced out of their jobs by energetic white people." Not too shabby a racist remark. In actuality Wilson's election was a real setback for blacks, segregationist policies were instituted in Washington D. C. Longtime black supervisors were replaced by whites and even separate buildings were built to house black workers. This was all happening 48 years after the War of Northern Aggression and 36 years after the compromise of 1877. Many would say these were long memories if the Southern vote was still fighting this issue in 1914. But hey, it gets worse.

OK the Solid South vote was racist and so was President Wilson and we also had racism running rampant in the Democratic Party. So what? What does this have to do with Dixiecrats? Glad you asked. Let me explain a little more. Some of you probably remember a small incident called World War II. There was a President during that time called Roosevelt. Now he was a Democrat, a northern Democrat and whether we want to debate it or not, he did get in primarily because of the 1929 Wall Street Crash. (Those Wall Street boys cause a lot of crashes, 1873, 1893, 1929, 2007. You'd think somebody would sit on them.) Well he was the first Democratic president since Woodrow Wilson and broke a twelve year string of Republican presidents and was the third Democratic president since the War of Northern…well, you know when, a period of 65 years. There were only three Democratic presidents in 65 years, 72 if you include the war years. You get the picture, the Republicans ruled, baby.

Well if the Southern Vote was so strong, why didn't it get more presidents in office, you ask? Well, because for 12 years reconstruction prohibited it and we kept growing as a nation. In 1910 the continental US filled out and we had a whole lot more states than we had in 1865. This reduced the influence of the Southern Vote in choosing national candidates and its influence within the Democratic Party and Congress, but it was still a powerful voting bloc. Plus the Democrats had the two thirds rule.

Two thirds rule, you ask? What was that? Well, the Democratic Party in 1832 decided that no one would be their nominee for president unless they got two-thirds of the votes of the delegates to the convention. This rule held fast until 1936, over a hundred years. The reason for the rule was to ensure that the nominee had full support of the Party. But what it did in essence was nominate a whole lot of people that were second tier, basically not as powerful, commanding or domineering as we would like in our leaders. If you are a leader, you get enemies, just a fact. Leaders, true leaders, command dissent and discussion and rarely have the overwhelming support of anyone, let alone two thirds. So when Democrats met, the main leaders took to the floor to get nominated. But, so did those that opposed them. Since these dynamic people drew controversy, the side with the fewer votes waited them out; ballot after ballot, knowing their opponent couldn't get nominated. Those opposed to the nomination always controlled just enough votes to keep him from getting two thirds of the vote. The Southern Vote used this position often, as they voted as a group. This made sure the Democratic candidates supported South positions, and also ensured continued Southern power. So to get anybody to be the nominee, the South and others, frequently settled for a candidate they could all agree on. It was a consolation candidate.

But in 1929, the Great U.S. Depression got everybody on the Democratic page and in 1932 Roosevelt was elected. Now it wasn't as pretty as all that. Roosevelt had the majority of votes needed to be nominated to run for president of the Democratic Party, but he didn't have the two-thirds needed to clinch the nomination. Opponents were hoping for another long drawn out battle for votes that would ultimately allow them to choose someone else. In stepped John Nance Garner, Speaker of the House, candidate in his own right for the nomination, and from Texas, one of the Solid South states. Garner makes a deal to become Vice-President, and suddenly FDR becomes the candidate for the Democratic Party. The South is happy because they have a man in position to influence the agenda and the North is happy because they have their man. This was the beginning of 20 years of Democratic control of the Presidency and such a strong hold on the Presidency that the unthinkable could happen in the Democratic Party. Racist platforms and the Solid South could be shed.

The South was not only racist; many of the voters were also a part of the Progressive movement. Being racist and progressive do seem oxymoronic, but bear with me. It leads to the formal formation of the Dixiecrats. Progressives came upon the scene at the change of the century. They were formed of the new middle class emerging in the United States. They believed in science, all the sciences including social, economic and political sciences. They preferred professionals that had been trained in scientific fashions and educated in their fields. They were for purification of government and against political machines, bosses and the privileged elites of the gilded age. They supported women suffrage and prohibition. The Southern Vote particularly, besides segregation, believed in states' rights and limited government. This was in 1900; nothing new under the sun is there?

John Garner Nance was a Progressive and many of his views sided closely with Roosevelt's. Nance also had thirty years in Washington politics and knew the Senators and Representatives well. He was by far more powerful than Roosevelt and could get things done, even if Roosevelt couldn't. Roosevelt knew this and encouraged it. With the nation in disarray and any help needed Roosevelt and Nance had nearly cart blanch to do something, anything and they did. Using progressive ideals, they passed social security, Security Exchange Commission, National Labor Relations Act, and unemployment benefits. Roosevelt and company also removed 500,000 veterans and widows from pension rolls and reduced the benefits for the remainder, all to help balance the budget. (There's another eye opener for my many liberal friends. Roosevelt was a politician, not God.).

With all this goodwill and support from the people it was a good bet that Roosevelt was going to win another term in 1936. The Democrats were at the height of their power and support. So Roosevelt asked for something in the Democratic Convention that he was unable to get in 1932. Roosevelt asked that the two thirds rule be eliminated. Drawing upon the memory of over 100 ballots cast in the 1928 Democratic Convention, his current popularity, and his friendship with Garner, Roosevelt and his supporters convinced the convention it was an outmoded policy that didn't work. His supporters voted for the elimination of the two thirds rule and Roosevelt was freed from the constraints of the Solid South Vote.

After his election in 1936, Roosevelt started using his exceptional landslide victory and his lack of need to cater to the South to really institute New Deal reforms. Roosevelt was basically defining a whole new era of political movement which was later defined by historians by its moniker, New Deal. These reforms were heavy on support for Unions and more towards a welfare state. When the Supreme Court objected, Roosevelt even tried to "pack" the court to get his programs through. Garner thought Roosevelt had abandoned the progressive principles and gotten too above himself and stood against him. Garner led the defeat of the Court packing legislation and began to oppose more and more legislation sent by Roosevelt to Congress. This moment could be considered the moment when the Democratic Party began its split from the Solid South, their ideologies, and the beginning of Dixiecrats.

Garner and Roosevelt never reconciled to anyone's real knowledge. When the 1940 elections came around John Garner decided to run for President on the Democratic ticket, even at his considered advanced age of 72. Roosevelt was at the end of his second term and tradition held that he would not run again. Speculation suggested he might, although prior Presidents had tried to run for non-consecutive third terms and had been beaten because of the public's lack of tolerance for so blatant an act of ego. Roosevelt held back and said he would not run unless drafted. In a convention staged by his supporters Roosevelt was asked to run by the convention. Needing now, only a majority to win the nomination, and not needing the Solid South anymore, Roosevelt won the nomination and the Presidency. The New Deal was now official policy without internal debate and the reforming of the Democratic Party was in full swing. But so was the Solid South's work to regain its political prominence. Enter Harry Truman and Thomas Dewey.

The Solid South had been working to raise its influence since the 1940 convention. The war years kept them occupied, but also alarmed. With the war years the unemployment problem began to evaporate. In 1941 there began a great migration of southern blacks to the north to fill jobs in the manufacturing centers. This gave blacks, one of the major issues in the Solid South, economic influence and independence they had not known since right after the War of Northern Aggression. They sent their ideas and money south to their families and began the unrest that many Southern whites feared. Add to this was the service blacks were performing for the Armed Services. These factors were giving blacks position, status, votes and potential political power.

All this came together in the 1948 convention. Harry Truman's popularity was at an all-time low. The Republicans had taken over the House and Senate in the midterm elections of 1946. Some polls showed Thomas Dewey, the Republican nominee was ahead of Truman by double digits. The Progressive had already split from the Party because the government under Truman wasn't going to the left enough for them. In the middle of all this walked a Mayor from Minneapolis called Hubert Humphrey pushing a platform for Civil Rights for blacks. Humphrey proclaimed that the Democratic Party had to shed states' rights and support human rights instead. This was a call to arms for the Solid South. Humphrey was asking Truman and the Democrats to go against the very foundation of the Solid South movement, a movement they had spent over 80 years perfecting and defending.

The reason for Humphrey's motion was clear to many northern mayors and big city bosses. The growing black vote in their cities, due to the southern flight caused by the war, had created a political base that they needed and wanted to exploit. What the Solid South had feared by the blacks moving north for jobs had come to pass. The blacks had political clout and in their own party. Truman was indifferent to the adoption of the platform, but he wasn't indifferent to his need for the big city vote. Truman did not intercede and the platform passed. This action literally caused three dozen delegates to walk out of the convention led by none other than South Carolina Governor Strom Thurmond. The remaining Southern delegates nominated Georgia Senator Richard Russell for president as a rebuke to Truman, but Truman still won the convention by a majority of votes.   Russell only received votes from the south.

With the Civil Rights platform in, unable to support any Republican, and unable to back the Democrats, the Solid South had only two choices, abstain from any action or nominate one of their own for President. They chose the latter option and convened in Oklahoma City under the banner of the States Rights Democratic Party. Their nickname was "Dixiecrats" and thus the name if not the movement was born. They weren't a Reagan fantasy or a Republican dodge; they were real people with a real organization. They continue today, although their organization does not. (Well not in FACT, anyhow).

SO DIXIECRATS EXIST, WHAT OF IT?

In my exploration of the current political polarization in the U.S., the confirmation of Dixiecrats as an organization is a confirmation that political parties or ideology demanded loyalty above the country. The establishment of the States Rights Democratic Party, Dixiecrats, for the primary purpose of continuing a racist policy against confirmed citizens of the United States smacks of personal issues, not national issues. There is no patriotism or honor in this personal belief, no matter the size of or flag in which it is wrapped.

It can be acknowledged that if a person or organization believes strongly that a country is being led in the wrong direction by those in power, it is their right, if not duty, to mount opposition to those in charge and their policies. But there is a fine line here. When does your concern about the direction of the country become a preferred ideological belief rather than a concern for country? Specifically, I may believe strongly that Republicans should wear a red star on all clothing to denote them as Republicans so sane men and women can avoid them at all costs. I may even believe that by doing this it will make the country better and is therefore a better direction for the country. But is this not my own personal ideological belief? Republicans may wish Democrats wear a red star. Not only to denote Democrats from others, but in the hope the red of the star will somehow make those that wear it gain by osmosis a better sense of direction. (Liberals are known to wander.)

The argument as to what is good for the country cannot be based on a personal ideology, no matter how strongly we feel about it. (Believe me some in the political arena really feel strongly about giving identifying signs to the opposition.) The argument about what is good for the country, and what we must as citizens therefore embrace, is: "What is good for the whole country?" How can we move the whole country forward, all genders, all races, all economies and all beliefs?

The States Rights Democratic Party, or Dixiecrats, did not do this. They did not follow these simple criteria. Dixiecrats created the party to specifically ensure the exclusion of blacks from full participation in the United States 83 years after the war that created their full inclusion. Dixiecrats created a Party to further the supremacy of states' rights over the federal government. These were personal ideologies that did not further the country as a whole. In fact these beliefs, in practice in their own states, proved a hindrance to the furtherance of a race and their own economies.

There is an issue in this instance that is larger than just ideological belief or party partisanship and must be considered in this evaluation. Those that set up the Dixiecrats did so from a foundation of a defeated people. Their forefathers did not acquiesce and give in to a better argument. They were forced at gunpoint to accept the terms. Winning a war is not the same as winning the minds of an opponent. Those that formed the Dixiecrats still believed in States rights over Federal rights. They still believed that they should be able to determine who they associated with and who was a member of their society. They did not accept the loss of the war as the loss of their beliefs, nor should they be expected to do so. They lost, true enough, but they still thought they were right and the country was wrong. It was not only the injustices of the reconstruction that drew their ire, but the imposition of others beliefs upon them. There was no vote in agreement with Northern polices and beliefs, there was forced acceptance.

But let's not give too much of a leeway, based upon the War of Northern Aggression, to Dixiecrats in this evaluation. It has been three generations and 83 years since that war ended. There is a time to move on and no longer give leave to prejudices and constructs born of another era. A great depression, industrialization, and two world wars had passed since the Civil War. Blacks had proven themselves in combat and in business. Their efforts had saved lives and improved the country. All had been done without the leave of their white masters. The reasons for the establishment of the Dixiecrats were a furtherance of outdated prejudicial beliefs and personal power. There was no patriotic defense of country to attend this formation.

Now some may wish to debate the issue. For rebuttal is the platform of the States Rights Democratic Party. The platform quickly seeks adherents and patriotic acceptance in Section 1 which states in its entirety: *We believe that the Constitution of the United States is the greatest charter of human liberty ever conceived by the mind of man.* Pretty powerful and easily accepted by all United States' patriots.

Section 2 is a call to arms. It gives the impression something is being attacked that must be defended. Here is section 2 in its entirety: *We oppose all efforts to invade or destroy the rights guaranteed by it to every citizen of this republic.* Now we had just fought and won a war. We were acknowledged by all as a prominent power in the world for the first time in our history and somehow we must stand watch against attack. Fear rears its ugly head in this comment and becomes the basis for the foundation of the party.

Section 3: *We stand for social and economic justice, which, we believe can be guaranteed to all citizens only by a strict adherence to our Constitution and the avoidance of any invasion or destruction of the constitutional rights of the states and individuals. We oppose the totalitarian, centralized bureaucratic government and the police nation called for by the platforms adopted by the Democratic and Republican Conventions.* Now if this isn't a call for states' rights again you haven't been paying attention. And the idea that the Constitution must somehow be immortalized in its original form forever, when even the founding fathers thought it necessary to amend it because of flaws in the original document, is just self serving. (As a liberal I must state this part reminds me a lot of some group parading around right now. Hmmm... let me think on that.)

We get down to the segregation and the meat of the platform in Sections 4, 5, and 6. Section 4: *We stand for the segregation of the races and the racial integrity of each race; the constitutional right to choose one's associates; to accept private employment without governmental interference; and to earn one's living in any lawful way. We oppose the elimination of segregation, the repeal of miscegenation statutes, the control of private employment by Federal bureaucrats called for by the misnamed civil rights program. We favor home-rule, local self government, and a minimum interference with individual rights.* Gets right out there and says they want to segregate the races. Not only separate the races, but prohibit them from cohabitating and having children. These are personal ideologies. What is impressive is their strength after so long. They have obviously been handed down generation after generation and taught with fervor.

Section 5: *We oppose and condemn the action of the Democratic Convention in sponsoring a civil rights program calling for the elimination of segregation, social equality by fiat, regulations of private employment practices, voting and local law enforcement.* Now you gotta understand, Democrats were beginning the process of stopping poll taxes, literacy tests and other forms of black voter intimidation. This meant blacks would have a say in Southern politics again, a prospect that had been cleansed by white southerners for over 70 years. This section is a declaration to retain a power base, nothing more.

Section 6: *We affirm that the effective enforcement of such a program would be utterly destructive of the social, economic and political life of the Southern people, and of other localities in which there may be differences in race, creed, or national origin in appreciable numbers.* Well you have to give Dixiecrats credit for honesty. This is all about them, Southerners, or to be specific, white southerners. It is not for the good of the country as a whole.

Section 7 is more of a call to fear: *We stand for the check and balances provided by the three departments of our government. We oppose the usurpation of legislative functions by the executive and judicial departments. We unreservedly condemn the effort to establish in the United States a police nation that would destroy the last vestige of liberty enjoyed by a citizen.* If this isn't a personal opinion, what is? For anyone that would care to read it, this section just presents so emphatically that our very freedoms are in danger from those other ner do wells and we must get our guns and stand in defiance.

Section 8 is more long winded, but is another call to arms to defend their right to segregation: *We demand that there be returned to the people to whom of right they belong, those powers needed for the preservation of human rights and the discharge of our responsibility as democrats for human welfare. We oppose a denial of these by political parties, a barter or sale of those rights by a political convention, as well as any invasion of violation of those rights by the Federal Government. We call upon all Democrats and upon all other loyal Americans who are opposed to totalitarianism at home and abroad to unite with us to ignominiously defeating Harry S. Truman, Thomas E. Dewey, and every other candidate for public office who would establish a Police Nation in the United States of America.* Now we might go for this as a call to do what's right for the whole country, if what they defined as right wasn't the subjugation and isolation of a whole race of citizens of the United States. This is where the personal opinions and personal power issues are gussied up for respectability and wrapped in patriotism and the American flag. But a monkey in a silk suit is still a monkey. This is still a personal call for segregation and return to state's rights. It is a power play on the behalf of the South to regain what they had lost in the Democratic Party and in the United States politics in general.

The final section calls on Americans to vote for J. Strom Thurmond, (yes, THAT Senator. He only seemed to live forever.), for President and Fielding H. Wright for Vice-President. It was a simple straight forward platform that required duty to party above duty to the country. It relied on fear to gull people into action and it relied on anger to keep those people committed to the cause.

The results of the 1948 election are well known. This was the election that Truman won and held up that famous though erroneous headline, "Dewey Defeats Truman". But while the results of that election were important in the effect that Truman overcame divisions among the Democratic Party on the right and the left. (We aren't even getting into the Progressives and their movement. Liberal left, you have no reason to be smug. You are just as bad as the right.) What is important to this discussion is the results as concerned the Dixiecrats. The Dixiecrats carried a number of states and succeeded in garnering 39 electoral votes.

Dixiecrats carried Louisiana, Mississippi, Alabama and South Carolina. They also received one electoral vote from Tennessee. (Progressives you didn't get one vote for all your trouble.) Now it was easy to get some of those votes. Truman wasn't even allowed on the ballot in Alabama. The States Rights Democratic Party was declared the Democratic Party in Alabama for purposes of this election, so Truman didn't even get a chance. In Louisiana, Mississippi and South Carolina the State Rights Democratic Party was listed as the main Democratic Party and the actual Democratic Party was listed as a third party candidacy. (My county in Florida actually carried for the Dixiecrats even though the state did not.) So while the results were interesting the South was still voting solidly Democratic, just clerical manipulations had them vote for a different Democratic Party.

With a failed election behind them, a loss of power for the Dixiecrats within the Democratic Party and the nation followed. This unsuccessful exercise for power and a prominence of personal ideology laid bare what had been known but not acknowledged. In some ways it gave a bit a freedom to the Dixiecrat movement that they had not had before. They could now go forth openly with their beliefs and not obfuscate them under the cover of more acceptable ideals. The Dixiecrats could preach and solicit like minds more openly after this effort, than at any time before. Their movement, while more localized in the South than ever, actually gained strength in its convictions and its memberships as the defenders of the Southern traditions and ideologies.

The Dixiecrats spent the next sixteen years trying to rebuild their influence and power in the Democratic Party and did succeed on some levels. One of the failures of the Dixiecrats during the 1948 election was not gaining full support of all the members of the Solid South. Some leaders in the South were accepting and in agreement with the new direction and ideologies. There was no longer a complete acceptance of Dixiecrat ideology in southern Democrats. Other leaders simply did not join for political strategy reasons. Either way the Southern leader's refusal to support the Dixiecrats helped lead to defeat of their strategy. After 1948 the South still controlled a considerable number of state houses, governorships and U.S. House and Senate seats. They still voted almost solidly Democratic, but cracks were beginning to show after this election between the Southern Vote that was Democratic and the one that had a Dixiecrat bent.

However, Dixiecrats refused to leave and refused to give up as shown in the courtship of their vote in 1980 by the Reagan campaign. Although diminished in stature over time Dixiecrats remained a significant voting bloc. The election of 1948 gave us, through the results, a geographic area we can safely regard as Dixiecrat territory. It also gave this voting bloc an identity that they carry with pride and defiance, a part of, yet independent of, the Party to which they belong. They also continue to contribute, sometime with pride, to a polarization in American politics.

HOW DO DIXIECRATS AFFECT US TODAY?

Born of segregationist's attitudes and the beliefs of states' rights that could not be diminished by a loss in war, Dixiecrats still seek to influence the United States political agenda towards their beliefs. Some may argue that too much time has passed for Dixiecrats to seriously believe that a reversal in civil rights and states' rights can be accomplished. To this argument can be applied the violence in the Middle East. It cannot be doubted that many Jewish people believe Israel is the Holy Land given to them by God thousands of years ago. Nor can it be doubted that Arab beliefs believe this is their sacred and Holy Land. It has been fought over for millennia, despite the fact that ownership of these lands has been held by one or another of these groups for hundreds of years, before taken away by fiat or war, held by the other side for hundreds of years and then reversed again. If these groups can hold onto a belief over this time, why couldn't a Southern voter hold onto the belief that states' rights will prevail and segregation will return over a matter of 160 years?

There is no doubt that attitudes have adjusted. But based upon whether you are white or black, how much adjustment has been made in the South is subject to debate. It has only been forty-six years since the passage of the Civil Rights Act, but in this county the signs that warned blacks to be off the island before dark were taken down barely over 16 years ago. While prejudice does exist, this doesn't mean that all Dixiecrats are prejudiced. What has happened is a redefining of the positions of those associated with Dixiecrat sentimentalities.

Dixiecrats believe that they should be allowed to associate with whom they want and where they want. They now believe that blacks have the rights of every American citizen and (almost all) do not wish to return them to slavery or even the Jim Crow era. But Dixiecrats do not think they should have to be with blacks if they don't want to be with them. Dixiecrats don't believe they should have to be with anyone they don't want to be with from blacks, to Jews, to Muslims. Denying them segregation and discrimination in public places such as schools, restaurants and shops, is denying them their Constitutional rights to free association. In other words defending the rights of minorities prohibits their rights as the majority.

Dixiecrats also still believe strongly in States' rights over Federal rights. While Dixiecrats are, in their way, immensely patriotic and believe in the United States, they feel that when there is a disagreement between the states and the Federal government, states rule. These two basic beliefs translate into a voter that is a very conservative, independent, and isolationist in their views. Things are simple and they do not know why it has to be so complicated.

But Dixiecrats are no longer an organization, you say. The States Rights Democratic Party dissolved shortly after the 1948 election. If they are not organized how are they a voting bloc? True enough, they are not organized in fact. There are no monthly meetings or yearly dues under the Dixiecrat banner. They do not put up candidates for president or even state legislator. But they do exist. For 16 years after the 1948 election they worked to regain their power in the Democratic Party. Their organization existed in and through the southern Democratic Party. If you were in the Southern Democratic Party you were most likely a Dixiecrat. Their leader Strom Thurmond and others continued to get elected based upon those that believed as they did and through the local Democratic apparatus. Local Democratic parties in the South were led by those who actively supported Dixiecrat ideals. The Dixiecrat base was the southern Democratic Party. So while the Dixiecrats didn't exist as an entity in fact, it existed through its auspices in the southern Democratic Party.

Dixiecrats had built up a strong base of power in the Southern Democratic Party, not only politically but economically and socially for years. For almost a hundred years after the War of Northern Aggression if you wanted to get elected to any post in the city, county, state or federal government in the South you had to be a Democrat. While blacks could vote, Jim Crow laws and intimidation made sure there were always a majority of whites voting in these counties. To be white and in the South meant you had to be a Democrat. Democratic primaries were the preeminent, if not only, way to be elected. Support from the Chair of the local Democratic Party, could almost guarantee your election. The general election was a formality. Many times there just wasn't a Republican to be found to run. Over these hundred years tradition or habit or both created a base of power, a social and economic structure, in the local Democratic Party that allowed the allocation of county jobs, contracts, and position. As an individual, when you became of age, you became a Democrat. This was bored into you by peer pressure from family and friends until it just was a fact of being a southern white voter.

Being a Democrat and Democratic Party member in the South was has been likened to being a member of a Mafia family. While not dedicated to racketeering to build their personal fortunes, Southern Democrats in the mid 20th century did exert influence in elections and patronage positions in a similar vein. You had to be a member to be accepted and you didn't waver on your vote to remain in good graces. Economic and peer pressure kept you in compliance. Southern Democrats were Dixiecrats, they voted as Dixiecrats and Dixiecrat ideals were the only ones permitted to be taught.

Eventually national Democratic policy veered sharply from Dixiecrat values. When they did Dixiecrats had a choice leave the Democratic Party or stay. With their base of economic and social power built up over more than a hundred years, and a tradition requiring voters to register Democrat, the disruption to the local Dixiecrats in power and their personal economies would have been too great. So Dixiecrats remained in the Party, but voted conservative. Dixiecrats like to say that they are the original Democrats and the Party left them, they didn't leave the Party. They are right.

But how did and do Dixiecrats control who gets their votes? Shortly after the departure from Dixiecrat values in the Democratic Party a new phrase was coined by knowing Dixiecrats, "Party doesn't matter." When Southern Democratic voters wanted to know who to vote for in an election they asked those in charge. If the return was "Party doesn't matter" they voted Democrat. Otherwise they voted Republican. This way the local Democrats, or

Dixiecrats, kept the local offices to themselves and their friends, which kept the jobs and contracts inside the Party and with the Dixiecrats. But the state and national offices, where Party mattered, went to Republicans. This adjustment allowed Dixiecrats to remain Democrats and keep their base of power and economic strength, but stay true to their stated values.

The proof in the power of Dixiecrats and their continued involvement in and registration with the Democratic Party is in the Presidential elections in Florida in 2000 and 2004. While most current readers are aware of the debacle of the 2000 Presidential election in Florida, we don't concentrate here on the voter intimidation, covert and overt, practiced in Florida during that time. Our point is the heavily Democratic Voter registration in some of the smaller counties and their solid support of the Republican presidential candidate. In the instance of Holmes County in Florida in 2000, there were 10,304 registered voters. Eight thousand, five hundred and eighty-nine, (8.589), were registered Democrat or almost 83% of the voters were Democrats. Yet in 2000, 5,011 voters voted for the Republican and only 2,177 voted for the Democrat. In 2004, with a voter registration of 10,974 and 7, 983, or 73%, registered as Democrats, 6,412 voted Republican and 1,810 voted Democrat.

The stark contrast between the number of registered Democrats in this county and the voting results caused a concern towards the validity of the results in the recounts. But many counties in Florida with similar voting registrations reported the same results. Pollsters began questioning their statistical formulas based upon the registration numbers and the results. Democrats in other parts of the nation cried foul and believed their election had been stolen, (It was. But for that commentary you can read a whole pile of other books.)   It just couldn't be believed that with that such a great majority these counties would go Republican. It was only in a contest on the national stage that was this closely monitored, and with so few votes separating the contestants, that the reality that Dixiecrats still existed was evident.

Still, after 135 years since the end of the Civil War and 52 years since the results of the 1948 election, this group of conservative Democrats, the Dixiecrats, exist and continue to support the systems their fathers, grandfathers, mothers, and grandmother created. Impressive that in a country largely convinced of its own enlightenment, that this group could maintain with startling efficiency, a group of voters that delivered, without any structure, organization, or outward appearance, votes on a regular basis for the candidates they wished and the causes they support. Yet here they are, in counties all over the south, delivering large blocs of votes for local Democrats and national and state Republicans. But the question becomes how do they continue to have local voters conform in a political climate so diverse and with such external influences? Another question is how do they do so in an era where the actual dominate local political committee is dissolved and has been for a number of years?

The probable answer to both these questions is a closed society. Holmes County like so many other counties boasting a Dixiecrat background doesn't grow much. It is an agrarian community not an industrial center. The county lacks much of the amenities that people look for when moving to a new location, shops, malls, schools and the like so it often gets passed by. Even in the last census including the recent building boom of 2001- 2006, Holmes County increased its population by a little over 1400 residents. It has taken Holmes County roughly sixty years to double its size from 10,000 residents to just less than 20,000. This gradual growth and its ability to indoctrinate those moving into the county into the dominate Dixiecrat culture was a factor in the perpetuation of the mindset and organization.

To show contrast, and in support of the assumption of slow growth, Flagler County in Florida, which actually voted with the Dixiecrats in 1948, is now considered at best a swing vote county with a heavy support of Democrats even in national and state elections. The overriding variable is the population growth. Unlike Holmes, Flagler was the fastest growing county in the United States for two years running between 2000 and 2010. Spurred by the effects of a planned community designed by a major corporation for economic profit Flagler grew and with it came tens of thousands of Northern voters, black and white. In the 2008 election Flagler was the only smaller, (rural), county to carry for Barack Obama. The population grew so fast and quick that the ingrained political structure could not overcome the change and a new political fabric was created. This has not removed Dixiecrats from the voting system, but has reduced their influence and power substantially.

Dixiecrats are diminishing, but only through time and the pressure of ideas thrust upon them by outside influences. They are not gone and despite external pressures they hold fast to their positions as long as practicable and often longer. They and their forebears had the ideology instilled in them for generations. Dixiecrats still believe in being able to associate only with those they wish to associate. They still believe that the state has more power, and should have, than the Federal government. They have not deviated from these founding principles. While many have mitigated their beliefs to not abide discrimination because of color, segregation has not been abandoned by all.

Because of their history, where they live and have lived, and the efforts they have gone through to preserve their community and society, Dixiecrats are more isolationists than worldly. They think locally and have more concern about US policy as it attends to preserve, protect and defend the United States and are less inclined to care how the US attends to other countries. They are less concerned with social issues. They feel strongly the government has way too much influence in personal lives and will support any candidate or policy that works to remove that influence. Dixiecrats wish to be left alone. If called for help or service to the country they will come, but when done they will go home and expect you to do the same. In essence they feel they are the embodiment of the independent American. Individuals and the United State should stand on their own two feet. They are what Americans should be and should do. They teach these values to their children and expect others do the same. They stand confused when policies, economic or political changes arise that do not embody these beliefs and normally vote or work against them as a matter of principle.

This belief structure and the persistence over time has made the Dixiecrats, whether by name or idea, a solid strong voting bloc exerting formidable political pressure in United States politics. It is a voting bloc and a society that has tremendous draw for many outside the historically organized counties and groups. It speaks of simpler times that should not have been abandoned and a hierarchy that was understood. When difficulties seem too hard to handle, such as the recent recession, this can be a siren song for many.

But Dixiecrat policies by design create the polarization that is anathema to our country. The promotion of their ideas relies strongly on the process of creating fear. The fear of what is going

The fear of what is going to happen if the "blacks marry our white women". The fear of what will happen if we have to pay for "all those bum's drugs". They live in the belief and sell the fact that someday there will be someone go down to their state, then to their county, then to their town, down that country road, turn onto the path and park in their yard just too personally shoot them or their family. Someone "out there" is getting ready to do that right now. They, whoever they are, the black, Muslim or Jew, is out there planning right now just to get them personally and they have to be ready. The only way to respond is to be ready and the only way to attack is with anger. Anger at anyone, anything or any institution that they perceive may let "them" do their dirty deeds.

Dixiecrats formal creation was one to continue the segregation of the races and deny blacks a place in our society, because of their fear of what could happen. Some would say after "redemption and reconstruction" they had a right to this fear. But it has been 145 years; the people that lived through that era are long dead. The war is long over. Let it rest. That should not be our battle. There is no profit in continuing the hate or fear. Only personal animosity gains here.

Segregation is still a part of the Dixiecrat platform as shown through the insistence that we must be allowed to only associate with those that we wish to associate. States rights are still a part of the platform. Isolationism is a part of the platform. For the recognized most powerful country in the world this is denial. The United States cannot fight and go home. We cannot isolate our citizens into dens of unique cultures. We cannot send blacks "back home". This is their home. The Unites States very existence requires attendance and attention in world politics, societies and cultures.

Dixiecrats are self-serving in that the United State can only exist as they define it. In their view there is no room for opposing views. While independence of thought and standing for what you believe is something to be admired in this country, stubborn adherence to an outdated belief system that seeks to marginalize other citizens based on race or religion is not. This attitude, fought for with polices of fear and anger over tens of decades, contributes to the polarization of the current political climate in the United States. Their parochial views are consistent with what they want, but are not and have not been consistent with what is good for the United States. In their view what is good for the Dixiecrats is good for the USA.

But the rejoinder should be what is good for the USA is good for the Dixiecrats. They are members of our society; we are not members of theirs. As they benefit from the largesse of the USA, it is not for us to measure up to their standards, they should measure to ours.

T.E.A Party, Do We Really Have To Go There?

Well yeah, I guess. I mean it is in the title of the book. I really don't want to and it's not what you think. I was all ready to jump on the TEA Party. Man was I ready. Had all my conspiracy gear out and I was gonna rake them babies for what they did to our country. BUT, what I thought I knew about the TEA Party wasn't what was true. Now I know how crow tastes, like vinegar.

I mean I am a liberal, (did I mention that? Good. Didn't want to mislead you.) TEA Party people and liberals are like oil and water, they just don't mix. I was sure the TEA Party was a commercial construction of the FOX News Network, (Fair and Balanced, my sweet Aunt!). But the TEA Party is a true grass roots movement and in spite of Sarah Palin, FOX, MSNBC, Michelle Bachman, and a whole slew of other politicos, billionaires, and external influences, remains grassroots. The quotes "Never doubt that a small group of thoughtful, committed individuals can change the world. Indeed it is the only thing that ever has." is attributed to Margaret Mead. While I can confirm the "committed" part of this quote to TEA Partiers, (In all its pun intended connotations.), it is also a real description of what the TEA Party has done and the TEA Party is a confirmation of this quote.

To best understand the TEA Party is to go to the beginning, not Boston in 1773, (sheesh, will you hang in there with me a bit? Really!), but Seattle Washington in 2009. Generally acknowledged as the first TEA Party event by leaders in the group, Keli Carender, a Seattle blogger, (about 28 years old at the time for those of you that think all of the TEA Partiers are just "cotton tops") organized the first TEA Party event on Presidents Day, February 16th. It wasn't called a TEA Party then; it was called a Porkulus Protest. Now for those of you just taking notes, President Obama had only been in office 27 days and she was already throwing a protest. (I don't know if Michelle Obama even had their things unpacked yet. Talk about not giving a guy a chance.)

Now Keli is not uneducated, as in the point of having received a formal education from an accredited institution of advanced learning. She has a degree in Biology and Math, studied at the University of Oxford in England, and worked in four other nations. This is not a woman of limited experience and background, grinding out hate emails, in curlers, in the cluttered third bedroom in some trailer in a mobile home park, (talk about promoting a stereotype!, lol). She has a brain and thoughts. She thinks that those in the United States have a limited knowledge of economics and don't remember or realize their individual rights. Her blog is dedicated to disseminating knowledge and information on those subjects from her viewpoint and in her view, defending America. Keli is completely altruistic, and unfortunately for my criticism, patriotic, as she is working for the betterment of the whole country not just her own agenda. Now as a Liberal, I am not a fan. As a citizen, I am impressed. Well done. But Keli didn't do it alone. She, like all grassroots organizations, had help.

This is where it begins to stink, and in some ways it shouldn't. Rick Santelli, a CNBC Business News editor was broadcasting from the floor of the Chicago Mercantile Exchange, (Chicago Stock Market. What, you didn't know there were more stock markets than Wall Street?), on February 19, 2009. (Just 30 days into a new presidency, mind you. Michelle is definitely unpacked by now.) Using his pulpit he criticized the government plan to refinance mortgages which had been announced the day before. He said the plans promoted "bad behavior" and the country was going to subsidize "loser's mortgages." (Yes, I watched the video. You can to. It is on YouTube. They never delete anything, even this crap.) He said that in protest the traders should have their own tea party and dump the derivatives in the Chicago River on July 1st. His video rant went viral on the Internet and was featured on the Drudge report, a conservative news web site.

Now the reason the TEA Party idea began to stink here was the venue and the personality. Rick Santelli was using his position as a personality on TV, (OK a minor personality, but a personality), to promote a personal belief. There was no place for argument or debate of his rant, he was the show. He used his position to his and his agendas advantage. It was a shallow display. But it wasn't just the personality; it was the venue, on the stock exchange in a major market. This was the group that created these derivatives that depended on bankers and financers selling mortgages to people that couldn't afford them so they could make huge personal profits. They preyed on the losers they are now deriding and when their finances and banks faced bankruptcy they ran to the United States Congress, Republican President and Republican Treasury Secretary and pleaded for taxpayer help to save them. They got it, saved themselves and then racked up huge profits at taxpayer expense. But when the taxpayers wanted a little hand up, well those taxpayers that saved them and they bilked, well they were just losers not worth the time. No matter how you look at it, it was tacky and ungrateful. Reminds me of the old adage "never give a sucker an even break."

Now for those of you that think this is a little unfair of me to attack Santelli and not give him a chance to speak for himself in my book, or not allowing another viewpoint of his attack, well maybe you get my point. For those of you that didn't, think about it a minute.

But even with the Santelli stink, OK, hypocrisy, (my book, you think I could call this hypocrisy a stink.) the TEA Party idea was still grassroots. Even during the rant Santelli was calling on the traders in the room to join him in protest. This wasn't planned or orchestrated. It was one man with an opinion and a rather loud bullhorn, calling people to protest what he hypocritically thought was a government wrong.

This is the very definition of grassroots. This wasn't the actions of an organization, even though it was on cable. (And it was on cable, come on, not like this was mainstream.) It was the actions and opinion of one man. Fox News, that bastion of all that is right, only reported on the TEA Party idea the day after this rant. They were still following the trend, not making it. They had their own personalities making up news and ideas and were not looking for outside contractors.

After Santelli's rant a series of websites began to pop up, including reTeaParty.com which were used to coordinate TEA Parties protests. Now we are talking, that within 12 hours of the rant on February 19th, web sites were up and running to coordinate TEA Parties for protesting government actions on April 15th, what we all know as Tax Day. (This is the power of grassroots and the Internet, not corporate deities. That group can't get a committee together in that time.) In other words, thirty-one days after he took office, TEA Parties and people in the TEA Parties were lining up to protest the actions of the government and the president. I'll grant you that President Obama was leading one of the most aggressive agendas since Roosevelt, but even this level of protests in this few days was exceptional and reason enough for liberal bloggers like the Huffington Post to believe it was all staged. Huffington Post even ran an article delineating how it was all a conspiracy, but sorry, no. It really was grass roots, conservative right wing grassroots, (the distinction is important, this was a nationwide grassroots, but the whole nation didn't agree), and still is. Those political personalities, parties and wealthy businesspeople were trying like hell to make it their idea and control it, but all they could do was hang on.

Well what happened then? All that you can expect of a grassroots movement and more. Grassroots movements, if successful, become a bandwagon. Everyone wants to jump on board and claim they built the movement. It is hard to dispute any claims because in a grassroots movement, everyone does contribute to the organization. You can't exclude businesses, or politicians, or even news organizations from a grassroots movement just because of whom or what they are. There are no rules to who can join and be a part of the movement. Any one or any organization can be a part of the movement and contribute any asset they may have to make the movement successful. So those that joined did just that, added to the bandwagon and the movement.

Now why is that so terrible? Well to those in the TEA Party movement, it isn't. But to those opposed to the TEA Party position, a grassroots movement is one of the worst things that can happen. Nobody knows how to really handle a true grassroots movement. As has been said there is nothing more powerful than an idea whose time has come. So it is with TEA Parties. Liberals desperately want this to be a conspiracy, because then they can attack it and expose it and defeat it. But to attack a true grassroots organization is tough because you are attacking real people, with real concerns and real ideas. Worst of all a dedicated organization, even one that is a small percentage of the whole population such as the TEA Party, can change the outcomes of elections just by voting en mass, particularly in a low turnout election. TEA Party grassroots organizations filled all the requirements and the 2010 election was projected to be a low turnout year. Everything was in place for a major disruption and it happened.

TEA Party organizations continued to grow after Santelli and Keli. The idea was just too powerful for a group of people that felt disenfranchised from their government. Abigail Adams organizations, 912 organizations, any organization that rebelled against the supposed status quo rallied to the TEA Party ideals. All these organizations were, in effect, TEA Party organizations though their founders and members would rail against the comparisons. These organizations grew and conservative organizations joined them.

They gained an early and loud bullhorn when the FOX News Network decided it was a good idea to give them plenty of attention. The addition of a former Vice-Presidential candidate that had a penchant for expressing her opinions loudly and often didn't hurt either. Rallies were held and passions were enflamed. Those that wanted to win read the polls and the tea leaves and saw that the odds were in favor of those that embraced the movement. As more embraced the movement, the movement got bigger, until you couldn't distinguish one from the other. It really wasn't anything but a grassroots movement and it should be looked at for what it was. It is and was a social phenomenon to be understood, but not condemned, because what happened for the right can also happen for the left. It would be nice to declare it uniquely American, but we are witnessing the same sort of process in the fall of governments across the Middle East right now.

But for my fellow liberals that are rocking in despair, there is good news. Grassroots organizations usually burn out very shortly after they have passed their goals. Like a grass fire, grassroots start with a spark, build quickly, burn hot, destroy everything in their path and then burn out. The fuel just gets eaten up and the furor can no longer be sustained. However, we do have to live with the destruction for many years after the event. It takes awhile to restore what needs to be restored and often organizations are altered permanently after the grassroots affect.

The evidence suggests that this is what is happening to the current TEA Party movement. They have become institutionalized. They are no longer grassroots. The TEA Party movement is finding out what it takes to sustain power and influence long term is a committed organization. This is all part of the process of maturation. Republicans and Democrats have known this for years and have the organizations to deal with the process. It remains to be seen if the TEA Party does the same. Odds are against it.

Who is the TEA Party?

So who is this TEA Party? If they are going to stay around or even if they aren't maybe we should know something about them. If you say they are a grassroots movement, (and I do), what got them all riled up and why? Maybe there is something that they have to say that should be heard if so many people thought it was so important.

Well according to unknown authors at the New York Times/CBS News Poll, *TEA Party supporters are wealthier and well-educated than the general public, tend to be Republican, white, male, and married, and their strong opposition to the Obama administration is more rooted in political ideology than anxiety about their personal economic well being.* Well, as a liberal if it is in the Times it must be true! Well actually this poll is true, others confirm it, but the summary is way to general. Makes it look like we have a bunch of well-heeled cottontops running around bitching because they didn't get their way in the last election. (OK for those of you that don't know cottontop is a word that describes people over 65 or retirees. It alludes to the fact most of them have white hair, if they have any at all. Got it? Good.)

TEA Partiers are not just old rich white guys and their wives. TEA Partiers run the gamut of the social network in the country and demographically they represent the public at large in the United States. (I got this from a Gallup Poll done April 5, 2010 and available publically on the Internet.) Yep, liberals, they represent the country, rich, old, poor, middle class, white, black, Hispanic, women and men. I'm sure that made many of you reach for the antacid. Why, you are asking yourselves. Why?

Well let me tell you, this isn't the first time something like this has happened. Remember 1873, now put up your hands I know some of you did. Really, you are gonna cop to that? Oh well some people will swear to anything. For the rest of us 1873 included the Panic of 1873 which surrounded a severe international economic depression, including the United States and Europe. It was created by the fall of demand for silver when the economic powerhouse of the time, Germany, abandoned the silver standard in the wake of the Franco-Prussian war. In the US, major banks failed, the stock market took a dive and the depression ensued. Sound familiar, stock market collapsing, bank failures, government run amok? While the history lesson as to the fact 1929 wasn't the first depression in the United States is interesting we are not going to go into detail here. Let's suffice to say it did and it has very similar characteristics to now. What we are interested in is what happened to Congress in the next election.

The next election was 1874, barely nine years since the end of the War of Northern Aggression and as you would expect Republicans ruled the House. (Now as a reminder this was the time when Senators were elected by the State Houses so we can't use them as a gauge of the voter unrest, only the House can be used as a reliable measure.) But after the Panic of 1873, despite the recent victories in the War and support for those that waged it Republicans were ousted in large numbers. The Democrats took over the House by taking 94 seats from the Republicans. If this can happen in post Civil War United States there is no reason it couldn't happen in 2010. To give hope to the Liberals, two years later, the Republicans retook the House. Anger and fear propelled the elections of 1874 as it did in 2010.

This is a process in elections, particularly in the United States and follows almost every economic upheaval. In 1928 the U. S. House was heavily Republican. In 1930 after the Wall Street collapse it stayed Republican only through the Election Day by 1 vote. Subsequent special elections turned it Democratic and in 1932 the Republicans lost over 100 seats. In the words of the Clinton Campaign, "It's the economy, stupid." Whenever there is a great disruption in the economy, the voters in fear and anger strike back. So in 2010 the TEA Partiers struck back, as their forefathers did before them and theirs did before them. With this information and the polls we can draw some conclusions about what a TEA Partier is beyond an old rich white man and why they do what they do.

First, once again, TEA Partiers are as a group conservative, right wing. That does not mean that they are all conservative, right wing. It just means as a group the far majority (70%) are conservative right wing which makes the tenor of the TEA Party conservative right wing. Also not everyone supports the TEA Party or is a part of the TEA Party. Only 28% support the TEA Party according to the Gallup poll, the rest of us, 72% of us either don't care or oppose them. In other words they are a minority despite the attention they get. By the way, just because you support the TEA Party doesn't mean you are part of the TEA Party or vote in that direction. So TEA Partiers are much more a minority than even that number expresses.

TEA Partiers are by far white and over 50, (43% are white men 50 or older). White women over 50 make up 36% of the TEA Party. So 79% of TEA Partiers are white and 50 or over. Not representative of the up and coming generation baby, no way. This is the old guy's league, the baby boomers and their dads. These boys and girls are past middle age and looking for retirement of which 21% or more are already there. They have their money and their power and they are looking to keep it. The kids can wait. Actually, by the way, they do have money, 55% of TEA Partiers have an annual income of $55,000 or more a year. Quite a bit above poverty level.

But let's not be too harsh yet. Just to bring you up to speed 50% of all adults in the US make $55,000 a year or more and 47% of us are 50 years of age or older. Also 75% of us in the US are white so really, as was said, the TEA Partiers reflect the US population generally. What really strikes everyone when they see a TEA Party rally or organization is that those participating by far are white. I mean aren't they the guys in charge? What are they doing protesting? We see another group of Hispanics or Blacks protesting, or a group of college students, well that's what they do. But white people? Really? The world has to be off kilter.

Now to make this perfectly clear so we get along, for those of us over 50 and white males, we are not old white guys. It is everybody else that's old, not us. I just want to make that clear. The old white guys are those older than us. But those of us over 50 are definitely in middle age. We can accept that.

Forty-three percent of TEA Partiers are white men over 50 so you can understand why when we see a large group of TEA Partiers we think we just have a bunch of cottontops that have no understanding of what it means to be an American in today's world. But 43% of the TEA Party males are younger than 50 and white. The point were making here is that TEA Partiers are by far white, and that is what makes the organization so different. White people don't protest, especially our parents and grandparents. They are the ones in charge. So when a large group of the senior generation come out and stands up, the news and us, take notice of them and ignore the others. But the TEA Partiers are not all one cultural group; they represent the population of the country.

What is different about TEA Partiers are their beliefs. They are conservative. Some would say they are on the right of conservative. They are mostly Republican, (by 49%) and those that are not are classified as Independent, (43%). The remainder (8%) consider themselves Democrats. (Really they are Democrats, but us liberals sent them over there to spy. We're so clever!).

Now when we say Independent, this does not necessarily mean one type of open minded, clear thinking, issues considering voter. Not that there are not those included in this group. Independent does not mean liberal, left leaning or informed voter. It just means that these people chose not to be affiliated with a major party. In our county there are 23 political parties listed, including the Motorcycle Silly Party, which would be listed as Independent in this survey. So listing yourself as Independent is not an automatic patriotic badge of honor. Independents run the gamut, just like the population of the US, from conservative to liberal. When we say that 43% of TEA Partiers are Independent, this does not automatically give the group the badge of free thinking intellectualism. TEA Parties are conservative and this means that at least 75% of those listed as Independents are conservative independents. The rest claim moderate status, which could mean anything. They just don't feel they lean as far right as the rest. But when you are so far right, moderate can still be pretty far right.

TEA Partiers are not desperately poor. This has to be noted as well. That is not to say that TEA Partiers don't have those with limited income, but only 19% have an income less than $30,000 a year. This puts them above poor, but just in lowest middle class. When you see TEA Partiers marching and meeting you are not seeing those that have missed many meals. Tea Partiers are comfortable in their economic position, comfortable in their social position, and comfortable in their community standing. So, what you may ask, are they protesting about? They aren't poor, hungry, have aids, Black, Latino, immigrants, poor housing, or any of the standard social issues that constantly come banging at our door for attention and help. These guys are middle class Americans that have got the American dream? What could they possibly be complaining about?

Short and simple? Fear and ideology. TEA Partiers do have most if not all of the American dream and they want to keep it. If you had the American dream wouldn't you want to keep it? TEA Partiers are afraid that the current policies of the United States government will jeopardize our country's security and financial future and lead to a deterioration of their personal gains. In short they feel a real sense they could lose what they have. They worked hard for it and want to protect it and who could blame them. These are the children of parents who lived through the Great Depression and World War II. Some of the older ones did live in the Great Depression and fought in World War II. The Great Depression started only 82 years ago and World War II started only 70 years ago, an easy reach age wise for those over 65. These are real moments burned into the memory of this age group, either through their own personal experience, their parents experience or grandparent's experience. They or their families saw or lived through bread and soup lines and watched as wealth was reduced to dust. Status was something you once had and now someone else had it. They saw brothers, uncles and fathers die in faraway lands and the tears that followed and tore families apart.

For those that did not have the advanced age of others they lived through the horrors of Vietnam, gas prices of the seventies and the high interest rates of the early 80's. In short they saw what bad national economic policies can do to a small family in a single town. They worked too hard to get where they were and they were not going to go quietly into that good night. They were afraid and they were fighting back. TEA Partiers wanted to retrench and reset the course and policies of the country to what they considered delivered the American dream they had accomplished. In doing so they embraced the ideology they believed had made the country and wanted it re-imposed, (as if it had ever been imposed) on the

American people and its government. Ideology had made them and a return to that ideology would save them.

What was their ideology? Easily seen in the many web pages of these organizations. They place it often right on the front page. Limited federal government, individual freedoms, personal responsibility, free markets, and returning political power to the states and people are the leading ideologies. Oh and of course it must all be done according to how the Constitution and our forefathers intended it. The Constitution reference is a big ideological issue with the TEA Party and especially returning us to the original intent of the Constitution. But least we not forget, the final issue is taxes, for how could you have the TEA Party without taxes being included. After all, some TEA Party acronyms use T.E.A. to mean Taxed Enough Already.

Not really a bad platform. But then again the Libertarian Party has been expressing the same thing for forty years. The Libertarians were formed in 1971 in Colorado Springs and their platform expressed on their web page mirrors the TEA Party movement. Still it is not a bad platform, limited government, lower taxes, and personal liberty. Who could argue against that? Well, like everything else, it is in the interpretation. If limited taxes means no taxes, and you depend on taxes for food, then this is everything you need to stand against. Interpretation is everything. Plus ideology cannot replace reality and practicality in running a country. Guide it, maybe, but it cannot be used in place of it.

So What is Wrong, if Anything, with TEA Party Ideology?

Well if you are a TEA Party supporter, nothing. You can skip the rest of this chapter and move on. You obviously have all the answers and we liberals, (I am a liberal. I know I mentioned that) and the majority of the country are just a bunch of whiners that don't know how our country is supposed to be run. But to the rest of us it seems you have quite a selective memory about history and our country. I will give TEA Partiers this. They do not sit and pontificate with only personal opinion. They try to get information and teach this information to others. Well done and applause. I would challenge other organizations, even the Libertarians, to do as you do.

But, the information TEA Partiers choose to get seems only to reaffirm the positions they take. Sort of like religion. If you are Muslim you acknowledge Christianity, but know it is the wrong path to God. So you preach, teach and seek information that supports the Muslim position. If you are Christian, you know other religions need converting. As Christians, you also teach, preach and seek information that supports the Christian position. And why wouldn't you? This is what you believe, why would you teach something you don't believe. But this doesn't lead to a clear understanding of metaphysics. It only leads to a clearer understanding of your metaphysics. As a scholar, I know that unless you challenge your assumptions and are willing to change them based on unbiased evidence you will never gain knowledge. In fact you harbor the great disadvantage of destroying that what you seek to protect. TEA Partiers, as well as Democrats and Republicans all suffer this malady. But we will rag on the Democrats and Republicans later; this chapter is about TEA Partiers.

If anything can define TEA Partiers is that they are empiricists. Now, when I say they are empiricists I am probably not using the standard definition brought to you by philosophical scholars. My apologies. Empiricists for those of you not schooled in philosophical debate, according to Merriam-Webster, is someone that believes all knowledge originates in experience. For our definition an empiricist is someone that believes all knowledge originates in what they see or deduce from obvious experience or logic. For example gas prices are high. President Obama won't allow oil drilling in the Gulf of Mexico. Therefore, President Obama is causing high gas prices. Of course one of the main differences between TEA Partiers empiricism and academia is academia make empiricist conclusions after experimentation, TEA Partiers have empiricist conclusions first, support second.

It isn't important to condemn or congratulate this example of empiricism, it is important just to know that TEA Partier empiricism exists. There is a basis for TEA Partier beliefs and ideology. It is not a random set of issues just dedicated to the destruction of liberals and removal of President Obama. We liberals, no matter how we are confused by this empiricism, must get off our high horses and understand that there is logic to the process. TEA Partiers are not all fanatics, just like not all liberals are fanatics. We both have problem children within our groups and we should not judge the group by the actions of a few.

Let's take the personal freedom issue as brought by the TEA Party. TEA Partiers empiricism sees the number of laws being made telling them what to do. Seat belt laws, gun laws, civil rights, and a whole host of other laws are telling them what to do and who they must accept. Therefore the logical deduction is the government is interfering in our lives and violating our personal freedoms. But let's take a closer look at this issue.

Personal, or individual, freedoms are a nebulous rallying cry for the TEA Party. Many quotes are made but they boil down to the point that government is too intrusive in their personal lives and that the people, (now they are speaking for all of us here. Aren't you so glad.), want to just be allowed to govern themselves. Oh, as the Constitution intended. I can't leave that out. My bad. Now if this sounds a lot like the "family values" issue, you are right. Just like "family values", personal freedoms are not really defined, but the TEA Party knows they are being attacked. They believe strongly that the U.S. government is limiting our ability to make our own personal decisions, based on our personal beliefs, more and more each day. But they cannot specifically say where, except maybe in Health Care, but we will take that up later.

On this issue of personal freedoms they have a solid agreement, EXCEPT when it comes to any others definition of personal freedoms, or the ruling that gave the right of privacy to the people of the US. Eighty-two percent of TEA Partiers do not believe that same sex couples should have the right to marry. The large majority of TEA Partiers are pro-life, (as opposed to pro-choice, not pro-abortion as some would have it.), and are against anyone personally choosing to have an abortion. They are against Roe v. Wade because it allows abortions, but do not realize, or ignore, that Roe v. Wade is the Supreme Court ruling that guaranteed the right to privacy in the United States, thus preserving personal freedoms. Basically they are for their defined personal freedoms as long as their defined personal freedoms do not allow someone to do what they are against. Hypocrisy is the usual term.

But now wait, I am declaring the issue of abortion and same sex marriages as a personal freedom issue. To TEA Partiers they are not. They are another issue entirely. So there is no hypocrisy here. Oh, no. Abortion is about murder and same sex marriages are about morals, so they don't count as personal freedom issues as defined by TEA Partiers. Well, now we have to use their terms as to what is moral and whether abortion is murder. Aren't these definitions a personal choice? Well no, according to TEA Partiers, it is obvious and a matter of Truth. Empiricism. Well isn't their definition of Truth a personal choice? No, Truth is Truth, everyone knows what Truth is. Empiricism again. And around and around we go.

Philosophy and Religion are still trying to define Truth after centuries of searching, but TEA Partiers there is no issue. Truth is defined. There is no personal decision as to what is Truth so there is no issue of personal freedoms in this discussion. TEA Partiers are, enviably, secure in their beliefs. There is no need for wavering, so there is no understanding of why it is so difficult to resolve these greater issues. Just do what is right and we will all be better for it. Why can't we just see this?

The TEA Partiers position on taxes, deficits and budgets takes the same familiar turn as their position on personal freedoms. Now the tax issue is something that is confusing to liberals as well as knowing conservatives. The current administration and the one before it reduced taxes. Basically there has been a consistent reduction in taxes for 10 years. Yet TEA Partiers insist our taxes are too high and they have to stop the government from raising them. They also have to rein in the government debt. But they are going to do this by cutting spending on things like, oh I don't know, Health Care reform. (You know the Health Care law that will reduce the deficit by almost a trillion dollars. Yeah. We got to get rid of that deficit monster.) By the way Health Care reform hasn't really set in yet. Not due to go into full blown mode until 2014, just a little detail that gets in the way of the point.

Yes the current deficit, another TEA Party issue with a simple solution. Now the idea that we engaged in two wars a half a world away for more than 10 years and also had a large tax cut at the same time could have nothing to do with the deficit we are running, according to TEA Partiers. The position that even during World War II the United States sold war bonds to pay for the war, because guess what, war is expensive, but we didn't when we entered these wars is also beside the point. The deficit is too large and our taxes are too high and we have to cut government spending and shrink the size of the government that, according to TEA Partiers, is the problem and solution. Period. Problem is most don't know what the tax rate is or how their rates are calculated. Many don't even know how much they pay, although when asked 52% of TEA Partiers thought their taxes were fair. So if tax rates are fair, why do we have to cut them? Oh, I forgot, to reduce the size of the government. Hard to keep up some times.

For a bit of clarification for those that don't know, U. S. taxes are graduated, (That means there are different levels for different amounts of income. You know, income, the money you make and bring home.) and based mainly on two criteria, the amount of money you make and the tax rate for that category. In other words you could have a top tax rate of 35% but you won't have to pay that much unless you make over $357,700 and you only have to pay 35% on the amount you make over $357,700. The money you make up to that amount is another tax rate entirely. So when someone says we have a high tax rate because it hovers around 35%, you have to ask yourself. How rich is that guy that he has to worry about the highest tax rate? .

But back to TEA Partiers positions on taxes, budgets and deficits, here is a quick primer. Now when you have too many bills and not enough income, you have a couple of choices personally. You can file bankruptcy. Not an honorable thing to do and despite advertisements to the contrary it does have consequences in your future. Another option is avoiding eating, but that will only last till dinnertime. A third option is to reduce you debt by not spending as much. But unfortunately this only reduces future debt; it doesn't take care of past debt. The only way to get rid of that debt is to reduce your expenses, like moving in to a less expensive house, or turning in that too expensive car and getting a smaller one. Then you have extra funds to pay down your outstanding debt. But what if these efforts still don't bring in enough funds to pay off your debt? What if you still have more payments each month for debt than you have income? Well you can get a second or third job. In other words you increase your income to pay off the debts.

This is the checkbook economics that most TEA Partiers believe in, and it is not a bad ideal. For a lot of us the discussion is whether we get a job, (more income), before we get rid of the new car, (expense reduction). Now if getting a new job, (or raising taxes), comes before getting rid of the new car, (cutting government expenses) means that I have to pay for your new car instead of you paying for it then getting a new job is a very bad idea. I want you to get rid of the car. Why should I have to pay for your ride? I agree, if it was a simple a transaction as that.

Notice how I slipped in that subtle idea relating getting a new job to raising taxes? Clever aren't I? But that is the point. When it comes to government, raising taxes is one of their only means of getting new revenues to cover expenses they have incurred. They can't go and govern another country on a third shift to generate new revenue. (Efforts in Iraq and Afghanistan aside.) Question is do they really have too many expenses or are they just not getting paid enough? TEA Partiers would automatically reply that they have too many expenses. When you don't have enough money to cover your costs, you have overspent. Therefore you have too many expenses. But once again that is TEA Party empiricism. What if you budgeted properly, had adequate income to meet expenses and put money in the savings, then your income was involuntarily reduced? Like your job left town with the last hurricane. Now what if half of that income was to take care of your very sick child and you no longer have insurance? Did you really have too many expenses? Or did you just have the right amount for what nature had deemed were your costs, but it was involuntarily reduced?

Where we are going with this exercise is government isn't simple checkbook economics, especially a Republic government based on Democratic principles. We cannot use basic TEA Party checkbook budgeting in running a government. Follow along. In 1999 the government had adequate income to pay its bills and meet all expenses. Then the Republican Congress was elected and determined that we had more money coming in to meet expenses than was required and this was true. Congress decided, hey it's your money, we should give it back. Then they did through a large tax break for the U. S. citizens. But then we were attacked and entered into two wars. Question then becomes, did we really have too many expenses and not enough income? We had enough money before, but now when we go to war we don't. Wars cost, not only in lives, but in funds. Those Tomahawk missiles at about one million dollars apiece blow up. They don't get used again. They have to be replaced. So is the deficit a result of too many social programs, too many wars, or just bad budgeting?

Being a liberal, I know what I believe, but we are not talking about liberals yet. We are talking about TEA Partiers. I reiterate that TEA Partiers are educated and, for the most part, well off. The problem with TEA Partiers empiricism is that regardless of the number of wars, social programs or budgeting, the amount of money being spent is too high and so are the taxes. We need to cut spending and not raise taxes. Period. The government has and always had had too much money and it needs to be cut and so do their programs because they interfere too much with personal liberties. The government is ten times bigger than it was in say 1945 and keeps growing each year regardless of whether we have wars or not. Every year, regardless of who we elect the government budget grows so the government is too big and has too much money, simple straightforward TEA Party empiricism. I mean step back a bit. The government budget is in the trillions of dollars. Do we have any idea how much a trillion is? Any government ought to be able to handle all of its obligations if they have a trillion dollars to spend.

But can they? Is the government too big or is it just the right size? Using historical budget records it seems the TEA Party has a point. But really, as my grandfather used to say, the only difference between a 100 and a 1000 is zero and that ain't nothing'. In other words the budget is in the trillions but we could just as well understand it in billions or millions. The amounts are all relative and especially relative to the times they were recorded. We are frequently referring to 1970's money in "today's" terms. This isn't because today's money is worth any more or less than 1970's it is just a different measure. We added the zero's to adjust for inflation of our currency not because as a percentage of our government we are spending more than say in 1985. So is the budget too big are the TEA Partiers right?

In 1990 we had our first trillion dollar budget. Right now the budget is 3.4 trillion. (O.K for all you numbers geeks, yes I know this can be disputed based on a number of factors. But I am using Office of Management and Budget charts EVERY citizen has access to on the Internet. My interpretations and my point. The exact amount is not as important as the concept so pay attention and get off your high horse.) Ahem, we continue. Yep, you heard it right. The budget presented to Congress in 2010 wasn't for 1 trillion dollars, but 3.4 trillion. But what is that relative to? I know I hear you all out there. Back in my day (or "back in the day" to use the current vernacular), government was way cheaper! But was it? And this is the point. Was government cheaper back in the day or are we paying the right amount for the size of the country we have now? The question has to be asked and answered to defend or deny TEA Party positions. So here is my analysis.

To make comparisons we have to look at a standard of measurements. (Sorry but we have to use a little math. Try and keep up, it's a little tough for those of us that haven't been to school in a couple of years. OK, OK, maybe more than a couple.) We can't all be saying different things. The U.S government made it easy. It looks at everything as if we lived constantly in 2005. So no matter what year you actually choose everything monetarily equals the same value as if it was 2005. (Personally, I can think of better years, but I can think of a lot worse years. But to continue.) So using that standard lets create another measure. Pundits and think tank experts like to look at deficits and spending and large numbers that can be debated. Let's look at lower numbers you and I can understand. Let's divide the budget for every year by the number of people living in the United States.

Now a budget is more than a list of things to spend money on. A budget is also the money we get and how we split it up. You know what I mean. Tom and Tracy get $1000 a month in and they spend $980 a month. Tom gets $150 after they pay the rent and food and Tracy gets $200. (She's the girl. She always gets more guys, get used to it.) That complete system, how much they get, how they spend it and how it is split up is a budget. So when some pundit or television personality opens their yaw and says the budget is $3.4 trillion dollars, understand they are speaking about only one portion of the budget, what is to be spent, not what is taken in. That portion, the $3.4 trillion, is the amount we expect to spend in the next year. It is not the part we did or will spend. It is the amount we expect to spend if everything holds together.

Now when I say I want to divide the budget for every year by the number of people living in the United States, what I am really saying is let's divide the expenses expected for each budget by the number of people living in the United States. This puts it down personal to a level we can handle and understand. So in 1941 the first year of the great war we had 132 million people living in the United States and we budgeted expenses, (or expected to spend), $163 billion dollars for the government. If we divide the expected expenses of $163 billion dollars by the number of people, (132 million), the United States government in 1940 expected to spend $1,237 on every citizen in the United States. Cool, let's line up and get ours! (Now remember we have already adjusted for a difference in 1941 and 2011 dollars by using a 2005 dollar standard so these are direct comparisons. No other adjustment needs to be made.)

Well you ask what about now? How does it stack up now? Wait a minute, bucko. You have to know the whole deal to understand. No shortcuts. I will cut it down so you don't have to look at every year, but you need to know a bit more. For instance in 1945 the expenses expected was up to $1 trillion dollars. Yep, in 3 years the government went from spending $163 billion to $1 trillion. The amount being spent on each person in the U. S. went from $1,237 to $7,760. What a gain! Now we really want to get in line and get ours. What was the reason and the difference? Well WWII of course. For those of you that didn't know, time for a trip back to

High School history or just flip on the History Channel, all WWII all the time.

Well, geez, didn't it ever go down? Well yes but not back to $1, 237. It held a steady progression upwards for 60 years, almost always making a large hiccup in the war years. Take 1968, another $1 trillion dollar budget, but it went up to only $4, 972 spent on each person in the U. S, way less than WWII, but still $400 more per person than the year before. Of course we went to the moon, had the space race, and fought in Vietnam.

In George W. Bush years we had the greatest expense per citizen increase in 50 years. We started spending $6,729 in 2001 and his last budget year we spent $8,773 on each citizen in the U. S., a $2,000 increase spent on each citizen in 8 years. The increase was during arguably one of the largest income booms ever in the U. S. but still it is quite significant.

As for now? Well we went from $8,773 in 2008 to $10, 848 in 2010. We are spending another $2,100 per citizen in just two years under the current administration. Impressive, cut the increase time by 75%. Now that is getting it in gear. Quite a feat, but it was caused primarily by the recession, two wars and a large tax cut.

Which is the point again, everything is relative. The original question is can't a government run itself just nicely with $1 trillion to spend or in this case $3.4 trillion? Is the government too big or is it just right? I mean these figures pretty much prove the TEA Partiers point don't they. Their point being there is too much government, too much spending and regardless of the wars and recessions, cost and expenses go up and we need to cut spending and taxes. And I would have to agree it appears to do so, except for the big but.

The big but is, "But what are we spending the money on?" There is a reason why I used spending on each citizen as a measure. The largest part of the Federal budget is not the defense bill, NPR, or welfare. It is Social Security, Medicaid and Medicare, a total of $1.7 trillion dollars. These three mandated programs are 50% of the current budget. So the Federal government, while taking in money through taxes, actually spends a large portion of that money right back on its citizens. Understand in 1941 Social Security was just making its first payouts and was less than 1% of the budget. After the war, the current TEA Partiers, or at least their Dads and Moms, got busy and created the baby boom. Now the chickens have come home to roost and it's time to pay up. So we are spending more on each citizen because we are supposed to. It is our earlier contract with the TEA Partiers and their moms and dads.

If we didn't spend one dollar on the President, Congress, or Supreme Court, not one dollar on defense or any other program. If we didn't spend one dime paying for any government salaries, we would still need an annual budget in the Federal government of $1 trillion dollars just to pay off Social Security. We add Medicare and Medicaid you would need another $700 billion dollars. In other words no matter what, you need a Federal budget of at least $1.7 trillion dollars just to pay the citizens what we owe them to keep healthy and have a secure retirement life. You want to spend less on the Federal budget, take away the Social Security, et al and you suddenly only have a $1.7 trillion dollar budget. Using the absence of Social Security, Medicare and Medicaid to set the standard expenses we are only spending about $5,519 on each citizen in the U.S. Quite a bit less than what they spent on each citizen at the height of WW II and we have two wars plus a recession.

So are we paying the right amount for the government we have now? Uh, maybe, but it definitely is not as simple as TEA Party empiricism. Basically the budget is big, because our country is big. Just look at the difference between the population in 1940, (132 million), and 2010, (308 million). We grew as a country almost 230% in sixty years. We got more roads, cars, technology, and became the largest and only superpower in the world. And this is one of the flaws with TEA Partier ideology. TEA Partiers have no perception of how big we are. Baby, we are big! Number one with a bullet! TEA Partiers only use parochial benchmarks, local landmarks, and personal references to evaluate their positions and our country's size. They deduce what the U.S. needs based on their own experiences. Their view is limited by the television set through which they viewed and do view the world. In many ways they have become the television generation the country feared, relying on thirty or ten second sound bites for their information and not utilizing the extensive information sources available to them.

Are we paying the right amount for the size of the country we have? That is always debatable. But we cannot just assume an empiricism that the government is too big, no matter what, and it is taking too much money regardless of the costs of war and recession. We must understand our costs and revenues before we make blanket statements about how to solve our problems and this is not a TEA Party forte. Our government budget is a lot more complicated than that and affects too many citizens directly. A lot of them are TEA Partiers. Serious thought must be given to this issue, not bumper sticker logic, which seems, to us liberals, a hallmark of TEA Party activity.

OK then. The budget is complicated and not subject to TEA Party empiricism. Still can we and should we cut spending? Are the TEA Partiers wrong on this. You betcha we can cut spending. That deficit has to be reduced and it ain't gonna do it itself. But we should also adjust taxes. Unlike TEA Partiers empiricism, this is not an all or nothing proposition. You gotta do both. Even in the famed WW II, we raised taxes. We knew that wars are expensive and we were no fools. Why anyone thought we could go to war and make money is beyond the pale. And for those that are screaming "Our taxes are too high!"get a load of your Dad's or Grandad's tax rates. (Once again ladies, I know you pay or helped pay taxes, but the period we are talking about is before the feminist movement. So I was not being chauvinist.). In 1941 the high end tax rate was 81% and $5 million. That means that everyone that made anything above $5 million dollars had to pay 81% of the amount above $5 million to the U.S. government. Of course in those days that basically meant Rockefellers and no one else and did we really care? In 1942 and 43 the rate was 88% and $200,000. Now you were getting serious, 88% and dropping the income level to $200,000? You might actually get someone else to pay besides Rockefeller at this rate. Not the President mind you, he only got paid $100,000 a year back then.

But hey it gets worse. In 1944 and 1945 the rate went up to 94% and $200,000. Compare that to the current rates of 35% and $357,700. Let's face it granddad was not only tough; he knew to cough it up and quit complaining. When the country was in trouble he was there in body, mind and paycheck if needed. And for those of you that think I am only bringing out the top brackets, bottom bracket in 1944-1945 was 23% and $2,000 compared to today's 10% and $16,050. I mean even the people on the low end knew to pay up. Not that they didn't complain, but compared to today, no contest.

But don't get me wrong, I didn't say raise the tax rate, I said adjust the taxes. One of the problems with TEA Party empiricism is that any adjustment that will cause more revenue to come in is a tax rate increase. Sorta makes it hard to come to terms with taxes when there is such a broad spectrum of definition. No, I mean adjust, not raise, taxes. We can raise more revenue just by LOWERING the higher income level to $250,000 from $357,700. That means that the difference of $107,700, ($357,700 minus $250,000 equals $107,700) will be taxed an additional 2% or add another $2,154 to be sent to the government per income that makes that much. Doesn't sound like much and if you are making over $250,000 in INCOME you can afford it. (Income, that is the money you have to spend on you and your family after ALL deductions including housing, medical, and personal exemptions. Basically it is the money you have left over after you paid for all your basic needs.) But you multiply that number by 4.6 million, (the approximate number of people with incomes over $250,000 in the U. S.) you get over 9.5 billion dollars. Lower the rate to $150,000, get $7,270 dollars more and add $33 billion dollars to the economy. Add this to $70 billion in cuts and suddenly we are cutting our deficit by $100 billion a year, starts to bring that deficit baby down quick without hurting people of little or no means. And best of all we didn't change the tax RATE, we just changed where we applied it.

Nice I just solved the deficit problem. Well, no, I presented a solution, one I might add has been presented quite often over the last couple of years. But TEA Party empiricism prohibits even discussion of such a fix, let alone consideration. It is one of the problems with TEA Party ideology. Like the Libertarians they so closely follow, they rely on this empiricist ideal that has no basis as a final solution in actual real world applications or problems. We have to realize there are no simple solutions and seriously consider the breadth and complexities of the problems and the number of people that will be affected by the solutions we choose. It is not simple. Just like solving the deficit or finding which part of the budget to cut is not simple. Each choice has a consequence. TEA Partiers do realize their choices affects people, but they do not know who or how and most importantly they do not know how many. Their limited vision of the size of this country assures them that their solutions will have narrow impact on the citizens and no important adverse effects on them. But to their credit they do so with the belief they are helping and working for their country. They are true patriots in that sense.

But no discussion of TEA Party patriotism and ideals can be complete without a discussion of the ideals and beliefs that TEA Partiers ascribe to the United States Constitution. For this portion of their ideology they are fervent. There whole belief structure heretofore considered has no basis without their standing on the Constitution. TEA Partiers believe. But they believe as they interpret the Constitution, not as it is interpreted for them. TEA Partiers are strict interpreters of the Constitution. Hermeneutics professors would have a field day deciphering the meanings TEA Partiers get out of five pages of documents written over 220 years ago. (Hermeneutics. The study of meanings in writings. I had to learn what it means so you get to learn also.)

Now a nice recap of the Constitution is in order. First and foremost it is not Holy writ. Second it is not the Articles of Confederation. Finally it is not the Declaration of Independence. Well, yeah, you say. You would be surprised how many United States citizens do not get the distinction, including many, if not the majority, in the TEA Party. The terms "life, liberty, and the pursuit of happiness" are invoked all the time as rights enshrined in the Constitution, but no, they do not exist there. They exist in the Declaration of Independence. Not in the Constitution, not law. Nope, there are no other laws or amendments written to include them as law. However, the whole quotation is, *We hold these truths to be self-evident, that all men are created equal, that they are endowed by their Creator with certain unalienable Rights, that among these are Life, Liberty, and the pursuit of Happiness.* So it doesn't matter to Americans if these words are in the Constitution, our Creator gave us these rights. They are not subject to human law. They just are. (Note that Thomas Jefferson said Creator, not God. Allows for more than a Christian definition. Also, ladies, once again, I did not write this, women only got the vote in the 20th century, so don't get mad at me because just the men were mentioned.)

But back to the Constitution recap. In actuality there are only seven articles in the Constitution, three of which deal with the organization of the Congress, Executive (read President), and Supreme Court respectively. The final Article deals with the requirements of ratification and cleans up some scriveners errors. The other three Articles talk about how the States will treat each other, how the Constitution can be amended and that the new

Congress will recognize debts of the old Articles of Confederation. Rather simple legalistic stuff really. In actuality it could be the basis of a common contract. It even has the requisite boilerplate. And that's all the Constitution is really, a contract between the states on how they will govern interactions. We look at Washington D.C. and all its marble, shrines and buildings of authority and can't help but think that what created this, (the Constitution), had to be some wondrous divinity inspired Word. But it wasn't. The guys in charge were writing the bylaws for a new organization. They didn't know if it would work and even provided for amendments to it because they were pretty sure they didn't get everything. In fact before the paper was even accepted they had to go back and redo it ten times!

But that is the issue isn't it. The TEA Party wants to return the United States to the way it was designed and written in the Constitution. They believe the Constitution has been usurped and we must return it to the founders view. They even demanded the Constitution be read on the House floor at the beginning of the 2010 – 2012 session to stress the importance. But what the founders, those same people that the TEA Party reveres, really thought about the Constitution went along these lines, "Well I think we're right. Sounds good. Better than the Articles of Confederation at any rate." Actually many of the members of the convention thought so little of the Constitution they wanted to form a new convention and begin again. They asked to do so for two years after the original convention ended!

But, if TEA Partiers want to return to the founders writing of the Constitution, the day it was written. Well we have to get rid of the first ten amendments along with all the others. The Constitution was approved and ratified without them. The Constitution was approved on September 17, 1787 and the necessary votes for ratification were accomplished on July 2, 1788. The Bill of Rights, the first ten amendments to the Constitution were not even presented to the states for ratification until October 1789. These amendments were not approved until December, 1791. The Bill of Rights was not even a part of the Constitution until four years after it was written.

Let's face it the Constitution was written because the Articles of Confederation were a colossal failure. If you want reality, the guys that wrote the Constitution wrote the Articles of Confederation. The Constitution was the second effort; those guys failed the first time around. Doesn't make the document a premise for greatness does it. So why did the Articles fail and why did they write the Constitution? Because, my curious friend, the Articles put the states before the central government. The Constitution put the Federal government before the states. Yep, for all intents and purposes the Constitution does not embrace states rights, it restricts them. The states agreed to it in 1791 and confirmed it in the War of Northern Aggression, so much for TEA Party ideology embracing more state's rights.

Why did the Southern states voluntarily agree to the Constitution if it supported a strong central government? Because they made the Devils bargain to keep slavery for at least another 20 years. I'll tell you. This country has made so many changes based upon the prejudice against the black race over three hundred years; the blacks could make a darn good case for claiming they made the United States what it is today. (For my part, continuing to allow a minority to decide the course of the country because someone doesn't like the color of their skin has gone on too long. Equal rights are here. Blacks are equal. Now let's move on and put this behind us for gosh sakes!)

The whole point of this narrative is that we have to understand what going back to the Constitution the way it was written really means. The Constitution was written by men who knew it had to be amended and wasn't right the day it was written. They specifically put a whole article; out of only seven they used, to set up a means to fix what was wrong with the document. To paraphrase a thought from a group of text book authors, Tea Partiers have to understand that their strongly implied assumption that the Constitution can be entered into the Book of Eternal Certainties as ever abiding Truth is just misleading. Those that wrote the Constitution felt it had many errors and needed revision. They did not believe it as ever abiding Truth and neither should we. In fact going back to the way the Constitution was written removes the ten amendments that embed the rights U. S. citizens hold most sacred. Going back to the way the Constitution was written allows slavery and makes slaves only three fifths of a person. Going back to the way the Constitution was written removes all those changes that our fathers and their fathers created because what was written in the Constitution wasn't working.

Take Amendment 17, a favorite of the TEA Party for repeal. This amendment makes election of Senators a direct popular election and takes the election of Senators away from the state legislators. Why did our great grandfathers do that in 1913? Well because the Senate never knew how many Senators were going to be there in any session. There was so much politicking going on in the state legislatures to appoint Senators that sometimes there would be months if not years before a Senator could get himself elected to the Senate. Senate seats were literally vacant. Laws were passed, taxes raised and lowered, treaties passed or denied, and wars declared and some states and their citizens, a lot of them, were underrepresented and not heard. It was a major flaw in the Constitution and had to be fixed so that every state had an equal voice and the U.S. Senate could do its business. If we went back to the original Constitution we would face and fight the same battles our more learned grandfathers fought and fixed. They would think us fools to break what they had already fixed.

Going back to the way the Constitution was written also endangers many of those rights we find most sacred, but aren't in the Constitution or amendments. Many of the faithful, of which a good number are TEA Partiers, are quick to point out that there is no separation of church and state written into the Constitution. They are correct. But there is also no right to privacy written into the Constitution either. There are many rights and beliefs we, as citizens, take for granted that are not in the Constitution. The right to privacy is something we all expect and demand from our country. With this we expect freedom in our homes and the government not telling us what to do and when to do it. But the right to privacy, and protection from those that violate it, isn't there. However, like the separation of church and state, the right to privacy is written in the rulings handed down by the Supreme Court as it interpreted the Constitution and intent of the authors when it was written. Returning back to the Constitution as it was written also jeopardizes the standing of those precious rights as the rulings of the Supreme Court that made those rights explicit would now be in question.

Too often when asked many citizens look at the Amendments as an addendum to, not a part of the Constitution. This is forever wrong. The Amendments, as intended, are a part of the Constitution as if the founders had written them into the document themselves the day it was drafted. What we have now is the Constitution as it was written over two hundred years ago. Our forefathers knew they had gotten a lot wrong and made provision to make it right. Over time we have done so and honored those men by making the changes. By making the changes we have preserved the Constitution and kept it the way those who wrote it intended. To go back to the original is to dishonor their document and do dishonor to them.

Are TEA Partiers Racist and Other Musings.

Well yeah, they are, but so are Democrats, Republicans, liberals and conservatives. I've been to more than a few black neighborhoods and get not too subtle a vibe. Also when I go to south Florida, and not being able to speak fluent Spanish, I get disgusted racist looks and comments. (Well I think they are racist comments. I don't speak Spanish.) I mean there is racism everywhere. Now if you mean is the TEA Party movement as a whole racist against the black population? Well, no. They have better things to be upset about. They do have a higher racism factor than the general U.S. population, but the organizations themselves are not racist. When surveyed those that strongly support the TEA Party organizations showed a much more racist attitude than the general population by as much as 25%, which gives the strong impression the TEA Partiers are racist. But here is a caveat, not all members of the TEA Party can be classified into the definition of "strongly supporting". The TEA Party organizations are just like any other organization. They have varying degrees of support ranging from "Hell, yes" to "sounds interesting". Now considering the "maybe/maybe not" group is the middle ground, it is usually here you find your greatest organization population. So, as a whole, the TEA Party is not racist against the black population. They have racist leanings because of those "strong support" groups, but to condemn all for the leanings of a few, well is stereotyping, a form of racism dude.

What does this mean for TEA Party policies and ideology? Well, considering those that really support an organization are usually the ones driving the organization, racism is a factor in TEA Party organizations. So this is a problem for the TEA Party if it wishes its policies and agenda to be taken seriously by the general voting population. TEA Party organizations whether they like it or not, have an issue to deal with when it comes to racism. The organizations as a whole are not racist. TEA Party organizations real concern is about the direction the United States is taking, no matter what liberals, like me, think of their ideology. The organizations were not created to destroy Civil Rights or dominate minorities. But ignorance or turning a blind eye to the racist attitudes within the TEA Party movement will bring serious problems to the organizations, if these organizations continue to thrive. It often looks and feels like TEA Partiers are just against President Obama, not his policies or programs, just him and just him because he is black. This fact obscures a lot of the points they are trying to make, and even if I dislike their empiricism their points do need to be heard. But they need to be heard sans racism.

So TEA Parties attract racists. Doesn't this mean they have an organization that nurtures racism, therefore they are racist? (Some of you just don't give up. But good point.) No, they do not nurture racism. But the nature of their positions does attract one group that happens to be racist in large numbers, particularly in the South. Remember the Dixiecrats? If not go back to the beginning and read again. (Shortcuts, always with the shortcuts. Have to read the last chapter first. Why do we bother? Someday I am putting the ending at the beginning and really confusing these people.). Anyway, if you recall the definitions of Dixiecrats, they are by design racist. It is what their platform was built upon and what they believe in. They are also white, often middle class and meet the TEA Party demographics. They are also heavy on state's rights and government intrusions. Without a platform to hang onto, the Dixiecrats banner being extinguished in 1948, and Democrats no longer holding to the Southern Vote, Dixiecrats, in the TEA Party, have found a home for their values. Just like the Democrats after the Civil War, Dixiecrats seem to have joined a group that puts up with their eccentricities because of their similar positions on other topics. (Hey, each marriage has some adjustment problems.)

Now. Now. I didn't say the TEA Party was just another form of Dixiecrats. The geography alone says the TEA Party is not the Dixiecrats in a new uniform. TEA Party and the various incarnations have chapters all over the United States from Main to California. What I said was that the Dixiecrats, for a lack of a place of their own, gravitated and joined the TEA Party movement. The Dixiecrats natural inclinations to be racist to the black population, and their membership in the TEA Party, tilt the group towards a more racist attitude than the U. S. population as a whole.

I hear some of you say I'm splitting hairs. If a large portion of TEA Partiers are racist and they are a strong element of that organization then the TEA Party is racist. I disagree. A large portion of the United States is black, about 13%. We have a mix of other groups and the white population is about 60% of the country. To say we are a black nation because a large portion of our organization is black and strongly supports black issues is on its face just wrong. The same analogy applies to TEA Parties. However, for members of the TEA Party to ignore inherent racism problems is just as wrong as the United States ignoring the black population. It is there, it is a part of us. We must come to terms with it.

Now that we dealt with TEA Party racism, are you done ragging on these fine people? Well, almost. I do want to point out their Yankee can do attitude. One of the problems TEA Partiers have is they just don't understand why it things take so long and why the bureaucrats are always in the way. Why can't we cut the damn red tape! Let's get things done.

What, you ask, is wrong with that attitude? A little more of it if you please. Well, it sounds good but we have to remember a caveat, a rule about rules. Rules or laws are made because someone took advantage of a situation. We went shopping and some grocer used a bad scale to measure the food so he could make more money. So we pass a law that says you have to have accurate scales, a penalty for having inaccurate scales and a bureaucracy to make sure the scales are accurate. We also have to have a bureaucracy to take the bad grocers to court, fine them and then collect the fines. All of this happens because someone wants to make another two cents a pound on bananas without letting us know they are cheating us.

TEA Partiers are empiricists. I know I mentioned that, but I just wanted to note it again. Too many immigrants in town? Have the Sherriff round them up and ship em back to where they came from. Simple. Let's do it and get on to supper. Of course us liberals immediately see problems with this quick fix. Like how do you know this person's an immigrant? Oh, he looks Mexican and picks tomatoes. So that is the criteria? Round up anyone that the Sherriff, or you, think looks Mexican and picks tomatoes and ship em out. Well how about due process? What if this guy has a green card or even is a legal immigrant or what if he was born here and is a U.S. Citizen?

Now we are getting to the problems we have with the Yankee can do attitude of the TEA Party members. Take Representative Steve Womack of the 3rd Congressional District of Arkansas, TEA Party candidate and elected to the House of Representatives for the first time in 2010. Before that he served as Mayor of Rogers, Arkansas. He got elected to that job on a get tough policy on immigration. The city under his tenure ended up in Court for racial profiling. A court settlement ended the policy. Now while that bit of history is interesting it is not the reason for bringing Rep. Womack to the forefront of the TEA Party Yankee can do attitude problem.

We have shown that Rep. Womack just wants to get it done. Bravo! Hurrah for him! But this attitude caused harm to some citizens of the town he was Mayor of wouldn't have ended up in Court. Now he is in the House of Representatives and he wants to make an impact now. Womack wants to end this budget charade and get on with fixing this country. This budget issue was just dragging on so he creates a solution. In his eagerness to resolve this problem Rep. Womack introduces House Resolution 1255, the Government Shutdown Prevention Act. This little bit of lawmaking would have altered the Constitutionally mandated budget process so the President and Senate would have to pass a budget on the House's time table and take away the President's veto power and the Senates power to vote on the United States budget. Now how is that for Yankee can do, let's get it done action? We just sidestep the very Constitutional authorities that the TEA Party fervently supports.

Uh, what? Yes, you read that right. Being empiricists TEA Partiers believe that they were elected to get things done their way, now. Therefore, they make decisions on how to get things done. Even if it means stepping on the very law they swore to defend. Now, obviously the law didn't pass. The President and Senate had to agree to the law and of course they wouldn't. It didn't even make it out of the House. The point is we cannot be governed by empirical TEA Party, Yankee can do attitudes. The TEA Party scored some significant victories in 2010, but they didn't win a majority of the House, Senate or even Republican Caucus in the House. The TEA Party for all its hoopla is still a minority in the government of the United States and State governments. A large majority of the people of the United State do not want them governing them or the country.

The reasons are vast and varied, but for some voters, the reason they don't want TEA Partiers anywhere near the government is they fail to understand or learn why laws were passed and rules made. TEA Partiers are offering nothing new to our government. Good men and women before them have taken the same tasks and offered just as many solutions. The danger of the TEA Partiers is the rash dismissiveness of those gone before and the victorious arrogance many practice working in the government. Take time and read your history, or better yet the law. Every decision over the last two hundred and thirty years was not made by an uniformed, liberal legislator.

There were reasons for the laws that were passed by your fathers, mothers, grandmothers, grandfathers and their forebears. Even with the vested interests laws passed, and the corruption in various shapes and forms, the vast majority of the men and women that serve in the State and Federal Legislatures did and do so because they too are patriots. They care and care deeply about our country and states. TEA Partiers are the newbie's here. Have a little respect. Understand that we are here because someone took advantage of the system and tried to get something for nothing, and our past legislators reacted. The former legislators, liberal and conservative, didn't sit and ignore the problem; they worked, found a solution and then got the votes they needed to pass the solution in both houses and signed by the President. It is called compromise. It is being heard by every citizen's representative, not just those that agree with your opinion. It is the way we do government in the United States. The TEA Parties' revered Constitutional founders understood this. TEA Partiers need to take the time to learn it as well.

As a final thought on TEA Partiers I note I have learned something about them. They are yelling loudly because they think no one is hearing. They are not driven by a racist agenda or refighting the War of Northern Aggression on a new front. They care deeply about this country. They are a real grass roots movement that even the conservatives that court them cannot control. Their votes are dependably conservative so they are much more of a concern to the Republican wing of the power structure. They are also unique in the fact that they are a protest group basically made up of those that are large and in charge of the United States, white, middle income, older Americans. They are not a poor or marginalized constituency seeking favors. They are also patriots.

They are also frustrating in that they seem to want to refight every decision made since the Constitution was written. They are empirical in their thoughts and ideology. Their decisions and rhetoric give credence to the belief they do little research on the history or reasons for prior decisions. While not being racist, they do have racist leanings due to their membership. In other words, they are uniquely Americans. They are a part of us and we need to pay attention. Not because of their fleeting fame, but because they represent a real part of the United States that is working to make America better.

Republicans. Really? Yes, Really.

Abraham Lincoln was not a Republican when he was elected President in 1864. No, really, he ran under and was elected under the National Union Party banner. The National Union Party was formed in 1864 so Democrats, known as War Democrats, which supported Lincoln, could vote for him to be the Presidential nominee. That was the only way Republicans that supported Lincoln could get him the nomination, to get help from Democrats. Now doesn't that make your lips pucker?

The Republicans were severely divided in 1864 since the Civil War was still in doubt and many wanted to nominate another candidate. Many Republicans thought Lincoln was incompetent and couldn't be re-elected. The Republicans nominated John Fremont in a Convention in Cleveland. They took the name the Radical Democracy Party. So really we had two Republican parties in 1864, one with Lincoln as the nominee and one with Fremont as the nominee. Sorta blows the whole myth about Lincoln's sainted stature in the Republican Party don't it?

On top of all that Lincoln was primarily a Whig Party member. He was actually a Whig longer than he was a Republican. Republicans didn't even show up on the membership roles of the United States House of Representatives until 1854. But that year they actually won 46 seats in the House. Zero to 46 House seats in one election is really moving it. So who were these super politicians that garnered so much support so fast?

Well actually they were mostly former Whig Party members. Let's face it. Slavery was a big issue. I commented on the outsized influence blacks have had on the direction and formation of this country before and this is a perfect example. The destruction of the Whig Party and the formation of the Republican Party was a result of the stance, or lack of stance, of the Whig Party on the slavery issue.

The Whig Party was formed to oppose the policies of Andrew Jackson. Its members included Daniel Webster and Henry Clay. The Whig's enjoyed membership across the sectional divides of the country, so it had many Northerners as well as Southerners in its ranks. Whig's Party emphasis was on a modern, market-oriented economy. Basically they supported merchants over agrarians, (Farmers to the rest of you.) Whig's wanted to modernize the interior of the United States and expend money to do it. At that time the interior that the Whig's were referring to were in states such as Illinois, Kentucky, Ohio and Michigan. Lincoln being from Illinois, you can imagine why he supported and was a part of the Whig Party. This platform would especially benefit Illinois.

Whig's elected two presidents and had four serve. Now this would seem weird, but by a quirk of fate the two presidents nominated and elected by Whig's died in office. So their Whig Vice-Presidents took over and served the remainder of the elected official's terms. So the Whigs elected two presidents, but had four serve. Neat, huh?

So we know that Whig's were a strong Party and a National Party and Lincoln was a Whig. But why did the Whig's die and the Republicans become a Party? Well as I said previously, slavery. As we started growing as a country through expansion out west, economy and legislative power were becoming issues. The Southern politicians, in their ever unyielding stance on slavery, were very concerned about whether new states would be slave or free. More than once legislation had been proposed in the Congress that would eliminate slavery in the United States. So if more states came in as Free states than came in as slave states the political shift in power could allow one of these legislative pieces to pass. So a balance was required as far as they were concerned.

Well many Northern Whig leaders were ambivalent about slavery, which allowed Southern Whig leaders comfort within the Whig Party. However, many northern Whig members were against slavery. An unsteady truce ensued for awhile until the Kansas-Nebraska Act of 1854. This allowed self-determination of slavery by the settlers in the territories of Kansas and Nebraska and repealed earlier understandings and compromises on slavery. This spilt the

Whig Party in two. Northern Whigs abandoned the Party and joined the newly formed Republican Party. The Whig Party in the South vanished and the 1856 elections saw no Whig Party members in the House of Representative. From 60 members to zero in one election.

So was the Republican Party just a new Northern Whig Party? Well, no. The Republican Party was already forming before the destruction of the Whig's in 1856. And according to the Republican Party website, the first Republicans, (although they did not call themselves Republicans yet.), met in Ripon, Wisconsin in the early 1850's. The first official Republican meeting took place in Jackson, Michigan in July of 1854. (My family is from Michigan! What the...?) The same year the Kansas-Nebraska Act was passed. (Sounds like a grass roots movement taking advantage of discontent of the people that don't think Congress is listening. Tea Partiers, Republicans, and liberals take note.)

The Republicans got better organized in the next two years and became a national Party. They ran John Fremont for President in 1856 and, although defeated, he received 33% of the vote. (See Lincoln wasn't even the first Republican presidential nominee.) Now the big news out of this election wasn't even Fremont. It was the ascendancy of Republicans to the House of Representatives. This solidified them as a political power in the United States and a legitimate Party. It also solidified them as an anti-slavery, business oriented, Northern Party.

It took the Republicans just one more election cycle to take control of the House of Representatives in 1858, displacing the previous majority Democrats and beginning a decade's long rivalry that spans more than a century. We pretty much know what happens to Republicans at least in the next four years. The Civil War, (Hey, we are talking about the Northern guys now. It can be a Civil War.), erupted and the Republicans pretty much ruled the government for the next four years. But implementation of any Republican policy was put on hold until the resolution of the conflict. The Republicans continued to hold onto the House and the political power until the election of 1874 when Democrats took back control of the House following the Panic of 1873. (Dude Democrats didn't disappear during the Civil War. Democrats were always in the House and Senate. They just couldn't get past the Republican victory image until everything collapsed.)

The election of the Democrats in 1874 marked the end of reconstruction and concentration on issues of the Civil War. It was time for the Republicans to solidify a position of economic recovery and leadership. With the primary issue of slavery gone and reconstruction becoming an issue of the past many were wondering where this two decade old party was going and what it was intending to accomplish. But it had to wait for its chance to define itself. From 1874 until 1894 with just two minor hiccups in 1888 and 1880 the Democratic Party controlled the House. (Remember, guys and gals, we are only using the House as a barometer of political influence as the Senate was still at this point elected by the State legislators not the popular vote.) However, except for Grover Cleveland, from 1885 until 1889, the Republicans did control the Presidency. But this still portends a party not quite sure of its direction. Without having the historical background like the Democratic Party, the Republicans were relying on Whig Party doctrine to guide its fortunes and members. That is until the election of William McKinley in 1896.

The Progressive Era hit the United States at the end of the 1800's and lasted about 20 years. Now the Progressive Era is not my term and research has not shown who really gave that time frame its tagline. But the Progressive Era is what it was and recognized by historical researchers. Now if you recall, the Republican Party formed because it was all about change. They wanted to free the slaves and spend more time building up the interior of the country. So when the Progressive movement came along it was a good match for the Republican Party. So what was the Progressive movement and what did it do you ask?

Well good question, and for you ladies, an excellent question. The Progressive Era in the United States came about because of the large changes taking place in the country. The industrial revolution of the last century moved millions of people from the country to the city. Immigrants were moving into the United States at record paces and a new thought process was sweeping the educated. Philosophers were debating the writings of Karl Marx and working on the underpinnings of positivism, a philosophical theory based on the scientific method. The sciences, rationalism and efficiency were now the watchwords in the economy and culture. In short the United States was becoming in many people's views more "modernized."

What the Progressive movement did was bring about efficiencies in government, including if you can believe it, the idea of having a budget. Progressives pushed city managers, bureaucracies, exposed corruption, created family assistance programs, worked to clean up food and water, created child labor laws, supported public education, and got women the vote. In a lot of ways the Progressive movement sounds like the Democratic movement of today. In fact there is a Progressive Democratic wing of the Democratic Party. But the Progressive movement back then was embraced by the Republicans, particularly Presidents William McKinley and Theodore Roosevelt. In fact the Republicans were able to control the House from 1894 until the elections in 1910 and controlled the Presidency from 1901 until 1913. So progressivism was very good for the Republicans. And yes, ladies, we have the Republicans and the progressive agenda to thank for getting you the vote only fifty-six years after black men won the vote. But the Democratic President Woodrow Wilson gave voice and backing to support that put the Nineteenth Amendment over the top. (Truth be told though, it was all the ladies that got it done. Us guys still don't have a clue. My wife confirms this belief.)

Now the Democrats did control the House from 1910 to 1916, but from 1918 until 1932 Republicans controlled the House and except for the final 3 years of the Wilson presidency, Republicans also controlled the Presidency. As an added bonus the Senate was now elected popularly and the Republicans controlled the Senate from 1918 until 1932. Basically the roaring twenties were the Republican years. Progressivism paid off for Republicans and they embraced it for awhile. More conservative elements in the Republican Party were working to restore prior Republican culture. But still, as long as Progressive presidents such as Theodore Roosevelt and McKinley were in office Republicans Progressivism ruled. During this time Republicans still held onto their business centric backgrounds, but the Republicans were also movers in what many would call "social" or "domestic" issues. The economy was strong and Republican ideals and agendas were paying off. Although with hindsight, it seems much of the Republican agenda of that time reflects current day Democratic agendas.

Then the Party, (pun intended) was over. The great depression hit and blew the Republicans away. The people wanted help and believed that the Republicans had no ideas or platforms on how to deal with a crisis of this magnitude. The wanted a new sheriff and they got one with Franklin Roosevelt and the Democratic Party. The problem when you are a minority party is no one really looks at your ideology and agenda, because, well, it's not gonna be implemented, so who cares. This is what happened to Republicans. After years of being the top dog and pushing an agenda everyone agreed with, suddenly they were second and nobody wanted to hear it. For all intents and purposes the Republicans could have truly changed their platform and belief system during the Roosevelt and Truman years, but few cared and few believed they had. All they believed was the Republican agenda got them in the Depression and they wanted no more of it. Now to be fair, Democrats helped this belief along with their programs and policies, but Republican agenda was dead on arrival for most voters during this time.

In fact Republicans controlled the House only twice during a span of sixty-four years, 1930 until 1994. Those years were 1946 when the country was a little fed up with Truman and 1952 when Eisenhower was elected President. The Republicans ultimately lost the House in the years subsequent to those elections. In the Senate the Republicans did a bit better, controlling the Senate in 1946, 1952 and also controlling it in the years 1980 until 1986. Presidential wise, Republicans were able to get their message and agenda out, faring better there than the legislative branches. Five Republican presidents served a total of 28 years during that sixty-four year Democratic House reign.

So how did they get back in the game? Well the Democrats made some shifts in their policies and the Republicans took advantage. Also Republicans started to redefine themselves and their ideology, especially their economic ideology, and distinguished themselves from Democrats. Now let's not give all the kudos to Republican initiative. Democrats helped a lot, particularly in 1964 and again in 1980. (We'll get to the Democratic issues later. We're gonna beat up on Republicans for awhile. Besides I'm a liberal. I got to have SOME fun.). But the Republican leaders in the Party made sure they were ready when the fall happened and took advantage of it. Bravo Republicans. But if you haven't noticed a pattern here let me enlighten you. Usually a significant change in Parties leading Congress only happens when something bad hits the U.S. voter personally. Wars don't even affect the change in

Congress or Presidency as much as a personal hit on the voter. The personal hit I am referring to is the economy.

All major changes in the way we are governed have a basis in personal economics. Some take hold like the 1929 disaster and some are good for a few years like the 1874 elections. (Ok, you could point out the Civil War was about slavery. But you can make a real case that the war was first about economics. Slaves were property.). This said, the changes the Republicans were ready for was the inflation, recession and depressing, (as opposed to depression), of the 1980's. Let's face it even Nixon and the Vietnam War did not change the Party leading the U.S. Congress. But 21% loan rates, long lines at the gas pumps and personal wealth in jeopardy made Democrats vulnerable and Republicans took advantage. In 1980 they elected Reagan and a Republican Senate. Then the Republican initiated their new economic ideology, the supply-side economics. Many would argue this new economic program saved the United States and there is a good argument for that position. But we will debate that point later. Right now, the Republicans were in charge of the Presidency and Senate, but could not wrest the House from the Democrats. This lasted a whole six years until 1986. Then the Democrats took back the Senate while continuing to hold onto the House. Like, what happened?

Well large deficits and social inequalities in income were some of the reasons, but basically Senators that were elected with Reagan had to run for re-election and lost. But this did not stop our intrepid Republicans. Sensing that they did not have to remain the minority party indefinitely, (A taste of the top can keep you hungry.), the Republicans continued to prepare for their chance once again. And like clockwork, it came. At the end of the Bush presidency, (the first President Bush, not the second, keep up will you?), another recession hit. It helped propel Bill Clinton to the presidency, (Remember the line, "It's the economy, stupid"?) and kept a Democratic Congress. But the economy didn't turn around like it was supposed to and the Democrats introduced a major Health Care Reform bill, (Now this sounds eerily familiar.), Republicans jumped on the chance. In 1994 they took over the House and the Senate for the first time since 1952.

The Republicans kept control of both Houses of Congress this time for a total of twelve years, losing both houses to the Democrats in 2006. Once again, you guessed it; the economy started taking a nosedive. Dual wars didn't help and things only started to get worse. The Republicans rode a wave of bad news and mistakes up until the 2008 elections when the huge recession hit in the middle of the 2008 election cycle. Democrats were able to pin the whole fiasco on the Republicans and hit the trifecta, taking both Houses and the Presidency. Of course, as expected, but not wanted, the economy didn't recover with a single election and the Republicans were able to come back from the devastating defeats in 2008 and regain the House in 2010.

So from the beginnings as a protest movement against the Whig Party, a growth spurt through the War of Northern Aggression, proponents of Progressivism in the early 1900's, loss of national political control through most of the last century and finally a return to power in the late 1990's the Republicans have been a force for change in the U. S. They have embraced the abolition of slavery, women's right to vote, child labor laws, unions, and a plethora of social issues. They have always been and remain a supporter of main street business, one of the single strong threads that continue in their heritage. They have made and remade themselves to adapt to the changes of the economic and political environment. Republicans have a proud and strong history. But are they contributing to the fear and anger that now consume the political discourse? What is their ideology now?

Republican Ideology. Is it Comprehensible?

Ok, I admit I made that last line up. But I am a liberal, you gotta know I was gonna take a shot. But seriously, we all believe we know what Republicans stand for, small government, deregulation of business, lower taxes. But do they really and how did they get where they are now? Was there a beginning?

After looking through articles, books and book abstracts, stopping to read the more serious extracts, I was able to discern a political ideology, beyond the conservative moniker, for Republicans. However, one of the best, although I could not trace its origins, showed up in a Wikipedia article on Republican ideology. While most articles and books related to slogans of the various era's and platforms from the conventions, all well and good mind you, this article stated the philosophical bent of Republican Party beliefs. Clearly stated they were classical liberalism, paleoconservatism, and progressivism.

Now many of you may ask, "Doesn't the Party platforms tell us the ideology of the Party?" Well, no. Now I don't mean to diminish the Party Platforms. These documents spell out the positions the Party has adopted in the party member's own words for anyone to read.   But what are these stated positions foundations? What is the general philosophy of the membership of the party? This is the Party ideology and it determines the course of the Party and how it will affect our government, so it is a much more important point than the propositions of a Party platform. For the Republican Party classical liberalism is their beginning ideology.

Classical liberalism, as stated by Richard Hudelson in his book "Modern Political Theory", was a philosophy committed to the ideal of limited government, liberty of individuals, freedom of religion, freedom of speech, freedom of press, freedom of assembly and free markets. Pretty much sums up Republican stated political beliefs for the last hundred or so years. Yes, liberalism was the basis for Republican ideology. Bet that hurts. Of course it isn't all that simple.

To understand the distinction between ideology and the platform let's go back to the first couple of Party platforms for the Republican Party and hear from the Republican founders themselves. The 1856 platform, (Can't get much earlier than that. That was the first year Republicans ran a presidential candidate.), was all about freeing the slaves and letting Kansas come into the Union a free state. The final two resolutions were about building the Trans-Continental railroad and building canals in the interior. The Republicans were in favor of both. Considering the birthplace of the Republican Party this is to be expected. The voters in the Michigan, Illinois, and Ohio area wanted greater emphasis given to developing the frontier, which at that time was them. They also had an economic interest in freeing the slaves as well as a moral interest. Many Republicans thought having slaves reduced costs needed to produce crops and manufactured goods and believed it gave Southerners an unfair competitive advantage. Not near as saintly, but as always, the Republicans were for main street business.

Things changed a bit after the war. Most notably the platform got longer. The burdens of success I guess. But some interesting things were in the 1868 Party Platform. In the eleventh declaration of principles the Republican platform states that *"Foreign immigration, which in the past, has added so much to the wealth, development of resources, and increase of power to this nation-the asylum of the oppressed of all nations – should be fostered and encouraged by a liberal and just policy."* Now to a liberal like me, sounds a bit at odds with the stated intentions of building walls around our nation as current Republicans wish. Of course there were some harsh things said about Andrew Johnson and an equal measure of great things said about Lincoln. But little was said about developing infrastructure. Most was concerned about paying our debts and rebuilding our national credit.

As you can see these two Republican platforms tell us what the Republicans want and on some measure tell us what they support and why. But they do not tell us the basis of their belief system. The Party platform addresses those issues that are prevalent at the time, at least for the Party, and state the position of the party on those issues. In other words the party states, in general terms, how they think those issues should be handled. Platforms also are frequently used to set the agenda for an election and draw attention to an issue that otherwise might not be prevalent in the upcoming debates. So, Party platforms can serve multiple purposes. But Party platforms are merely a presentment of the issues members feel need to be addressed. They are not a statement of the base ideology of the Party, its founding members or any subsequent members. Just like Dixiecrats and TEA Partiers, there lies a basis of belief for the Republican Party.

Can Party platforms help in analyzing ideology? Well, yes. But only over an extended time frame. We can look to the Party platforms to detect trends or changes in the base sentiments of the Party. Changes in the Party platform may indicate a shift in Party ideology. But to know Party ideology is to know how the Party, when in power, will govern. To govern the Party membership must have a base idea of how government should work. Republicans believe, at least in 1856, in small government, deregulation of business and lower taxes, or the philosophy of classic liberalism. This shouldn't be surprising since classic liberalism drew upon Adam Smith, (He of the "invisible hand" argument.), John Locke and Jean-Baptist Say as well as others, seminal thinkers of economics and the individual. But this classical liberalism was grounded on four assumptions about human nature. Namely that people were: 1.) Egoistic, 2.) Coldly calculating, 3.) Essentially inert, and 4.) Atomistic, (Atomistic means that the sum is no greater than its parts). All essentially logical and straight forward, easily categorized and placed in their proper cubbyhole. (Sounds so regimented and logical. Gives you a warm, fuzzy feeling to know everything has a place don't it?)

It is the belief of classic liberalism that man, (once again ladies, this was 1856 and we are denigrating men here so be patient.) was solely motivated by pain or pleasure. Motivation to work was through either reward or fear of hunger. Of course there was a special exception for the men of higher rank, (you know the ones that wrote the theory and thought the thoughts.), THEY were motivated by ambition. Everyone else, (meaning the working man, essentially everyone, but aristocrats) were only motivated by base requirements. Classical liberalism also believed government was created to protect people from one another; it wasn't there to provide for the general welfare of the people.

Other beliefs of classic liberalism were that poor urban conditions were inevitable and starvation would help limit population growth. (Now there is a nice thought, sanctioned government starvation.) The profit motive would ensure products that people desired were produced at prices people could pay. Also individuals should be free to obtain work from the highest-paying employers. And government only had three functions: protection against foreign invaders, protection from wrongs committed by other citizens, and building and maintaining public works that the private sector could not profitably provide.

Now many of you liberals and not a few of you conservatives are asking "Why is this ideology different from Republican ideology of today? And should it be?" Well, for a lot of conservatives it is not. But clinging to an ideology that was developed in the late 18th century and by many accounts is over 235 years old is to ignore a tremendous amount of information and work that's been done during that time. Much of that later work has totally dispelled the theories by which these works were based. It goes to the point that things change. New knowledge is acquired and cultures change.

When Adam Smith wrote his book *An Inquiry into the Nature and Causes of the Wealth of Nations*, (Yes this is the whole name, not just *The Wealth of Nations* as some undereducated believe is the title.) the United State was not yet a country, aristocrats were still believed to be given by birth the right to rule over peasants, and the King ruled over all by divine right. There was not a democracy in sight. The closest thing we came to a conglomerate was the East India Trading Company. Nothing lasts forever and while we may revere Adam Smith and others for their seminal works it doesn't mean these thoughts were entered into the Book of Everlasting Truths. Smith, by the way, during his life wasn't unopposed in his beliefs. Shocker isn't it? Once again we come upon a position that some hold as absolute, accepted by all men, when in fact, even during its original presentment, it had its detractors.

What then is wrong with the classical liberalism that Republicans first embraced? Well, for one people are not machines able to be pigeonholed into a nice formula. I know we like to think everyone, but us, is predictable. However, we aren't. Statistically we can prove a large population will probably do something, like vote for the wrong guy at election time. But we cannot, with any certainty know what any individual will do at any given moment. So classifying human nature into four sterile categories is not only wrong but highly arrogant. We also know through a lot of research that people are motivated by many things other than great reward or fear of hunger. Sex, security, and power are just three quick examples. (Now the debate rages. What if sex was your great reward? Really? Sex for a tank of gas is a great reward? Get real.)

One of the bigger beliefs in classical liberalism is non-regulated markets. But Adam Smith, the icon of classic liberalism, business, and many Republicans, warned against the nature of businessmen to collude and fix prices. (So what happened to the "invisible hand" argument? As always it comes with caveats. Nothing is fixed or absolute truth dude, especially that made by man. So give it up!). Business wants to make a profit. It wants to reward its owners in cash. Therefore, it is not in the nature of business to compete as much as it is in the nature of business to remove competition. By doing so, business can fix a price as it chooses not as the markets choose. By setting its own price business creates substantial profits. The idea of competition is a theorist's perspective and a necessity of the governed and government. It is not the ideal or practicality of business. As evidence has shown through monopolies, trusts and recent episodes of publically displayed greed, (think Bernie Madoff and Enron) the idea of un-regulated markets as expressed by classic liberalism cannot work. Government regulation on some level must be employed to ensure competition and prevent destructive greed. Adam Smith agreed.

While classical liberalism still has adherents, mostly those adherents are misinformed or under educated as to the problems and limitations of the philosophy. But in 1856 it was a major shift in government philosophy that was dictated by the industrial revolution and the Republicans embraced it. So "Huzzah!" Republicans. I mean they were embracing new thoughts, new ideas. Ideas that encouraged our most cherished freedoms. So, Bravo.

But while a current of classical liberalism continued in the Party, the Republicans ideology did change. A lot of it had to do with wanting to stay in power, but economic and cultural changes were a great influence. By the power of energetic leaders Republicans embraced Progressivism in the early 20th century. Progressivism, as a philosophy, continues to this day but instead of being a part of the Republican ideology it is a major part of the Democratic Party. Now doesn't that make a Republican wince? They actually shared similar views with Democrats. Worse Republicans were a strong influence in this Progressive movement's creation and survival.

Why did the Republicans embrace Progressivism? Well, consider the times, early 1900's. The country is booming. The war is behind us, railroads are being built and connecting the whole country in days instead of months. We are almost, but not quite, a power in the world. We are expanding at a great pace. From 1889 until 1912 the United States adds 10 states to the country. National Parks are being added. Industry is thriving. The United States is moving and many believe it is time to stand up and be taken seriously. So the Progressive movement came along with its hallmark belief in efficiency, eliminating waste, eliminating corruption and environmentalism. The movement got added emphasis in the nation and Republican Party by a primary sponsor of Progressivism, President Roosevelt. (Not Franklin, Theodore.)

Progressivism in a way was antithesis of the current Republican Party. Well at least as some stereotypes describe Republicans. Progressives were all for the concept of positive government. They believed in a government that directed the destiny of the nation at home and abroad. On the other hand, Progressives did not like a strict interpretation of the Constitution, especially those interpretations that would restrict the national government to work against social evils or extend democracy.

Progressives wanted power out of the hands of elected officials and placed into the hands of professional administrators. Progressives and by extension Republicans believed in the public education system and wanted education compulsory. Progressive Republicans wanted regulations of large corporations and believed in trust busting. Worse for some of the current purification legions of the Republican Party, Progressive Republicans supported labor unions, workers compensation, minimum wage, and the eight hour work day. Can you say Democrat about here? Which Party are we really talking about? Yes, we are still talking about Republicans. But don't worry it didn't last.

Certain Republicans did believe in all those Progressive ideas and more. Don't forget they were the Party that gave women the vote. But the base Republican ideology did not abandon classic liberalism. There were a lot of elements in the Republican Party that did not support Progressivism. The strong support by Presidents McKinley and Theodore Roosevelt gave Progressivism its foundation in the Republican Party. Teddy Roosevelt understood that Progressivism did not have the total support of the Party and worked to ensure its adoption after he left presidential office. His support of William Howard Taft was an effort to continue the Republican embrace of Progressivism. However, Taft was not as ardent supporter of Progressivism as Roosevelt and in the 1912 election this ideological conflict within the Party caused a schism. Republicans nominated Taft again over a return of Roosevelt. Roosevelt, in response created his own party, The Progressive Party, (nicknamed the Bull Moose Party), and ran for president again against Taft and Wilson. The party split allowed Wilson a Democrat to take office.

With the defeat of Roosevelt, Progressivism declined in the Republican Party. Those that opposed the radical change of Progressivism moved the Progressive ideology more to the side until it was no longer a major Republican ideology. But Republicans never totally abandoned Progressivism. They adapted some of the Progressive ideology into their ideals. Republicans still believed in the independence of man. (Once again ladies, it was early 1900's. We are still denigrating men here.) Republican ideology believed that man, especially the United States man, a Yankee Doodle Dandy, worked, worked hard, and was responsible for his own circumstances. Republicans believed that when the shackles of big business and the government were removed from a man that man would flourish and create his own fortune. His fortune would then grow and add to the wealth of America. Republicans believed all men were created with this innate drive and it only had to be unfettered. Those men that didn't create their own fortune had no value. This was Progressivism as well as classic liberalism.

Even during the internal divisions over Progressivism, Republicans still believed in the power of main street business.

While efficiency and stemming the tide of corruption required the Progressivism ideals, government regulation was more for those large robber barons that corrupted their cherished system than the local hard working man and his main street business. Government regulation could be tolerated, but only with a very light hand. Individualism, hard work, and innovation were the name of the game for Republicans and in reality the whole country. But, why not? The United States was flourishing. Who wanted a government telling us what to do and how to do it? We beat the Kaiser and the roaring twenties were, well, roaring. Then something that wasn't supposed to happen, happened. The Great Depression hit the United States. Yes we had had financial crisis before, but nothing like this. Suddenly, there were no jobs, and no matter how much you wanted to work no one wanted your labor or your product. Hard work and industry just didn't have the value it once had. People were starving and dying. Those that had blamed the poor for their circumstance were now poor. Republicans though, stuck to their ideology. But the people didn't stick with the Republicans.

Republican ideology for the next sixty years didn't really change. Classical liberalism still prevailed in Republican circles but with modifications. Republicans never really adopted the next generation of liberalism, modern liberalism, (or social liberalism). This liberalist philosophy believed that it was a legitimate role of the government to address social issues such as unemployment and health care. Republicans were of such a minority in the government during these years that consideration of their ideology by the electorate was minimal. It was during this time that Republicans began to gravitate more and more to the conservative big business end of the spectrum. They were the one group that listened to them. The people had effectively abandoned the Republican position of independent hard work as the only means for success. This philosophy hadn't worked for them and it appeared more and more that the only ones benefiting from anyone's hard work were the large businesses.

As business men gained money and influence, they still believed strongly in the Republican philosophies. Many thought, (some by right, most by personal deception) that their personal industry is what created their fortunes. These businessmen, from their perch of prosperity, believed that moving away from modern liberalism back to classical liberalism would engender a stronger

United States and not coincidentally reduce their tax burden and increase profits. However the sting of that failed policy was felt so strongly for the next two generations, it was never adopted again.

Even though the Republican ideology of classical liberalism wasn't governing the nation during this time, its influence hadn't gone totally away. As Republicans gravitated towards big business, they also became more conservative. Having little position in the way of representatives in Congress to move their beliefs and agenda, Republicans, particularly Senator Taft of Ohio, formed a coalition with Southern conservative Democrats. It was through this coalition that the classical liberalism philosophy was still projected onto the national stage and the complete adoption of all social liberalism policies was thwarted. It was also during this time that a renewed call for state's rights, balanced federal budgets, and opposition to labor became a mainstay of Republican ideals. Not surprising considering that the Southern Democrats of the Conservative Coalition were Dixiecrats, (we already talked about them. Go back and reread that chapter if you forgot!), and the businessmen who made up the Party were suffering the sting of large organized labor. These positions became mainstays of Republican ideology during this time.

But Republicans did want to get back in the game. After all you don't create a political party to govern from the back seats forever. (Well, I wouldn't think so, but I'm a liberal, not a member of the Green Party.) So members of the Party began to embrace neoliberalism. Neoliberalism is in fact an extension of the ideals the Republican Party was embracing through the last 60 years. The classical liberalism embraced limited government, freedom of press, freedom of individuals. Its emphasis was on main street businesses and the individual. Neoliberalism is a market-driven ideology where the emphasis is not on main street business but private enterprise. Social policy and economic approaches are developed to maximize private enterprise and shifts risk to the individuals. How is this different from classical liberalism? Primarily the difference is on its approach to letting business guide the government and society. In classical liberalism the emphasis was on freedom of the people, allowing individuals through hard work to achieve greatness, and on removing business from government oversight. In neoliberalism business doesn't remove itself from government, it is government. Government, the actions of the people, and society are defined in the terms of markets and business. There is a whole lot less emphasis on the individual as in classic liberalism and a whole lot more emphasis on business.

To give a better insight to neoliberalism, in the play and movie "Li'l Abner" there is a character called General Bullmoose. This is a very rich industrialist that controls a large corporation. The catch phrase in this movie is "What's good for General Bullmoose is good for the USA." That is an essence of what neoliberalism is about. What is good for business is good for the USA. This adaptation of neoliberalism and its influences led many to worry and wonder about a corporate takeover of the countries of the world. Many movies and books were written about the possibility. Some began to believe the book 1984 was prophetic. Some still do.

But there is obvious reasoning beyond a desire to regain power that caused Republicans to embrace neoliberalism. The shift to more conservative leanings caused by the years in the minority and an embrace of the large business community during that same time period created a natural bond to this ideology. Also, the Keynesian economic philosophy that had driven the nation for over sixty years was beginning to crack. (Here is an update folks. Keynesian economics says we give the money to the masses and they spend it as opposed to supply-side economics where we give money to those that already have it. More later.) Stagflation, long gas lines at the pump, recessions were all beginning to pound at the Keynesian model and we are talking 1970s and 80s not 2006. The fall of communism and the growth of new countries through revolts and decolonization began to really grow the global market. The United States could no longer deal with its economic policies in an isolationist mode. Being the only superpower in the world demanded that every action the United States made had a reaction throughout the world. Business and markets seemed the only common language and neoliberalism seemed to answer that need.

When Republicans adopted neoliberalism they began a road back to power and governing. Ronald Reagan was elected and we lived through six years of Republican control of the U.S. Senate. Republicans finally controlled the House of Representatives and Senate in 1994. But while gaining position and power this adoption of neoliberalism has cemented the Republican Party as the party of business, but not just business, big business. This bonding of Republicans to markets has made them vulnerable to the charge of being out of touch with the common man and woman, materialistic and the Republican Party as nothing more than a tool for business. (As a liberal I have to say, "Well said!" Wait a minute. I said that. Well, "Well done me!"). But unfortunately I don't get off that easily. Enter supply-side economics.

Yes, Republicans embrace neoliberalism and the market based governing structure. But to many, this is foresight and leading the way. As we said Keynesian economics faltered. The world economy came into our bedrooms. (Think the Internet.) To continue to be great and protect ourselves we have to be willing to embrace new economic models, new ways to insure our democracy. The supply-side model pushed by Republicans is considered by many the means by which we can continue to lead in the future and protect all citizens of the United States. In this way the Republicans are very much concerned with common man and women. If this is so, attention must be paid and we must gain an understanding of supply side economics. (Now doesn't this topic sound so boring? Give it a chance. Grab your favorite beverage and settle in to finish reading this part.)

Let's put this theory out where most people, even Republicans, can understand it. (Another jab, I love being the author.) Many, if not all of us, have heard of supply and demand. This is the idea, or theory, that if you need, (or demand) something, like a tank of gas, someone, the oil companies, will provide it for you at a price, (supply). The more gas you demand, the more the price should increase. The less you demand, the more the price will decrease. Now, I can hear all of you economics professors and others out there groaning. Yes, I know there is more to it than that. But we are talking about the basest definition for purposes of illustration so get a life.

When we talk about supply side economics, we are deciding to work with only one part, the supply part, of the supply and demand theory. This is where we get the name supply side and yes there is another theory called demand side. Now that we have stripped away the mystery and reduced it to nothing more than a name let's get on to describing the theory.

Supply side economics basically says that if you create a product you will sell it. Because why would you want 2000 bottle caps in your desk drawer? If you don't sell the product, you will go broke and become a Democrat. (Short Republican joke. Hey I didn't say they were funny.) But supply side also means that once you get paid you will also buy something because money has no value sitting in your mattress. So you will buy other products. In order to make more money to buy even more things you have to supply more products. The more products you supply the more money you have and the more products being bought. Around and around it goes in an ever exponentially expanding circles bringing wealth to all members of the society. In Cincinnati, Ohio there is a radio station with the call letters WEBN, cool station, wicked rock and roll. But they have an advertising gimmick that sort of encapsulates supply side economics. It is a fictional company called Brute Force Cybernetics and its motto is "We create a need, then fill it." Not too far off from the definition of supply side economics.

Now obviously there is a whole lot wrong with this theory, not the least of which you have to have something to use to purchase the product that was supplied. Supply side economics contends everybody has something of value to purchase what is supplied. Not just the base money needed to survive, but real discretionary income. For those of you not used to big words, discretionary income is money you have left over after buying groceries, paying the rent, car payment and the gas bill. Basically the money you have left over after meeting all your needs in order to live. Now to be fair, in supply side theory, products can be purchased with something other than money, (barter comes to mind.). But you still have to have something of value to get the product. If no one has anything of value, like money, to buy the product, well we all go broke. Sorta like what has been happening since 2006.

The second problem with supply side economics is you have to create something that someone wants. Just creating 2000 bottle caps in a world that uses pop tops doesn't mean you are going to sell the bottle caps, regardless of what Brute Force Cybernetics claims. A third point, and not by far the final problem with supply side economics, is some of us have realized that putting money in our mattress really might actually be creating value. At least it is far better than giving it to people who buy bulk mortgage securities.

Now I hear a lot of you saying, "Isn't this the trickledown theory that Reagan started?" Well, yes, yes it is. Good catch. It is also claimed to be Reaganomics after the erstwhile President that introduced this system to the country. But economists will tell us we are mixing up our words and meanings. Trickledown theory is really nothing more than a "rhetorical argument" and should not be used to define supply side economics. Also Reagan introduced supply side economics, he didn't create it. So to smooth hard feelings, avoid argument and further understanding, we'll continue to call it supply-side economics.

Now we can't hit all the things wrong with supply-side economics. This is not an economics text book. Suffice it to say that most learned economists have dismissed the theory. Now I say learned economists for a reason. While the supply-side theory has a basis in economics through learned economists Jean-Baptiste Say and Arthur Laffer, what we now have is a theory presented to President Reagan by a professional journalist, (yes, what we call a news reporter,), Jude Wanniski. Jude Wanniski was self taught in economics and did not have a classical education in economics. In fact after presenting and advocating supply-side economics, Jude Wanniski continued a journalist's profession. (Now here is a solid lesson in the way one man can influence a nation, or a world. Don't ever think you can't.) This does not mean that Jude Wanniski's learning was diminished. But it does cause you pause when those that study economics for a profession, and have studied supply-side economics as presented by Wanniski, say supply-side economics is "crank doctrine." It also causes you pause when, even with this determination, by no less than the Congressional Budget Office, we still have legislators pushing for its acceptance.

If supply-side economics has such a dubious background, why is it still advocated? Well, because despite its troubled birth, it does have solid credentials in Say and Laffer. Also, many claim the theory worked and resolved the economic crisis of 1980, leading to seven years of prosperity. But many, including liberals and conservatives, believe it is still advocated because of self-serving economic and political interests. Upon adoption of neoliberalism by the Republican Party, big business gained a political partner. Lower taxes mean increased profits. One of the foundations of supply-side economics is lower taxes. In fact many people believe, (and others point out those people want to believe) that lower taxes will increase tax revenues for the government. President George W. Bush and Vice-President Dick Cheney believed this even in the face of criticism from their own Chief Economist. The truth is the Laffer theory that supply-side supporters base this premise on, doesn't support this principle. In fact historical evidence doesn't support the theory. Actual evidence of this is the large deficit the country has in spite of 10 years of tax cuts. Republican or Democrats that expresses that reducing taxes raises government revenue do not know what they are talking about and do not understand supply-side economics.

What ever the reasons supply-side economics is still here, its premise is embraced by the Republican ideology and the Republicans acceptance of neoliberalism. Through this embrace of supply-side economics the Republican Party was able to overcome, to an extent, its perceived allegiance to big business and present a persona that embraced main street business and the average citizen. Average Joe and Josephine voter could work with this new concept and Republicans were able to shift voters to their camp during the financial breakdown of Keynesian economics in the 70's. This theory and neoliberalism, to the voters, seemed relevant to a world that increasingly relied on business as a means of communication and understanding, regardless of supply-sides theories larger failings.

But the acceptance by voters of this new ideology and theory was tenuous at best. Republicans were never quite able to resolve the issues where supply-side theory failed. Truthfully, they couldn't and deficits really began to rise. In addition the overbearing influence of big business in the party they molded could not be denied. Neoliberalism itself fostered inequalities in income and, as practiced by United States business, drastically changed the size and income of the middle class.

Neoliberalism is all about the business and businessman. Scant attention is paid to high income businessmen in neoliberalism. In fact these pay inequities are encouraged. This is the reason for the Republicans seemingly insensitivity to astronomically high wages and chasm of pay difference of the leaders of business and ordinary workers. If neoliberalism is working these high wages will be a product of the process. Neoliberalism is business centric and if you are head of a big business and recipient of the largess, you could not find a better ideology to justify your actions.

Neoliberalism, if practiced as preached, also led to greater privatization, lax environmental regulations and attacks on workers Unions. Because of these policies there became a push back from U. S. voters and fractures within the Republican Party as the Republican policies began to attack some cherished institutions and heretofore financial security. Those Republicans that strongly believed in neoliberalism and supply-side economics continued to dominate the party. But paleoconservatives soon began to appear in the Republican Party as well as those that wanted to return to the more classical liberalism that had defined the early Republican Party.

Understand that neoliberalism and supply-side economic theory are major shifts in United States governing policy. As much as these policies returned Republicans to prominence, they also redefined how we work and interact with each other and other countries. The emergence of barons of industry, reminiscent of the early 1900's did not sit well with many Republicans. Especially, since it was the Republican Party that led the charge against these types of industries and individuals. The Keynesian economic model that supported demand side economics was not universally dismissed by Republicans and the general population with the introduction of supply-side economics. The Keynesian model had provided security and prosperity for over sixty years and come to the rescue in one of the darkest times of U.S. history.

Many Republicans and others saw a "funnel effect" happening with the adaption of neoliberalism. ("Funnel effects" for those of you unfamiliar with the concept is the process by where you fill a funnel with too much or too quickly. That which you are pouring into the funnel, clogs, backs up and spills over. In essence preventing the substance you are funneling from passing through the funnel.) In neoliberalism it is expected that those on top will become richer and create more jobs through their prosperity. If you want to get the economy moving you give these men more money and resources and they in turn make jobs an products, (supply-side economics again). But the problem with this process is there are limited amounts of businesses and businessmen, they can only do so much. Pouring more money into these businesses get more and more decreasing returns because they just can't physically create more business. They get maxed out. In other words their funnel gets clogged. The businessmen and businesses get more money, usually tax money or money that would have been tax revenue, but they don't spend to create jobs. They just hoard the new money and job creation becomes stagnant and they become entitled.

This process is diametrically opposed to Keynesian economics where you give the money to the masses. There are far more masses than there are businessmen and businesses. In effect more funnels and a lot less chance for backing up or hoarding of the funds needed to get businesses moving. The Republican base was still mainstream America and they were not universally accepting of large corporations or businessmen calling the shots or directing government. These Republicans were not fond of neoliberalism and the economic aristocracy it was creating. It seemed to be against what they believed were the principles America was founded. While the return to prominence provided by neoliberalism and supply-side economics allowed Republicans to turn a blind eye to what was happening, elements of the Party were beginning to rumble, which could be said to lead to the emergence of the TEA Party.

Where does that leave Republican ideology now, are they patriotic, and is it a contributor to the current vitriolic discourse? Well, the answer to the first question is supply-side economics and neoliberalism still are the dominate force in the Republican Party, if for no other reasons than Ronald Reagan and big business. President Reagan brought back the Republican Party to prominence and revitalized America. He redefined the economic model of the United States and gave Republicans a road map to where they controlled the House, Senate and Presidency for six years. For many Republicans he has the status of a God. If it was good enough for Reagan it is good enough for us. So neoliberalism and supply-side economics are still strong in the base of the Republican Party.

Big business is the other reason neoliberalism is strong. Big business bonded with the Republican Party when no one would. There is no other economic policy that justifies and supports big business and business barons like supply-side economics. As long as big business continues its bonds with the Republican Party and finances its operations, supply-side economics and neoliberalism will be the ideology of the Party.

But the Republican Party is not, as opposed to popular liberalist viewpoints, a group of automatons. They are not all rich white men that live in mansions in the suburbs and employ Democrats to do their laundry so they can taunt them. Many people joined the Republican Party because of the basic beliefs taught to them and passed down from fathers to sons and daughters, (got you in their finally, ladies.). These are the beliefs of classical liberalism and the freedoms of the individual. Republican Party members do ask questions. They do challenge current ideologies and contrary to popular news media belief, moderate Republicans have not left the Party and become irrelevant. Some Republicans are working to return the Party to classical liberalism. Others are working to adopt paleoconservatism. Still others are working to redefine a middle that neither embraces the extremes nor excludes the benefits of competing ideology. Republicans still abide by the precept that a Republican ideology is better than a Democratic one, but they do not totally agree on that ideology. That is the why we see such a disarray in the current Republican Party.

Is this Republican disarray a contributor to the vitriolic discourse surging through the political climate and a reason for this book? Well, yes. Any tearing or reshaping of a major institution involves a lot of yelling, screaming and violence. If the Republican Party members don't think they are going through a conversion, they haven't been paying attention. Serious learned potential leaders of the Republican Party are doing a quick two step every time they meet with Party members to gain support. They must constantly question as to whether this group embraces TEA Party logic, paleoconservatives logic, neoclassical ideology or classical ideology. Trying to straddle all possibilities means that something has to give and it usually is the truth. This has led to the importance of special groups within the party and the rise of fringe leaders with a narrow value set and even more limited knowledge of government and U.S. history.

But does this mean that the Republican agenda is self-serving? Does this mean Republicans do not meet the definition of patriotic in their issues? A resounding, NO. Republicans are very patriotic and very committed to the success of the United States and its people. The adoption and continued support of neoliberalism and supply-side economics was an attempt, and some say successful attempt, to meet global economic needs and reverse Keynesian economic failures. Turmoil within a Party and public adherence to a failed policy does not mean that the Party is self-serving or unpatriotic. The actions of a few in the Party, even if in a leadership position, do not define the whole of the Party.

The intentions of most of those committed to supply-side economics are real. They do believe suspect evidence that gives credence to the validity of the theory. Since its adoption a body of research has been gathered that debates and argues the points of supply-side economics. The mere creation of this body of knowledge, whether it condemns or supports supply-side economics, to many, justifies the theory as legitimate. This has spawned many men of means and intelligence to work on the supply-side theory, as they would any other theory, to correct, amend or adjust the tenets of the theory to prove its validity. But after thirty years, a failure is a failure. No new adherents are clamoring to join this paradigm, which, even in scholarly worlds, is evidence of its failure. This adds to the clamor in the Republican Party and its antagonistic rhetoric without, because Republicans see the failure and want change. But change to what?

Adaptation of Keynesian theory means a return to policies that many Republicans, big business barons as well as main street merchants, strongly oppose. Supply-side economics and neoliberalism create, by their design, a chasm between the rich and the poor and decimate the middle class. These theories create an economic aristocracy and government only rich men can run. Supply-side economics is anathema to Republican sensibilities and beliefs and cannot continue in Republican guise. Republicans will force it out but only when a new direction can be agreed upon.

This is where Republicans have been in ideology and theory for the last ten years, at odds with themselves and those without. Those that have gained power in the Republican Party advocated neoliberalism and supply-side economics in spite of their own economist's advice against supply-side economics. As predicted by Keynesian economics, this adaptation of supply-side economics created a boom that went bust and left us with large deficits. Intelligent Republicans, (Oh, I gotta. No, no, too easy.), know the theory isn't working and knew this could happen. The problem is gaining the power within the Party to drive out those that adhere to failed policies of the past while advocating a change in ideology and theory that can be supported by Republicans as well as the American people. Because of the Republican prominence in the political landscape this internal debate will resound loudly throughout the country and influence the anger and fear that is our political climate. But this is not the only source that breathes fear and exhales anger.

Democrats. Finally!

The Democratic Party is the oldest continuous political party in the United States. Yes, the Party can trace its roots to Thomas Jefferson. Was Thomas Jefferson a Democrat? As opposed to conventional Democratic propaganda, in actuality, no he wasn't a Democrat. He was a founder and member of the Democratic-Republican Party, which is not, technically, the Democratic Party. But don't you Republicans get all excited either. Thomas Jefferson was not a Republican, despite the Democratic-Republican moniker; the Democratic-Republican Party did not become the Republican Party.   Also, as opposed to desired belief, the Democratic-Republican Party did not split in two in some evolutionary theater and become the ancestor of both parties. The Democratic-Republican Party as it evolved became known just as the Democratic Party. (Want to know how Republican's got here read the earlier chapters. Democrats so want to skip ahead!) So in this context the Democrats can claim Thomas Jefferson as well as James Madison as their charter members.

With this lineage as its marker, the Democratic Party can claim its foundations back to 1792, three years after the adoption of the Constitution of the United States, eleven years after the battle of Yorktown and nine years after the formal end to the Revolutionary War. Basically as of this writing the Democratic Party is 219 years old.

Well then who was the Democratic-Republican Party and why did they drop such as good name from their identity?   Actually the Democratic-Republican Party was the second organization that could be said to resemble anything like a political party. The first political party was the Federalist Party.

The Federalists were put together by Alexander Hamilton in order to influence the members of Congress and the people of the United States in passage of Washington's issues and Hamilton's own agenda. Hamilton, as you know, was the first United States Secretary of the Treasury and George Washington's right hand man during the Revolutionary War. The Federalists elected one President, John Adams. George Washington, although not a member, was considered a supporter of the Federalist movement. It was impressive that Hamilton knew early on the importance of support from the electorate to gain passage of legislation that was sympathetic to his causes. But let's not get too far ahead of ourselves, the Federalist Party was not the political party you know today, nor was the Democratic-Republican Party.

First of all President Washington opposed political parties and his position greatly restricted the growth of these animals. Secondly we are not talking a government with 535 members of Congress, 2,000 employees of the Executive branch or even nine Supreme Court Justices. This Congress didn't even have lobbyists, (Oh, for those good ole days!). In fact this Congress met in Congress Hall in Philadelphia instead of the hallowed halls of Washington D.C. There were 15 states, 30 Senators, and only 105 Representatives. Basically you could have a meeting of the whole government in a couple of school classrooms.

The Federalist Party, like the Democratic-Republican Party, reflected this level of political involvement. The Federalist Party was more of a loose confederation of like-minded individuals kept informed by Hamilton on the state of legislation that was important to their position. When necessary the Party did favorable editorials printed, (the members owned the newspapers), and pressured members of Congress towards passing certain legislation. But the Federalists did not solicit donors, have a national headquarters, elect a Chair, delegates, pass out literature, stand on corners waving signs, mail letters or make incessant phone calls. In fact, the Post Office was only about sixteen years old and phones weren't even invented yet.

The Democratic-Republican Party was, initially designed in the same format as the Federalist Party. Since Hamilton was so successful in getting his agenda approved with use of the Federalists, it didn't take Madison and Jefferson too long to decide to fight fire with fire. They formed the Democratic-Republican Party to stand against the policies of the Federalist Party in the same methods employed by Hamilton. Mostly Democratic-Republican members has editorials printed in local newspapers, (they owned newspapers also. Hey, everyone seemed to own newspapers back then.), and tried to influence members of Congress to vote for their legislation and against Federalist legislation. There was delineation in membership in the Parties though; the Federalists had men of industry, merchants and bankers while the Democratic-Republican Party gained support from farmers, planters and the common man. (Sorta reminds you of the divisions of today's major parties. Things change, but remain the same.)

Alexander Hamilton's policies were the main reason and the basis of contention for the founding of the Democratic-Republican Party by Jefferson and Madison. Jefferson was very concerned that Hamilton's policies were monarchist, (meaning that they favored a monarchy, you know, a king or queen) and that the Federalists were too close to Britain, the enemy they just defeated. (History lesson folks, not everyone wanted to leave England and be a new country. There were a lot of English sympathizers know as Tories, during and after the Revolutionary War. This was a VERY tenuous time.) Hamilton and Washington favored the Jay Treaty and closer ties to Britain, where Democrat-Republicans favored honoring the ties with France, even after the French revolution. Jefferson and Democrat-Republicans were for strict interpretation of the Constitution and state's rights and sure that Hamilton's creation of the National Bank was unconstitutional. Basically the arguments were over how we were going to build this nation. It wasn't all peaches and cream after the revolution was won, you know. (Did you know, or are you just nodding your head in agreement?)

Things started heating up in party politics in the election of 1796, the third election of a President of the United States. Washington refused to run for President again, (Hey, you could be President, three, four or five terms back then there were no term limits. So Washington refusing to run was a big deal.), and the first contested election for President took place between John Adams and Thomas Jefferson. So you knew this had to be good. Two of the country's founding fathers, both part of the writing and passage of the Declaration of Independence, going toe to toe to see who was going to build the foundation of this new nation. The ideas that made this country came from their heads! One from Massachusetts and one from Virginia, one a Northerner one a Southerner, one a Federalist and one a Democrat-Republican, this WAS the first Presidential political contest. It was not civilized. It was a fight for power and the direction of the country. The most base of our country's formation and longevity was at stake, and Jefferson lost. Yep, he lost to John Adams, the Federalist and became Vice-President. (Now back then all the elector votes were counted up and the top vote getter, as long as his vote was a majority, got the Presidency. The second most votes got the Vice-Presidency. So Adams was stuck with his nemesis as he tried to govern, talk about tough.)

It became evident that Hamilton's tactics at creating a Federalist Party had carried the day. Hamilton's connections, editorials and efforts pushed Adams over the top by 3 votes over Jefferson. Jefferson, Madison, and the Democratic-Republicans noticed and learned. Boy did they ever learn. The Democratic-Republican Party started inventing campaign strategies that we use to this day and the first campaign strategies of its kind in world history. John J. Beckley became a campaign manager in Pennsylvania, probably the first campaign manager ever. Handmade ballots were created and passed out to voters so they could just drop the votes in the ballot box. Editorial cartoons, slanted editorials, and get out the vote campaigns were created. In 1800, the fourth campaign for President was held again. This was also between Adams and Jefferson. It was even more rancorous, and this time Jefferson won. The Democratic-Republicans had invented modern campaigning.

The next 24 years saw nothing but Democratic-Republicans winning in the House, Senate and Presidency. It was so expected that this group would win it became known as the "Era of Good Feelings" because there was no real political dissent between political parties. The only real dissent was inside the Party itself. The Federalist Party finally died an ignominious death in 1815 when some members of its Party actually discussed succession from the Union. (Yes, Virginia, secessionism wasn't started in the South or in South Carolina. New England states actually began the talk first, so all you Northerners can get off your high horse when talking about the War of Northern Aggression.) The Democratic-Republicans were the only Party left. (Democrats ruled, baby! Take that,

Republicans.)

Everything seemed hunky dory and the U. S. won the second revolutionary war, (War of 1812, honey. Look it up.), when along came an outsider named Andrew Jackson. The Democratic-Republican Party and the Party system began to heat up. As usual the Democratic Party, even if it was known as the Democratic-Republican Party, was its own worst enemy. By 1824 the President and Congress were basically chosen by the caucus of the Democratic-Republican Party. (Now if that wasn't ironic. Jefferson and Madison created the Party to keep republican values and it denigrated into a simple caucus choosing the elected officials. Democracy it was not.) Well now, true patriots were not going to overthrow a king to have it replaced by a committee and in 1824 dissidents in the Democratic-Republican Party splintered the Party. This split placed four candidates up for the position of President of the United States; John Quincy Adams, Andrew Jackson, Henry Clay, and William Crawford.

None of them received enough electoral votes to win the presidency so it was sent to the House of Representatives. Jackson won the popular vote and J. Q. Adams was second, and not even a close second. The top 3 candidates went to the House; Jackson, Adams and Crawford. Henry Clay was not only fourth, but happened to be speaker of the House. Clay hated Jackson, favored Adams and through his support behind Adams. Adams was elected President by the House and Clay was made Secretary of State. Now for all you that don't follow history. This was a scandal, because in the beginning of the country, becoming Secretary of State was the same as becoming President in waiting. Adams and the three Presidents before him had all served as Secretary of State. Needless to say, with the popular vote and the plurality of electoral votes in his column before the decision went to the House, Jackson was infuriated at the House's choice.

The bargain made, or not made, by Clay to be Secretary of State, riled up much of the country. Many people believed that Clay had violated the will of the people for personal gain. It made Jackson the man of the people that had been robbed by the eastern aristocrats. Jackson, never one to take defeat well, resigned from the Senate, (yes, Jackson was a Senator. Actually this was his second time at bat in that body.), and decide to run for President again in

1828. This time, as any good general, Jackson was ready.

Martin Van Buren revitalized the Democratic-Republican Party, renamed it the Democratic Party and re-created a national organization. The first elections of these Democrats to the House occurred in 1826 with the election of 136 seats. The Presidential rematch was in 1828. Jackson against Adams and Jackson kicked butt and took names. The Democratic Party was reborn and so was the Party system, never to die again, unfortunately. With the rebirth of the parties came the rebirth of campaign tactics.

This campaign was notorious for its mudslinging. Jackson's wife was attacked for bigamy, (which she had unknowingly committed). Jackson was attacked for his court martial and execution of deserters, for massacres of Indians and his unique habit of dueling. Adams was accused of giving an American servant girl to the Czar of Russia and using government funds to buy gambling devices for the White House. Both groups played upon the opinions of Thomas Jefferson to advance their campaigns in spite of the fact Jefferson had died on July 4, 1826 and given neither one advantage over the other. Nothing different than we do today, (note to Republicans, Reagan didn't personally anoint any of you. Why not try someone ALIVE?).

Jackson kicked butt again in the election of 1832 beating the man that deprived him of the election in 1824, Henry Clay. Revenge is sweet. But with this election came the National Republican Party, (NO, it was not the current Republican Party. We already went over this.), the Nullifier Party, and the Anti-Masonic Party, (The Masons are blamed for EVERYTHING.) In the House elections of 1834 the National Republicans, which were led by J.Q. Adams and Henry Clay, was dissolved. Adams and Clay had made a new Party called the Whigs and they claimed 75 seats in the House.

The Democratic Party ruled from 1826 until 1840. The Whig Party was the loyal opposition, but Martin Van Buren's handling of the Panic of 1837 allowed them to overtake the Democrats. The Nullifiers and Anti-Masonic were still involved keeping about 10% of the House seats for themselves. Nullifiers died out in 1836 and the Conservatives grabbed a couple of seats in their place. The Anti-Masonic was still giving em heck until 1840. Democrats regained control in the elections of 1842. Democrats lost control again to the Whigs in the election of 1846 and regained control in 1848. As discussed earlier Republicans showed up in the House in 1854 and

Whigs became the 3rd party in Congress. Democrats continued their control from 1848 and lost it for the first time to Republicans in 1858. The Whig Party founded by J.Q. Adams and Henry Clay was dissolved in 1856 and never heard from again.

From Jackson's election in 1828 until 1858, the Democratic Party controlled the government of the United States for 24 of those years including five Presidents that also served 24 years. This included over 20 years of Democratic control of the United States Senate. Between the Democratic-Republican Party and its revitalization into the Democratic Party the Democrats controlled the U.S. government for forty-eight of its first sixty-seven years. The Party saw the creation and dissolution of two major parties that challenged them and many more minority parties that didn't. In effect an argument could be made that the Democratic Party, and its leaders, were the creating force behind the U. S. government. It took a war to dislodge them and it was a doozy.

The War of Northern Aggression, (yes, we are back to that again.), and the issue of slavery, dislodged the Democratic Party from control of the Presidency, House and Senate, but it didn't destroy the Democrats. Understand that the Democratic Party had its birth in the folds of planters, farmers and Southern Merchants. Thomas Jefferson, Author of the Declaration of Independence and James Madison, Father of the Constitution were founders of the party and southern gentlemen and plantation owners. The Democrats took a particularly serious blow when the War began. The War not only split the country it split the Democratic Party. But the Party still served in Congress, even in the War. In fact the War Democrats ensured that Lincoln remained President past 1864.

Now contrary to popular teachings in Junior and Senior High School American History classes, the United States did not divide up into two competing camps on the day South Carolina fired on Fort Sumter, Friday, April 12, 1861. And as opposed to conventional wisdom, the War of Northern Aggression was not all about slavery, (Slavery is big in the War, but it ain't all there is.). Many issues had been fermenting between the rights of the states and the rights of the federal government. The right to succession was still an issue. The right to nullification had not been resolved. (Nullification was a right by sovereign states to ignore or not abide by federal laws they declared unconstitutional.) In other words the vaunted Constitution caused quite a few arguments as well as united the country. Once again, the Constitution was not perfect and was not enshrined in the Book of Eternal Truths. These, and many other issues, that tore at the fabric of our country, were in fact created because of the Constitution and its ambiguity in expressly delineating powers.

It took six years, between 1858 and 1864 to get a final count of the representatives that belonged in Congress. The reasons, besides states from the South not sending representation, were many and bore some legal questions. Some of the questions were; if secessionism was illegal, did this mean the states that claimed to have seceded from the Union still had rights to representation in Congress? After the war, especially since the war's victory proclaimed the illegality of secessionism, how could the Southern states need "redeeming" before having full representation in Congress? If it was acknowledged that all members of the state did not support the ideas of secessionism, shouldn't only those that forced the issue on those that didn't want to secede be punished? Why, should the whole state be punished and could it, by the Constitution, actually be denied representation if it couldn't secede anyway?

These were very real issues and took quite a bit of debate, not only in Congress, but in the individual states as well. More often than not anger, born by the heat of war, decided the results. But these questions were especially important to the Democratic Party. The South was the Democratic Party birthplace, particularly Virginia, home to its founders, Jefferson and Madison. The South was also home to Andrew Jackson, Tennessee's favored son and the first actual President that bore the Party name, Democrat. The secession of the South caused the total number of recognized seats in the House to go from a high of 238 in 1859 to a low of 183 in 1861, a loss of 55 seats. Almost all of the seats were Democratic seats from the Southern states. The Senate suffered just as significant change going from a high of 68 seats to a low of 50 seats and or a loss of 18 representative seats. Once again almost all of the seats were Democratic.

To give a taste of the turmoil during this time, in the Senate 9 elected Senators were expelled by the majority of the Senate for supporting the rebellion, even though they wanted to serve. All of them were Democrats. Eight of the Senators were from southern, (not necessarily Confederate), or western states and 1 was from the

North, (Indiana). Six of those Senators were replaced by Unionist Party members. (Unionist Party was a Republican invention to reduce Democratic Party power and influence. In essence it was an attempt by Republicans to end the Democratic Party. Unionist Party died after reconstruction.) Seven Senate seats that had elected Democrats did not have those Democrats take their seat and were vacant for the duration of the war. These of course were all from southern or western, not necessarily Confederate, states. The same sort of issues prevailed in the House with at least 3 expulsions and five vacant seats, all of them Democratic. These numbers do not include the seats, House and Senate, from the Southern states that formed the Confederacy and hadn't had anyone elected before the secession. These seats were just declared vacant. Almost all of these seats also would have been Democratic.

In 1859 when the Republicans first took control of the House they had a seat advantage of 116 Republicans to 83 Democrats. Prior to that Congress, the Democrats had 133 seats to 90 seats for the Republicans. During the Party realignment in the House due to the war, the Democratic Party lost approximately 46 seats in the House of Representatives. (I say approximate, because well, nobody really knows how elections would turn out if they were held.) . This placed the Democrats at a 102 to 44 disadvantage to the Republicans during the war years of 1861-1863.

But did this mean the Democrats were a secessionist Party? No and No. President Jackson, from Tennessee, a slave owner and plantation owner vehemently denied the right of secession by the states. He is quoted as stating, "The Constitution …forms a government not a league…To say that any State may at pleasure secede from the Union is to say that the United States is not a nation." Once again ladies and gentlemen, this was stated during the times of the Hartford Conventions of 1815 when Massachusetts, Connecticut, Rhode Island, New Hampshire, and Vermont seriously considered the option of secession. Secession wasn't just a Southern thing. It was a real issue as to where the states stood in the scheme of laws and rights under the Constitution. These issues were not, as the debate showed, resolved with the passage of and agreement to the Constitution by the respective states. This debated right of states was one more reason the states went to war against each other. The winner determined the primacy of Constitutional law.

But as a Party, the Democrats suffered through the war years. Even within the Party there were divisions. War Democrats strongly supported the war effort and President Lincoln. Peace Democrats, or Copperheads, wanted a negotiated peace and believed the North was responsible for the War. Peace Democrats also believed Lincoln had become a tyrant and that Republicans were trying to establish equality against the wishes of the people. Surprisingly for most of today's Democrats, this group was centered around Ohio, Indiana and Illinois. Copperheads had an innate distrust for Eastern Democrats.

Democrats did make resurgence in the mid-term elections of 1862, but did not retake the House. Failure of a speedy end to the War, draft laws, loss of habeas corpus, and fears of four million slaves entering the workforce brought Republicans into disfavor. Democrats had 72 seats to Republicans 86. (Yes boys and girls, even in the midst of this terrible war Americans held elections and pressed issues close to them. The North was not blindly united under one banner. There was dissension. The most they agreed on is the war had to end.) However, the following election in 1864, Lincoln's time for re-election, saw Democrats take a huge hit losing 34 seats in the House and Republicans gaining 50. Successes in the South by General Sherman and successes by General Grant burnished Lincoln's credentials and lead to support for Republicans. These successes took the wind out of the Copperhead's support and delegated the Democrats to minority status until 1874 when the Democratic Party took over the House.

Democrats did have a President serve just after the War. Andrew Johnson, the Vice-President of Abraham Lincoln was in fact a southern Democrat. The combination of War Democrats and Republicans that created the National Union Party to nominate and re-elect Lincoln placed Andrew Johnson on the ticket with Lincoln. One of the few, if only times, both parties were represented on the same ticket. While Andrew Johnson was a Democrat, he stayed independent of both parties when he served out Lincoln's term.

Democrats had to wait until the South was "redeemed" during reconstruction to get any real traction in taking back their position of dominance in United States government. Republicans did their best to destroy the Democratic Party during "Redemption", apparently hoping to eventually enjoy the same superiority that Democrats had for sixty years. When destruction didn't happen,

Republicans did their best to make sure that even the redemption of the Southern State would not diminish their power. War Democrats were frequently run and supported by Republicans against regular Democrats. State legislatures of the South were packed with Republicans or Republican leaning legislators as these bodies of government still elected Senators. It wasn't until 1878 that Democrats could get enough state legislatures leaning Democratic to return the Senate to a Democratic majority. That year was the first year since 1858 that the Democrats controlled both the House and the Senate, a span of 20 years. The Republicans still controlled the Presidency during this time.

The next 20 years was a see saw for Democrats and Republicans. The establishment of the Solid South, (keep up now, we talked about this with the Dixiecrats), kept the Democrats competitive and the northern Democrats were making inroads into Republican territory. The addition of new states was adding to the mix and nothing could be certain in elections for some time. With the War over more than 20 years, slavery abolished, youth becoming voters, and the influx of immigrants, the advantage of the War victory for Republicans was diminishing. Economic issues once again prevailed. Constitutional issues were not a priority to most of the electorate. The War had established the Republicans as a major Party that could challenge the Democratic dominance of national politics. But the Democrats, devoid of internal fights over the slavery issue, were regrouping and getting stronger once again.

Bourbon Democrats made their debut in this period around 1876, and for a time changed the look and feel of the Party. Bourbon Democrats were a conservative wing of the Democratic Party that favored classic liberalism, the same as Republicans. Many thought the Bourbon Democrats were but another attempt by Republicans to assimilate or destroy the Democratic Party. But the Bourbon Democrats were successful and became a strong force in the Democratic Party. They favored business interests, banking and railroads, (can we say DINO's, Democrat in name only). They were instrumental in getting Democrat Grover Cleveland elected in 1884 and again in 1892. Many of the Bourbon Democrats were southern conservatives that just couldn't and wouldn't join the Republican Party after the War and Reconstruction. They were known for their adherence to old political standards and platforms, hence the name Bourbon. It referred not only to bourbon whiskey from Kentucky, but the old Bourbon Dynasty in France that was overthrown in the French revolution. Woodrow Wilson was claimed to have been a reformed Bourbon, before he was elected President. The movement finally collapsed with the death of its advocates by World War I.

It was in the time frame between the end of Johnson's term in office and Franklin Roosevelt's term in office, a total of sixty years, that Democrats elected only two candidates to the position of President of the United States, Grover Cleveland and Woodrow Wilson. However, the battle for dominance in the House saw the Democrats take charge in 1890 until 1894. The Senate battle for dominance saw Democrat's in power in1892 before turning once again Republican. Democrats didn't take charge of the Senate again until 1912. The House remained Republican until 1910. The Democratic Party saw a brief resurgence from 1910 until 1918, mostly under the administration of Woodrow Wilson. Democratic majority had more to do with Republican factionalism between conservatives and progressives rather than any accepted Democratic agenda. After passage of the 17th amendment in 1913, the U. S. Senate was directly elected by the voters. The first year of Senate elections by the voters saw a majority of Democrats elected, which gave some hope that the Democratic Party was back with national voters. Democrats continued to control the Senate through these popular elections until 1918.

Conservative regained control of the Republican Party from the Progressives about 1917. The stability allowed Republicans to rule the Senate during the 1920's right up until 1932, the middle of the Great Depression. Republicans took over the House in 1916 and controlled it until 1930, the beginning of the Great Depression. The Great Depression was a key moment for Democrats as well as Republicans. The prior sixty years saw constant turmoil in the Democratic Party. Southern Democrats were flexing their muscle making sure sympathetic candidates were the only ones to get nominated for President by using the two-thirds rule. (Once again, all explained in the Dixiecrats section.) Bourbon Democrats had tried to sway the Democratic Party more towards Republicanism and classic liberalism. Traditional Democrats were pushing for the traditional foundations of the party which had to do more with family farmers and less with mercantile and business. Into this mess came a New York Governor named Franklin Delano Roosevelt.

Franklin Roosevelt believed in ideals of Progressivism. The very ideology the Republican Party had embraced and through internal disputes had abandoned. His cousin was President Theodore Roosevelt. Teddy Roosevelt was the President who had advocated for turning the Republicans into a Progressive movement. Teddy Roosevelt was the Republican antagonist that had formed the Progressive Party in order to run for President of the U. S. against his own Republican Party nominee. Teddy Roosevelt was considered by many to be a hero of Franklin Roosevelt. With the election of Franklin Roosevelt in 1932, Theodore Roosevelt's Progressive ideology finally defeated all of Teddy Roosevelt's detractors. The conservatives took back control of the Republican Party from the Progressive movement supported by Theodore Roosevelt, but Franklin Roosevelt was there to embed it into the Democratic Party and the United States. (So now all you self righteous Progressive Democrats know your ideals have a Republican Party birthright.)

Franklin Delano Roosevelt, or FDR, not only supported Progressivism, he combined this philosophy with new ideas geared towards having the government take an active role in helping the people. This ideology became known as New Deal liberalism. The programs of New Deal liberalism, then the advent of and subsequent victory in World War II, returned the Democratic Party to power and position it hadn't known since prior to 1858. Democrats had found a place with the masses as champions against the greed of big business. This alliance with the masses provided them the votes to ensure another sixty years as the primary party in the United States.

Of course Democrats being Democrats, they began to sow the seeds of their own downfall. Moving towards the masses moved the Party away from conservative values of the South and brought about the Dixiecrat movement. Linden Johnson's advocacy of Civil Rights sealed that adjustment and the Solid South began to crumble as a reliable source for votes. Embracing the Unions saw an increase in Union power, but a backlash from business and main street businessmen. Regulations reined in abuses, but began restricting advances. Republicans began seeing shifts in national elections with the election of Richard Nixon. Jimmy Carter was able to reverse the tide with his election in 1976, but the malaise of the late seventies and early eighties saw the Presidency and the Senate eventually become Republican.

George H. W. Bush followed Ronald Reagan as back to back elected Republican presidents, the first since Calvin Coolidge and Herbert Hoover in the 1920's. Democrats took their first serious blow to their domination in 1994 when the Republicans took over the House and Senate. George H.W. Bush only lost the Presidency when Ross Perot entered the contest and siphoned voters away from the Republican column. Bill Clinton won a plurality of the popular vote, but did not win a majority of the popular vote when he won as a Democrat over George H. W. Bush.

The election of Bill Clinton saw a movement of Democrats to a new ideology in order to meet the needs of a more modern electorate, not sustained by the memories of World War II and the Great Depression. In the effort to reach out to voters formed in the failed policies of Vietnam and the economic troubles of the late 1980's New Democrats were formed. This was a more centrist group of Democrats seeking to unite the right-wing and left-wing social policies, or a third way of social policies. Third Way was actually a policy created and enacted in the 1980's in Australia. Bill Clinton and Barack Obama are identified as being a part of this movement. This policy is still advocated by a number of Democrats in the Party.

The Republicans were able to keep control of the House and Senate for 12 years. A Republican President, George W. Bush, followed Clinton in the White House and for six years the Republicans were the party of position and power in the United States. Democrats retook control of the House and Senate in 2006 and following the failed international and domestic policies of Republican President Bush took control of the House, Senate and Presidency in 2008. Democrats were back in control one more time and kept that control until the elections of 2010 and the advent of the TEA Party movement.

Democrats have been guiding the country for over 200 years. Through various incarnations and policy changes the Party has continued to exist and thrive. It has had virtually 120 years of prominent position and power in times of weakened opposition. It has maintained that position in many years of strong opposition. It is the oldest continuous political party in the United States with a pedigree that encompasses the very founders and foundations of our country. The Democratic Party's influence on the course of history and policy of the United States and its people cannot be disputed. It currently is in a strong position within the Federal Government and has more voters associated with the Party than any other political organization. But are they contributing to the fear and anger that consumes the political discourse?   And what is their ideology now? Where do they want to take the United States?

Democrat Ideology. Honestly, There is a Reason to the Rhyme.

I know. I know. Sometimes you gotta wonder if Democrats even know what they are all about. (Like herding cats, some say.) Well I agree. But after 200 hundred years you pick up quite a few dust bunnies and fragments of ideas. If you liken it to wandering around in your garage and trying to decide what to throw out and what to keep, you get a better idea of how hard it is to define Democratic ideology for the masses. (What is this thing anyhow? Honey, do you know what this red thingy with a handle on the end is? Well, back to Democratic ideology. The garage will have to wait.)

For all the bickering, Democrats like Republicans, have always had a thread of continuity in their ideology. Thomas Jefferson and James Madison created the Democratic-Republican Party to give a voice to the farmers and common men against the businesses and industrialists represented by the Federalists. This voice for the common man has been the ideological foundation of the Party and still continues. But in what form this voice is spoken is the cause for many conflicts and the aggravation within the Democratic Party and without. Just like other observations made, Democrats really have nothing written in the Book of Everlasting Truths either.

When Thomas Jefferson and James Madison, (You know, I never know why Democrats don't give him more polish.), made the Democratic-Republican Party, the country was only sixteen years old. It was only nine years since the Treaty of Paris, Britain's official recognition of our existence, and four years since the Constitution was ratified. What was primarily on these great gentlemen's minds was the avoidance of some entitled gentleman returning them to a monarchial type of government. In their minds the greatest fear came from men of money and position who were used, through customs carried over from the monarchy, to ruling and telling others how to run their lives. Preserving the hard won liberties for the common man was of utmost importance.

Jefferson, Madison, Monroe and others like them had a distinct distrust for Great Britain and monarchies in general. They also were well aware that the task before them was a great experiment. They were aware it could fail. Plus they were loyal to those that had helped in their efforts to overthrow the King. As wealthy and aristocratic as they were, they disliked the deference some men expected due only to their wealth or position. From this basis they created the Democratic-Republican Party and blessed it with ideology.

This ideology, known as Jefferson democracy, insisted upon strict construction of the Constitution. It brooked no quarter with activist interpretations of the document. If changes need be made, there was adequate provision for amendment that all states could debate and agree. Sounds a bit like current Libertarian and Republican ideology and it was. But as enlightened as Jefferson, et al, were they were practical men and dealt with those things in front of them. The ideas of expansionism and governing area's as large as a third of the continent of the northern Americas was theoretical, not reality. So demanding a strict construction was practical in their times. There were only 13 states, 65 representatives in the House and only 26 Senators. It seemed that getting 44 Representative and 18 Senators to send an amendment to the States was an onerous, but highly doable proposition. In their minds the states held the supreme power and should be consulted on any attempt at change to political power in the country.

Which lead to the fact that early Democratic-Republican ideology adhered strongly to states' rights. It also favored a primacy of yeoman farmers and planters over bankers, industrialists, merchants and investors. In other words with everything being equal, the deciding factor in any decision should go to the farmers and planters. Considering his own plantation and the South's reliance on planting this should come as no surprise. Neither

Jefferson, nor Madison was above playing to their advantage. All sounds sort of like current Republican doctrine. (Nothing is new under the sun.)

Other core principals and one of the basic philosophies were the belief in representative democracy, the duty of citizens to aid the state and resist corruption. Jefferson believed Americans had a duty to spread liberty, but shouldn't engage in entangling allegiances. The philosophy believed in national government, but considered it a dangerous necessity and watched closely. Separation of church and state was a big Jeffersonian principle along with ensuring the rights of individuals. Jeffersonian democracy also thought a standing army and navy were dangerous to liberty.

These principals of Jefferson and Madison drove the ideology and doctrine of the Democratic Party until about 1826, basically because in 1826 Jefferson died. This is not to say that there wasn't dissension in the Democratic-Republican Party. The Federalists had died out in 1815 and many were absorbed into the Democratic-Republican Party. Henry Clay and John Quincy Adams were listed as Democratic-Republicans, but with a very Federalist bent. John Quincy Adams was elected as a Democratic-Republican. Truth be told, during this time you couldn't get elected unless you were a Democratic-Republican.

This internal wrangling in the party tore at the basic ideology of the Party, but Jefferson, Madison and Monroe's presidencies during this time ensured that the party held to the basic ideals. However with the election of J.Q. Adams in 1824, the party began to take a new twist. J.Q. Adams supported a stronger federal government. He wanted to create a national university, and many internal improvements in roads, ports and canals, all at the expense of the federal government. This was an ideological shift for the Democratic-Republicans. The problems associated with J. Q. Adams election, his ideological differences, and his lack of political ability doomed his re-election and ushered in Andrew Jackson and Jacksonian democracy.

Now first off we have to give a big "Well done" to Andy Jackson. He was the first president to be elected who resided west of the Allegheny Mountains, (He was from Tennessee. Go big T!), and/or was not from Massachusetts or Virginia. Imagine that, over fifty years of being a country and the big Massachusetts and Virginia were the only states that ever had a citizen become president. Talk about privileged interests dominating a discussion.

Andrew Jackson was a frontiersman, a general, U.S. Senator, a self-taught lawyer, and he dueled. Yes he went out at dawn and fought duels. In other words he was his own man. He fought in the Revolution and believed strongly in the rights of the white male. Ladies, not only did you not vote at this time, but neither did white men that didn't own property. Yes, ladies and gentlemen, for all of you that believed that we the people were electing our representatives and guiding our country from the beginning, up until around the election of Andrew Jackson, only white men with property were guiding our country. So don't wave the "democracy" and "people rule" flag too hard when you insist on returning to our country's "core values", because most of you wouldn't be able to vote at all if we did, especially you ladies. But with the election of Andrew Jackson came a populist movement. Part of the Jacksonian democracy was a belief that voting rights should be extended to all white men. A few years after his last term in office and with a Jacksonian democracy advocate in Martin van Buren in office property rights requirements had been dropped.

Jacksonian democracy also had a strong belief in the United States "Manifest Destiny" to settle, expand and control the country from the Atlantic to the Pacific. Patronage was also introduced into the political system. It was believed by Jackson and his party that the winners get the spoils and was theorized to be good political and governmental practice. Strict construction of the Constitution was also a belief of Jacksonian democracy, but not so much as to protect state's rights from federal encroachment, but federal rights from state's encroachment. Jacksonian democracy also favored a hands off approach to the economy as opposed to the opposition favoring federal government in banking, railroads, and general modernization. As Jackson, like Jefferson was a slave owner and from the South, the slavery issue was avoided, which gave it tacit approval.

However, the biggest shift from Jeffersonian democracy to Jacksonian democracy was not only in the inclusion of a large electorate, but the shift of power from the legislature to the executive branch. This reflected Jackson's demeanor as a general. He wanted the responsibility and he took it. He was used to giving commands and having them followed. He was denounced as a tyrant by both sides of the political spectrum including his opponent in his re-election campaign, Henry Clay, and his former supporter John

Calhoun. Nonetheless his influence on the office of president ushered in greater participation from the electorate, a larger electorate, and a much stronger presidency. This ideology stayed with the Democratic Party until the War of Northern Aggression.

The internal issues of the Democratic Party brought their decline from power more than the political opposition. Jacksonian democracy purposed a policy of avoidance when it came to slavery. The Democratic Party had its birth in the South, its early leaders were slave holders, (Jefferson and Jackson) and its primary power base was in the South. This aversion to meeting the problems associated with slavery head on lead to more and more internal and external squabbles as Jacksonian democracy pushed forward with its belief in manifest destiny. The more land the country annexed the more states and territories that had to be divided into free and slave states. The more states and territories that had to be divided the more the issue of slavery came up in Congress. The Democratic Party would not deal with it and the Whig Party also took little position on the issue. When their leaders didn't respond, the electorate did and created the Republican Party. (Note to current legislators. This could be you.)

The War of Northern Aggression happened and the Democratic Party blew up. There were factions in favor of the war, factions against the war, factions that joined the Confederacy and factions that remained loyal to the North and geography often had little to do with what faction you supported. In no uncertain terms, the advent of the War removed the Democratic Party from the position of power and influence in the United States and ushered in the Republican Party. The Jacksonian ideology that dominated the Democratic Party was up to being challenged and it took thirty years for any semblance of cohesive ideology to take shape. Of course we have our beloved Republican friends to thank for a lot of the problem with reforming and regrouping. They did their share to eliminate the Democratic Party while it was at its weakest.

While the Democratic Party was at this weak point, business interests pushed a move to control the ideology and direction of the Party. Bourbon Democrats, (discussed earlier), pressed a business friendly agenda and ideology. The Bourbon Democrats were for mercantile, banking and railroad interests and opposed to overseas imperialism and expansion. They crusaded against high tariffs and high taxes. They appeared more Republican in their beliefs even then than Democratic, and moved away from the yeoman farmer, planter and average man that Jacksonian and Jeffersonian democracy embraced. They were successful though and kept the Democratic Party viable during these transformative years electing two presidents. But the Democratic Party in the 1890's, despite the success and influence of the Bourbon Democrats was moving towards social liberalism.

Social liberalism is not the classical liberalism of the Republicans. Social liberalism believes that there is a legitimate role of the government in ensuring social justice. Social liberalism believes that the well being of the community is in agreement with the freedom of the individual. In other words if the people are not shackled by ignorance, poverty or disease they will experience and participate in their own freedom. This goes to the times that the ideology was developed.

The late 1890's and early 1900's were a time of immense growth in the country in size, industry and power. This was the time of robber barons, the gilded age, immense wealth and extreme poverty in the United States. Philosophers were studying the human condition and in the United States a lot of the human condition was working in industries using child labor, long hours and inhuman facilities. The owners of these industries were using the ignorance and fear to control their labor force and increase their profits. Loss of health meant loss of job and starvation or death. Wages were barely survival and many wages went to pay high prices at company stores forever indebting the workers to the whims of the company. Slavery may have been eliminated in the War, but its institution was alive and well in the factories of the United States. Social liberalism sought to level that playing field by ensuring education, healthcare and security for line workers, middle class and farmers to allow them to freely exercise their freedoms they earned coming to America.

As Democrats adopted social liberalism they recommitted to giving a voice to the common man in everyday politics. But this didn't mean sections of the party went hand in hand merrily to a new future. Democrats in the South were rebuilding a strong conservative base that would last for over a hundred years and challenge Northern Democrats on many issues. The southern conservatives did not wholly embrace social liberalism instead they still believed in State's rights and in separation of the races, (See the Dixiecrat section, folks.) Much of this time was spent in only one unifying goal and that was unseating the Republican Party. Actual Party ideology fluctuated as to whom was in power at the time. It mattered little to the country as Republican ideology was dominant and in control. The country was booming and people were getting rich. Nobody really wanted a change anyhow.

But the Great Depression required a Democratic ideology and they received one with Franklin Delano Roosevelt. The Democratic Party embraced Roosevelt's New Dealism. New Dealism was an ideology that radically transformed the role of government. It embedded a large part of Teddy Roosevelt Progressivism, part social liberalism, and the concept of government regulation in business, labor and farming. Government was considered the great equalizer, ensuring competition, protecting interest groups and labor. It was not a government content to let business alone. New Dealism engaged in the direction and future of the country and its economy. The introduction of Social Security was created under New Dealism and Keynesian economics was embraced as an economic theory. (Keynesian economics kids, says give money to the masses instead of the rich. The economy will grow larger and faster. Hey it worked for sixty years.) The sheer popularity of Roosevelt, his four terms in office and his success in World War II ensured that New Dealism would be the ideology of the Democratic Party for well into the seventies.

Democratic ideology took a turn in the 1960's, but not under John Kennedy. (I can hear a bunch of liberals racking me over the coals for that remark. Heresy, they say!) Actually it was under Lyndon Johnson. When you get through trashing Johnson in every conspiracy theory regarding Kennedy, Vietnam and Cambodia, you will find he had a great influence on Democratic ideology and the United States. Johnson created and got passed a social program and ideology known as the "Great Society". In scope it could have matched Roosevelt's New Dealism.

Now this was a big deal in a lot of ways. Johnson was a Southern Democrat. I mean real Southern. Tall man from a tall state called Texas. For him to champion the elimination of racism, well, was huge. It was putting a target on his back in his home state as well as the whole South. A white Southern politician, a former Southern Senator of the Solid South, did not just turn his back on the Southern positions. But he did. The Great Society he created worked to eliminate poverty. It passed four Civil Rights acts that forbade discrimination and segregation. It also provided federal aid for public schools. It created Medicare and Medicare. It a word it was extensive. This program established the Democratic Party beyond the position of protector but avid activism in improving social interactions. But this program also fractured the Democratic Party and changed its makeup forever.

The Solid South no longer felt a need to remain tied to the Democratic Party. The embrace of integration by the Democratic Party that led to the Dixiecrat challenge in 1948 and the passage of the Civil Rights Acts alienated Southern Democrats. Looking for a friend they found one in Richard Nixon. He and the Republican Party embraced the policies and issues of the Southern Democrats and rode them to an election victory in 1968. The Democratic Party ideology stayed, but there influence and power in the South left and became Republican. (It was something a good Confederate thought they would never see. Embracing the enemy.) Democratic prominence and their ideology also took a hit 12 years later in 1970 when Ronald Reagan gained office.

The financial malaise of the late 1970's early 1980's allowed the Republicans to create a crack in the Democratic domination of the government. The population, tired of too many social programs, allowed the Republicans to scale back some Democratic programs such as welfare. The Democrats, rebuked in their attempts to take back the Senate until 1984 and the Presidency until 1992 kept their Great Society ideology, but factions were working to redefine the ideology of the Party.

Bill Clinton's election in 1992 began the remaking of the Democratic Party ideology again. In 1994 the Republican took over the Senate and the House in a repudiation of Democratic ideology. The South was voting almost solidly Republican by this time and the many of the social programs initiated under Democratic control were under attack. The inability to make retake the House and/or Senate in 1996 and the election of a Republican George Bush in 2000 with a Republican House and Senate forced the Democrats to re-evaluate their internal ideology. Clinton had moved to embrace the "Third Way" a centrist type of government that tried to reconcile right-wing and left-wing politics. His influence moved the party towards this ideology, but subsequent loses, especially in 2004, retarded the growth of acceptance of "Third Way" ideology in the Party. Social progressivism became more dominate in this decade with more

Democrats embracing social freedoms, balanced budgets and a free enterprise system tempered but not controlled by government intervention. Neither centrist ideology nor social progressivism has captured the ideology of the Party. Currently the dominate ideology of the Party depends on your location in the country. Progressives, liberals and centrists are all competing for ideological dominance. It remains to be seen which leads this grand old Party in the future. This recession and success, or lack of success, at resolving the problem will go a long way to determining which course the Party takes next.

Does this mean that the Democratic Party is contributing to this unholy mess of rhetoric and anger gripping the politics of this country? Well, not as much as I would like. The Democratic Party took it pretty much on the chin in 2000, 2002, and 2004. The knockout for a lot of them was the 2004 election. I mean if you couldn't beat George Bush who the heck could you beat? The yelling and screaming of the Democratic Party pretty much wore itself out in those years. The drum beat of Democratic victories in 2008 weren't as much the success of Democratic Party ideology as large mistakes by the Republicans and their ideology. Let's face it 2008 was another major economic shift. Parties out of power have been shown to come into power in economic shifts. (Or haven't you been paying attention. What am I writing this for? Wake up, dude!)

This doesn't mean Democrats aren't contributing to the noise, they are, but much of their internal bickering happened seven years ago when no one but Democrats were listening. They are not currently facing the same internal issues that Republicans are working out. So the Democratic contribution is more muted. But the development of their future ideology is at stake and divergent Democratic positions on those issues are feeding the arguments taking place in the country right now. The results of those arguments will lead the Party and possibly the nation so attention must be paid.

Changing Paradigms. What is a Paradigm and Why is It Changing Now?

With all apologies to Thomas Kuhn, (He is the guy that wrote *The Structure of Scientific Revolutions* and presented paradigms as an entity within scientific disciplines. Sorta the guy that started this perception of groups always doing things the same way because it is the norm stuff.), a paradigm for our purposes is a group of adherents to embedded ritual, oral traditions, and a basic school of political thought. In this respect it is a societal entity. Those within a paradigm do what they do and act as they do because they adhere to the rules and ideals of the group. They do this because of their learned belief that this entity is the correct entity. They follow these rituals and rules to assure the survival of the entity and their beliefs. In other words it is the accepted way of doing things, because it has always been done that way and it should always work, if done correctly. (At least as far as they know.)

Under this definition the Democratic Party is a paradigm. So is the Republican Party. Each has rituals for selection of leaders, representatives and members of their parties. Many of these rituals are embedded in state statute as well as prescribed by-laws and charters. Each has a basic school of political thought. Throughout history Democrats have strived to provide the common man with representation in government. Republicans have strived to allow Main Street business a voice in the same government. TEA Partiers have an internal shared political belief, but their school of thought and voting record suggest a Republican paradigm. The same applies to Dixiecrats and the Religious Right. Progressives have a basic school of political thought with Democrats and a similar voting record. This suggests a Democratic paradigm.

Could Progressives, TEA Partiers and Dixiecrats be paradigms? Maybe, but not yet. They continue to work within the prescribed parameters, (Okay, the same sandbox. Gotta quit talking all intellectual all the time.), of the respective parties to which they associate. Each of these groups takes on the ideas, rituals and oral traditions of those groups and works to gain influence in each respective Party. They work to change the organization to their way of thinking, not set up their own paradigm. Which brings us to the title, and thoughts, of this chapter.

In the Democratic and Republican Parties there are conflicts between groups. Not everyone is an automaton in the Republican Party and agrees with all the values of those in charge. In the same way the Democrats have internal clashes between those that are far left, the Progressives, the Yellow Dog Democrats and the supposed moderates. Each wants to control the direction of the Party and influence potential legislation. But, there is the overriding paradigm that controls each Party. These independent groups butt heads with this paradigm continuously in the chance of changing it in their favor. They do this because paradigms are not cast in granite and written in the Book of Everlasting Truths. Depending on extended success, or lack thereof, paradigms guide the Party, and its political ideology, or are cast out.

A strong example of this occurred in the last century under Franklin Roosevelt. Roosevelt initiated New Dealism. His personality, the success of the Party and the success of the country defined the Democratic Party and its principles for over forty years. Its dominance has continued to help and haunt the Party as it has changed and tried other paradigms including Bill Clinton's Third Way. In the same respect the lack of success and the perceived lack of response to the Great Depression regulated the Republican Party to reduced political status for the same forty years. Efforts to redefine the Party paradigm and re-establish its prominence put the Republicans on pace to adopt the values of Southern Democrats and supply-side economics. Both parties gained adherents and lost adherents as the party's paradigms took hold and strengthened. Factions in each Party continue to challenge the paradigms of each Party and remake the paradigms in their image. But the paradigms remained.

To understand the current paradigms, or any paradigm, you have to understand the backgrounds and influences of the people in them. What caused them to accept this paradigm? What influences in their learning and environment shaped their acceptance and their continued support of this paradigm? After all paradigms are nothing without the people who employ them and adhere to their rituals and norms. You also have to understand the primary influences within political parties, because these influences are the guardians and teachers of the paradigm.

Generally the dominate force, and primary influences, in political parties are the elders. Elders are the people who have been in the party for a number of years and are experts in the various rituals and oral traditions. They are keepers of the history of the party much as the elders of tribe are the keepers of that tribe's history. By virtue of their age and position, the elders are often the most powerful and affluent of the party. They, in essence, keep the party and party members in line by position, power and money. Of necessity, those that have achieved high political position, such as President of the United States, are dominate in the parties, but not necessarily elders. Often, those in high political position are, in fact, not as powerful within the party as the elders, unless they are elders themselves by virtue of their history with the party.

With this understanding the elders are well, usually elderly, and in the case of the Democratic and Republican Parties this is the case. The first set of baby boomers, or first boomers, run these parties now and to understand their paradigms one has to understand the era in which they grew up. This group of baby boomers became aware about 1955 or when the first batch of them reached 10 years old. This group's formative years, the ages of 10 to 30 years old, when they develop attitudes, principles and political leanings were 1955 through 1975. The majority of this group grew up, for the most part, in a country brimming with prosperity. The era between 1945 and 1975 was know as the "Golden Age" since a high number of countries experienced high levels of prosperity. It was also when these baby boomers went from kids to young adults. It was a time when the United States took its place as a world leader and superpower. This portion of the baby boomer generation had never known a time when the United States wasn't a superpower and major player in the world. There were big fast cars, sock hops, dances at the gym, and two week vacations. Mom was in the kitchen and dad was the breadwinner. In other words, life for these children was the American Dream.

There were great influences in the first boomers development, forces that had never before been present and some others that were omnipresent. Their fathers were members of the self-proclaimed "Greatest Generation." They had won a World War after being sucker punched in the gut in Hawaii. They had defeated the Great Depression and had heroes that were larger than life in Roosevelt, Eisenhower, and MacArthur. That generation had created the atom bomb and discovered the theory of relativity. In short the generation that created the first boomers was a hard act to follow and the pressure to be 'like the old man" was and is intense.

But first boomers weren't born in a void. First boomers often had older siblings, or at the least older friends and neighbors. These were the tweeners, born during the time 10 years before the War and through its duration. This group of big brothers was born in the Depression and knew privation, but were the immediate beneficiaries of the prosperity and success of the post war years. They often witnessed their fathers march to war or their mother's tears. They cheered and felt the great joy of victory in VE Day and VJ Day, but didn't have the chance to contribute to its success. Korea, the forgotten war, was their first war, the Cold War the second. Often overshadowed by their fathers War, but never outdone. This was a group that created high standards and demanded the same out of their siblings in order to measure up. Reluctant to leave the stage for fear of leaving something undone, they continue even now to exert their influence, running for office and working for causes even in to their late seventies. Having known poverty and prosperity, this group pressures first boomers to protect the lifestyle, and paradigm, that they know was so dearly achieved.

Religion was another heavy influence on the first boomer generation, either by adherence or rebellion. White Anglo Saxon Protestant, (WASP's, remember that term!), Christian religion was a mainstay of the former generation, often in conflict with Catholics and Jews, but always the dominate religion. Religion and Church was accepted as what you did. It was a part of your life and existence. There was no questioning of Religion, God, or the value of the Church. "In God We Trust" was placed on money and references to God placed in the Pledge of Allegiance with general agreement that it was just and right. Merry Christmas was a general greeting accepted by all, either by agreement or acquiescence, and no one complained about the religious bigotry it engendered. Nativities filled the town square and prayers were said before public meetings and football games. The overbearing, overarching, influence of WASP religion was a major factor in their paradigm's development.

Another great influence was Network television. Network television had its debut in 1951 and the baby boomers became the first television kids. These kids grew up on Howdy Doody and Saturday morning cartoons. The TV characters wore high heels and pearls in the kitchens and Dad never seemed to have to go to work. When they got older "the most trusted man in America", Walter Cronkite was their newsman. Television sold cigarettes, monster Detroit automobiles, and apple pie. It also brought the world, in a highly biased view, to the common living room.

But there were also unique problems with television. Unlike their parents who had grown up with radio and books, the baby boomers primary source of information became television. While their parents held television with the regard of a novelty and entertainment, this generation grew up believing what they saw on television was a true authority. They believed what they saw was true because, after all, they just saw it. Television had an inordinate amount of influence on this generation as it often was the primary babysitter in the house. This generation viewed and understood the world through the size of the television screen. Their world, in a time of increasing global awareness, had shrunk. For many in this generation, how we behaved, who we accepted and the societal issues of the times were all brought into focus and awareness through television. And television, as an entertainment medium, was presenting biased programming in order to gain acceptance within households so their programs would be watched. Belief in television and its entertainment characters and personalities is a learned lesson many in this generation adhere to today and gives credence to the power of Fox News, CNN and MSNBC.

Civil rights, women's rights, the space race, nuclear power, and the Viet Nam War all played heavily on the first boomers. From 1960 until 1972, in a span of 12 years we lost a president, his brother, a major civil rights leader and went to the moon. During this time we fought each other in the streets and lost four students to the National Guard as they protested being sent to die in a useless war. In the same 12 years, the first boomers wore flowers in their hair and posed naked on Broadway stage. They rocked to a superstar in Jesus Christ and railed against and hailed 'Black Power' in Mexico City. They burned their bras, loved freely, danced at Woodstock, and reviled Nixon. And as opposed to popular belief, not everyone was a flower child, smoked marijuana and took LSD in Haight Ashbury. (True, many of that generation can't actually confirm this. The whole period is sorta a blur to them.)

A lot of the tension of the times was intergenerational, first boomers against first boomers, as values were weighed and measured and many found wanting. Many first boomers insisted upon adhering to the values their fathers instilled, (or brow beat), into them. Other boomers rebelled at the intemperate requirements to behave properly because their elders 'knew better'. In either case, there was no universal agreement on the first boomers beliefs, or of the beliefs of the brothers and sisters that followed and were also part of the greater baby boomer generation.

The culmination of these influences converged and developed the personalities and people that defend the current political party paradigms. These influences, through the people, have become part of the paradigms. These molded people defend and attempt to pass down the basic rules, oral traditions, rituals and knowledge that are required to continue the paradigm. If they are successful like those before them the paradigm will continue unabated, like New Dealism did for forty years. Experiments can be tried, like the Great Society and Civil Rights were in the sixties, but these are additions to not changes of the basic paradigm. The basic values will not be challenged. As long as the system works the paradigm continues.

However, those that the first boomers are trying to instill with the accepted paradigm have learned other lessons and grown up in a different climate. The second boomers, those born roughly between 1955 and 1961, came of age about 1965. They grew up watching their older brothers and sisters protest against the Vietnam War, take drugs, smoke marijuana, fight each other, and question authority. They saw Congress continue to send their brothers to die in a useless war while reaping the bounty of that action. They saw the first U.S. President resign in disgrace and endured the great social experiment of busing for desegregation. Civil Rights was no longer a concept it was the guy or gal seated next to you in class.

They came to know the other races and segregation was an issue for someone else.

The second boomers learned to question faith and demand equality for all religions. Staying home on Sunday morning to rest became the accepted practice. Religion, if there was one, did not have to be practiced in a Church on a set and sainted day. They saw their mothers burn their bras and demand fairness in hiring. Daycare became a noun and many found themselves watched over by strangers as their mothers expressed the new found freedoms. Cell phones emerged in this generation as well as 8 track tapes, cassette players and the beginning of cable television. They saw the last landing on the moon in color and witnessed Space Lab and the birth of the shuttle program. Television was not a novelty and often was something mom and dad watched so they could sing songs with Lawrence Welk. When they watched television it was for entertainment, not news, and they had learned to recognize the difference. This generation finished tearing down the barriers their older brothers and sisters had breached. And like the middle child, they were not going to be told by anyone, especially their older brothers and sisters, how to behave or act.

This is the group the first boomers want and need to take the reins of the political system and continue the paradigm. But the rituals, oral traditions and political thought have little meaning to them. They have lived another life and the first boomers are finding it hard to instill in this group the need for the continuance of this paradigm. This conflict would be enough to shake any paradigm, but the changing of the guard in earlier generations, happened and the paradigm continued. What about this changing is different? What has caused this conflict to become so fanatical? To understand, a better look at the current paradigm as well as a study of the past paradigms in each Party needs to be examined in order to give us an answer.

The Democratic Paradigm. Or What <u>ARE</u> Those Crazies Really Up To?

I have presented that the basic premise of the Democratic paradigm is to provide the common man with representation in government. This for the most part, they have done and continue to do. That said, Thomas Jefferson wouldn't recognize his Party, and in my estimation, would probably begin another one rather than join the Democratic Party. (Oh and for you teachers out there. Teach your students that we did NOT begin with a two party system. We evolved into it. Yes, evolution exists even in political systems, Religious Right.) No, Thomas Jefferson wouldn't join the Republicans either. Put your hands down TEA Partiers, he won't go there either. None of us live up to the total ideals of Jefferson and Jeffersonian democracy, so quit trying to plant his flag in your turf.

We talked about Jeffersonian Democracy. (Under Democratic ideology. Go back and look it up. I am not redoing it here.) Jefferson was a strict Constitutionalist. He didn't abide activist interpretations of the Constitution. So, per the perceived paradigm of Democrats, he wouldn't join this Party. He was for farmers, planters and against the merchants and bankers. So, per the perceived paradigm of Republicans he wouldn't go their either. But if the founder of the Democratic Party wouldn't be a part of it, what happened?

Things changed. Simple and direct, things changed. When Thomas Jefferson began the Party, England was still A number 1 with a bullet. They had a King that was a King, not a popular figurehead subject to the whims of Parliament. The United States also had few laws and few states. Congress was considered nothing more in many minds than a local social organization and had just as few members. Jefferson's concern, and the concern of many of the early founders, was keeping the freedom they won. A sudden switch by France and Spain to reacquaint the new United States with colonialism and we could have done little to stand against them. Many, if not all, of the opinions and advice he gave during this time was for those that governed in his lifetime or would immediately follow. He was not speaking from the grave to those in today's times. He didn't even know if there would be a today's time for the United States. What he and his fellow revolutionaries did had never been done before in the history of the world. They had no basis for confidence it would succeed, let alone have time to send messages to the future.

On this basis Jefferson created the Democratic-Republican Party. It was to keep Americans free from the immediate possibility of monarchy, internal and external. Understand the Constitution was written out of economic necessity, not to embed personal freedoms into our government. Basically, the Articles of Confederation, agreed to during the Revolutionary War in 1777, and ratified by the States during the Revolutionary War in 1781, (Bet that was something your High School History teacher didn't explain to you. They formed a government WHILE they were at war. Talk about big ones.), didn't leave enough provision for the new United States to pay its bills. It also had no provision to administer disputes between states or standardize some simple things like money. As a result, debts were piling up, personal banks, in as many states, were issuing money, and if you wanted to cross from one state to the next you had to pay a toll and customs duties. In other words economically it was a mess.

But the formation of the Constitution also created the ability to craft a monarchy. In many ways it still does. So Jefferson, to defend against what he thought Andrew Hamilton was doing, creating a monarchy and aristocracy, formed the Democratic-Republican Party. Jefferson embedded it with the idea that all the powers the federal government needed were unambiguously written in the Constitution. (Air travel alone dispels that notion. Nice try though, Tom.) Jefferson believed, if they needed any more powers, they could amend the Constitution. Jefferson also sought out personal allies and those he felt most earned the freedoms, as they had fought and died in the Revolutionary War, farmers and planters. These people had the most to lose with the loss of their new found independence. So the first paradigm of the Democratic Party was a fervent opposition to singular authority and an embrace of the rights of the individuals that actually fought and died for our freedoms.

But this paradigm didn't last forever. As time passed and the United States became stronger, fear of a monarchy or re-establishment as a European colony faded. The experiment was working. Also the people that created the Democratic-Republican Party were dying and their fears were dying with them. Their ways, rituals and oral traditions were dying with them as well. (Hey, we went from breeches to pants, dude!) But, paradigms do not change as quickly as an election cycle. They do not turn off like a light switch. They do not even end with the death of the founders. New paradigms begin as it gathers adherents until the new paradigms rituals, oral traditions, and basic school of political thought, overtake and supersede the former. Adherents to the old methods are then ignored, or simply marginalized to the point they don't matter. The old adherents that still exist do advocate for a return to the "original" paradigm, but their positions are considered too out-dated to consider.

This is what happened to the Democratic-Republican Party. Their success basically killed them. They essentially became the only Party in the United States for twenty years. (For nine years they WERE the only Party in the United States. Can we say one-party system, teachers?) Internal dissension began to tear at the seams of the Party. Political caucuses by a few prominent men that basically chose the leaders of the country were being challenged. The country was growing and getting stronger. What were we going to do about the Indian problem, the territories that wanted to be new states, and the growing number of white males that didn't own land, but wanted a vote? These were issues of the day not the fear of monarchy or new colonization. The new issues weren't even a thought for the founders of the Democratic-Republican Party. So as the new paradigm gained more adherents due to its immediacy and relevancy to the times, issues, and experiences of the people; the original Democratic-Republican Party paradigm lost adherents and was superseded by the new paradigm. But what was this new paradigm like?

In the original Democratic-Republican Party paradigm, early settlers came primarily for land, so only allowing those that owned land to vote wasn't an issue in the beginning. As anyone that cared to vote owned land. (If they didn't own land, but wanted to, they just went out to the Indian territories and claimed it. Ticked off the Indians, but hey they WERE Indians. What did we care?) But in the new paradigm members of a mercantile society were here. Those citizens that made a living in commerce and trade and didn't own land or seek it. These gentlemen wanted a voice also and they had money. Suffrage for white men, (bet women never knew there had been suffrage for white men in the United States), had come and with it more influence in government affairs from the men and new money in the west. As the hard working frontiersman made his mark in the Party he had little patience for politics. The number of the states and the distance between them created issues towards getting things done in a timely manner. Opportunities or lives could be lost waiting to overcome practical matters such as walking through the mountains to vote in Congress. The new frontiersman wanted it done and done now. A stronger Executive Branch that could give quick action was required, with less attention to the meddlesome problems of adding amendments to the Constitution.

The Democratic Party as designed by Andrew Jackson stood in strong contrast to Jefferson's vision of the Party. Jefferson stood in opposition to anything that reeked of monarchy, but embraced a strong Executive Branch. Jefferson opposed the monarchy concept as he believed all branches equal. But, while Jackson was a strict constructionist of the Constitution, his concern was with the states usurping federal powers instead of the federal government usurping state's rights, a 180 degree difference as compared to Jefferson's concerns about the Constitution. Jefferson was concerned about states' losing their rights to the federal government, not the federal government losing rights to the states. Jefferson may actually have advanced that idea to the colleagues writing the Constitution.

Andrew Jackson also advocated for all white men be given voting rights, (Once again ladies, please! I wasn't there at the time.). Thomas Jefferson was a landowner and aristocrat. His land was a plantation, he owned slaves, and he was raised with the concept of position and station. Jefferson accepted the concept of landowners only voting. Jackson self-taught, raised somewhere in Tennessee and in all sense an orphan in the west had a strikingly different view of the privileged class. (The pun intended for Jacksonian scholars. You know what I mean. The others can look it up.)

With Jackson, the paradigm for the Democratic Party had changed. The founders had died. Those old adherents were being ignored. New rituals in the way of National Conventions, (First Democratic National Convention in 1832), for nominations of Presidential and Vice-Presidential candidates were introduced. Oral traditions involving deeds and actions in the West were replacing tales of the Revolutionary War. The basic school of political thought was changing as the Democratic Party was embracing a strong Executive Branch and President.

But to reiterate, paradigm changes are not like turning on and off a light switch or even through the election of one group of people. This paradigm change had taken thirty years to begin and another eight to take hold. It had also taken the death of the founders and the change of important social and economic issues to create the change. Even then former adherents served in Congress and sought returns to Jeffersonian democracy values well after Jacksonian democracy had taken hold. But the paradigm change did happen and the country was changed for it.

The strong influence of the Jacksonian paradigm stayed with the Democrats for thirty years. Jackson himself died in 1845. But the party's Jacksonian paradigm created a reluctance to address another major issue of the1850's, slavery. Thirteen years after Jackson's death, this reluctance caused the Party to suffer a challenge to its prominent position. This time the challenge was from outside the party and the Democratic Party's established paradigm. This challenge was from the newly recognized Republican Party.

Let's face it from 1858 until 1930 who really cared about the Democratic paradigm? Republicans were in charge and they were doing their best to stay in charge. They launched puppet political parties trying to manipulate Democrats and Democratic voters to join them and thus delete the true Democratic vote. They initiated the "reforms' in the Southern States to limit the influence of the strong Southern Democratic vote that had dominated the United States for the first part of its history. Republicans even tried to embrace Progressivism in order to stay in the top seat. They were so good at it that even the Democrats in the Democratic Party tried to shape the paradigm to resemble more of the Republican ideals and for awhile they did. The Bourbon Democrats were prominent from 1876 until 1904. These were decidedly business friendly Democrats that supported the goals of banking and railroads. They refused to subsidize them with federal funds and insisted that they suffer the slings and arrows of competition. Basically they were classical liberalists in the same vein as John Locke and Adam Smith. A lot of Democrats could be forgiven for thinking these Bourbon Democrats were nothing more than Republicans that lost their way to the Republican Convention.

But even though Bourbon Democrats had their moments of victory with the election of Grover Cleveland as President of the U. S., they never took solid hold in the Democratic Party and faded away. The paradigm they supported, business and banking over common man, faded with them. Democrats returned to supporting the paradigm of giving a voice and representation to the common man. The resurgence of the Southern Vote in the form of the Solid South ensured a very back to the earth movement of the paradigm for Democrats. The paradigm also took a decided prejudiced tone as white Southern Democrats heavily controlled the fortunes of the Party. But it wasn't until the Great Depression of 1929 and the election of Democrats in 1930 and Franklin Roosevelt in 1932 that anyone really cared what the paradigm of the Democratic Party had evolved into.

The election of Franklin Roosevelt ushered in a paradigm heavy on social liberalism, with a leaning on Progressivism. Not only did the Democratic Party feel a need to represent the common man over the banking industry and merchants, the Party also felt the need to grow the federal government to support the common man. This was a major departure from Jeffersonian and Jacksonian Democratic Party values. While both men believed the common man should be heard, neither believed the federal government should provide the common man a living. There was also a movement towards directing the states and more infringement on states' rights. The Solid South worked to restrict this, but was ultimately unsuccessful against the popularity of Roosevelt. This was a definite movement away from the founding principles of the Democratic Party and the subsequent Jacksonian paradigm. Also the inclusion of Progressivism meant more professionalism in the bureaucracy and less cronyism, the opposition of Jacksonian philosophy which believed "to the victor belong the spoils".

The Party also encouraged a heavy dose of a strong Executive Branch to get the job done now, a bit Jacksonian in a way, but definitely not Jeffersonian. The entrance into World War II encouraged the need of a strong executive branch. Democrats and the Democratic Party were becoming comfortable with the idea of the President as a strong symbol of the United States. The attempt by Roosevelt to pack the Supreme Court and extend his power, even though the effort failed, was evidence of his belief in a strong Executive which he embedded into the Democratic paradigm of this period.

By the end of World War II the Democratic paradigm was nothing like its conception. It had changed to meet the times and needs of its people. Stories of World War I were being replaced with stories of World War II. Oral traditions that emphasized the god like status of men such as Roosevelt, MacArthur, Marshall, and Eisenhower embedded the need of strong executives in the Party and presidency. The need to provide for the least among us created a welfare system never before seen in the U. S. and created the Social Security system that lead to a health care system, Medicare. Suddenly the expansion of the federal government wasn't a bad thing, it was necessary to protect the country and provide for the citizens. There had become a subtle shift in the Democratic paradigm that embraced the need for an all-encompassing government, a government that oversaw all ills and took care of all programs. Only one government with a standard of care could provide equally for all. The Democratic Party embraced these new concepts and distanced themselves even more from the foundations of their beginnings.

This strong central government, big federal government, strong president and social awareness embedded itself strongly into the Democratic Party as it reaped victory after victory for sixty years. The paradigm was so successful it also embedded itself into the minds of the general population. But the paradigm success also became its downfall. Roosevelt, because of his Progressive background and his popularity and success as President started trying to alleviate the problems of the least among us. And in his time this was the black population. Roosevelt began efforts to bring the races together. Truman followed with the integration of the

Armed Forces.

These efforts, of course, begat the Dixiecrats and their attempts to, "take the Party back". (Sounds familiar doesn't it?) Kennedy followed Eisenhower with a heavy emphasis on social programs. Johnson followed Kennedy and created the Great Society and Civil Rights while running a war to stop the spread of oppression by the Communists. In effect during this decade the country just decided it couldn't afford the Roosevelt paradigm anymore and replaced Johnson with Nixon. Nixon won again in 1972 running strongly against McGovern who was pushing the same embedded Democratic agenda and Roosevelt paradigm that had a heavy emphasis on social engineering.

This election foreshadowed another change coming to the Democratic paradigm. In 1972 the voters who had lived through the Great Depression were sixty-two or older. Those that lived in World War II were fifty-three or older. In other words the supporters of the original paradigm under Roosevelt were dying off or beginning to die off. Those that benefited by the Roosevelt paradigm were getting older and richer. They didn't particularly want to give their money to those that didn't work, "forever". Then the recession of 1980 hit and Reagan and the Republicans were elected to office.

In 1980 the core of the Democratic Party that held up the Roosevelt paradigm for so many years, those voters that were between 45 and 65 years old, if they were still living, had aged and were now 69 and older. These were the ones that had made the oral traditions, rituals and basic principles of belief of the Roosevelt era. They, by virtue of their infirmities or age no longer controlled the Party. The oral traditions now being presented were of the Vietnam War and the War on Drugs and the Civil Rights movement. The last Roosevelt paradigm president was Jimmy Carter. The new group had seen the malaise created by the Democratic programs of the past and but they also saw the benefits created by Big Government. Included in this group were a new influx of black supporters and an exodus of white Southerners. In effect it was a transition looking for a foundation. The Democrats and their paradigm were in flux during the era from 1980 until 1994. Policies of the past had propelled them to great heights and prominence so many wanted to hang onto that which had been embedded in them by their fathers, mothers and peers. But many more saw the recurrence of Republican presidents and Republican Senates and wanted to change. The old Roosevelt paradigm imposed on them by adherents not yet gone and those that still believed weighed heavily on the Party. Remember paradigms do not go quietly into that good night. They fight and this one, from Roosevelt, fought hard. It was after all a paradigm of great success.

But finally in the 1990 Bill Clinton was elected to office, the first President of the first boomers. With him came a new paradigm on what the country needed based upon the lessons he had learned in the sixty's, seventy's and eighty's. His time was not of the Great Depression and Great War. He faced strong resistance in the Party paradigm to changes that did not embrace a complete acceptance of Big Government and an overarching government. He did not believe that the government owed all Americans a living. He was a hybrid that searched for a Third Way and could accept new economic theories. His changes were resisted until the complete defeat of Democrats in 1994 which signaled the end of the Roosevelt paradigm.

But what was that paradigm that Bill Clinton introduced? Well who really cared? Bill Clinton only lasted six more years after 1994 and that was with the help of a right wing third Party. Bill Clinton was a good president, but, internally Democratic wise, he was not as strong as Franklin Roosevelt. Republicans took over the House, Senate and Presidency in 2000 and held onto it for six years, which launched another battle for the soul of the Democratic Party. The lack of interest in the Democratic Party for the next six years, since it was out of power, precipitated the same lackluster interest of the general populace in its paradigm as all the other times the Party was out of power. The major impact Bill Clinton had on the Democratic Party paradigm was ending the requirement to adhere to the Roosevelt paradigm. It took a major recession to kick Republicans out of power, not the will of Democratic voters, and the Democrats were still trying to find a foundation and an overarching paradigm they could all support. By now the first boomers were out and the second boomers were in.

2003 signaled a major argument for the paradigm that the Democrats were trying to create. The number of candidates lining up to run against Bush for the Presidency all represented a new paradigm and a new way for the Democratic Party. All failed to produce. Kerry was a byproduct of the first boomers as were the rest. In order to garner a coalition that could procure them the nomination, they embraced all venues of the Party from the extreme left represented by the Progressives and the right represented by Dixiecrats, (Which by this time was a complete waste. Dixiecrats were now Democrats in name only, DINO's, lol). This ambiguity didn't garner the support needed to win. Segments of the Democratic Party were still vying for control of the paradigm when the recession allowed them back in power in 2006. The lack of a dominate paradigm and seniority rights in the Congressional system allowed first boomers a powerful seat at the table. But even then the first boomers were unable to solidify an overriding paradigm because of the opposition from newly minted representatives that were members of subsequent boomer sets.

In 2008 enter Barack Obama. Barack Obama was by all intents and purposes a second boomer. He almost qualifies as a third boomer, being born in 1961, so he bridges the gap between second and third boomer sets. But to many Democrats trying to set an enduring paradigm he was a complete surprise. First of all he was not supposed to even get out of the primaries. Hillary Clinton was the favored daughter. First boomers were assured that she would win and they would return to establishing their paradigm and power for many subsequent generations.

Hillary was after all sincerely a first boomer, born in 1947, and carried the first boomer influences and beliefs. By the time she would have taken office she would have been 61 as compared to Obama's age of 47. But to many Democratic factions Hillary Clinton was a reflection of the failed Clinton paradigm and the heavily influential Roosevelt paradigm. These factions wanted something new and different, something for the future not from the past. Shockingly to the first boomers these factions looked for a leader and group of leaders that could make a heavy influence on a new paradigm structure, not of Clintonian and Rooseveltian heritage. Shockingly I say because the first boomers were not ready to leave the stage and were surprised anyone rejected their visions of the future. But first boomers were starting to age, just as Hillary was, and they were beginning to lose some influence. Just like the Roosevelt paradigm lost its influence with the aging of its adherents.

When Obama stepped onto the stage all factions of the Party were looking for a paradigm that could gain enough adherents to silence the nagging influences of both Roosevelt and Clinton paradigms. Opportunity met need. Many of these factions rallied behind Obama looking for a chance to make their mark on setting a new Democratic Party paradigm. They infused their perceptions and beliefs into the man and the Democratic Party and elected both. Then they were met with total disappointment. Obama turned out not to be the God they had voted for, but a superior man infused with pragmatism and love of country. Obama has not coalesced the Party or even garnered a majority of the Party into accepting an overarching new paradigm. He has not even formalized a new paradigm with which to argue. So the factions still contend for the high ground.

But Obama's reluctance to build some new paradigm is not surprising. Only a fusion of multiple paradigms can achieve electoral and political success. The characteristics of the Democratic Party are changing dramatically. An infusion of Latino's combined with the Black heritage has started a new rumbling looking for an outlet. The United States is changing demographically and so are its needs. White US citizens are not the only arbiters to be considered in these discussions. The paradigm will not be imposed by only one faction of race, but an agreement of the strongest factions of race and what they feel their needs are. So in the Democratic Party the paradigms still contend. One may stand stronger for a while until a new influence or need moves it aside. There is no one group teaching the rituals and oral traditions of the Party. What you learn is based on what faction you attend. Until a stronger, successful, proven paradigm takes control the Democratic Party will face a period of identity crisis. There will be changing and contending political paradigms and the lack of consistency will affect the country.

Do Republicans Have a Paradigm or are They Controlled by God!

Well for a lot of Republicans, they think the Party is the Party of God, so this is just a stupid question. But for a liberal looking in, (I told you I was a liberal didn't I? Good. I was afraid I had forgotten), I could believe them. At least that they believe they are driven by the will of God. But those darn historical facts prove otherwise.

Understand all paradigms are not created equal and not all paradigms are equally constructed. The values, oral traditions and political principles in one organization do not necessarily bear comparative value to another. After all they are distinct political positions often formed in different timeframes. What one group values may not even be a blimp on the radar in the other group. But in some ways political paradigms are quite alike as in the case of having base threads of beliefs carry through in all incarnations of the paradigms over the years. Just as Democrats have the thread in their paradigms that they always work to support the common man and worker, Republicans have kept a thread of principle in their paradigms. This thread has always been a support of Main Street USA. This is not to mean the big banks, large conglomerates and global companies so much associated with Republicans today, but the mom and pop stores, small businesses and entrepreneurs that make and made the economy of this country. Good on them, because this group needs to be heard. Until the Republican Party came into existence, this group had no organized representation and no voice at the table of power.

But against all popular beliefs the Republican Party did not build its first paradigm off the legacy of Abraham Lincoln. He wasn't there long enough. He wasn't even there when the Party was founded. Remember he was a Whig first, before he became a Republican. He was only a Republican for about 6 years and that was including the time he ran and was elected as the National Union Party President. In actuality John Freemont was more of an influence on the first paradigm than Lincoln. Freemont was the US Senator from California and the first presidential candidate for the Republican Party, running for the seat in the 1856 election. He actually came in second, (It was a three man race. Sheesh I heard all the sniggers out there. Give Freemont a break!), and garnered 114 electoral votes.

Republicans as we have shown, (Once again for all of you that did not read the prior chapters, quit jumping ahead. I will not repeat it here.), did not have the auspicious beginnings that the Democratic Party had. No founding father came forth to use it as a shield against possible future tyranny. It was a group of activists and individuals, simple United States citizens with grievances, who came together in Michigan to create an organization to represent their beliefs, present their issues, and, in the process, stand against slavery. There seems little record if any to denote who these intrepid founders really were. (I'm sure there are plenty of descendents willing to lay claim that their fathers were in that august body. I'll let others debate those facts. Just remember they had to be fathers. Mothers couldn't vote!) It was the subsequent actions of the Party they started that gained the prominence. In this respect the Republican Party is a true United States institution, the product of the people.

The original paradigm of the Republican Party was encapsulated in their first presidential campaign slogan, "Free soil, free labor, free speech, free men". Now as altruistic as this sounds there was a message behind the slogan that related directly to the basic Republican Main Street paradigm. (Like fathers, like sons. Seems current Republicans learned from their intrepid founding fathers on the ways to encode meaning in "doublespeak".) Main Street and the small businessmen known as local independent farmers were highly affected economically by slavery. Plantations did not have to pay wages to grow crops. Plantations were also the big business of the 1850's and were buying up all the good farmland

and leaving the leftovers to independent farmers. Plantations often used slave labor to build or make items for free that directly affected the Main Street artisans and businessmen's ability to compete and make profits. In short small business and farmers wanted to end slavery, not so much because it was morally wrong, but because it hurt business. The immorality of slavery was a big issue for Republicans, but confirming it took precedence over economics in the first incarnations of the Party would be hard to sustain as initial actions to form the Party evolved from passage of the Kansas-Nebraska act, not the actual institution of slavery itself.

Now the Kansas-Nebraska Act repealed the Missouri Compromise that had prohibited slavery anywhere north of the 36° 30' parallel except for the state of Missouri. The Kansas-Nebraska act allowed any new US territory to become a slave state based upon the popular decision of its residents regardless of where the state would be located, north or south. This infuriated the Free-Soilers and many other political factions because now slave labor and plantations could be introduced to farmland in the north taking away an economic benefit for many and giving power to the "Slave South". So they gathered together, threw off the labels of Whigs, Free-Soilers, and even Democrats, (Side note, Steven Douglas, a Senate Democrat, yep the one that beat Lincoln in the Douglas-Lincoln debates was the legislative leader that got this bill passed. So in a way Democrats could blame him for starting the Republican Party and maybe even the War of Northern Aggression. Don't that make you wonder what would have happened if Lincoln won that seat that year?), and began the Republican Party.

So the Republican paradigm from the beginning was about good old fashioned personal wealth and the average man's right to pursue wealth and protect his competitive edge. It was not about defense of the country from tyranny, or the rights of all men, or women, to vote. It wasn't even really about the morally correct ideal of ending the horrible institution of slavery because of the suffering of millions of human beings. The Republican paradigm was a defense of the right of fair competition. Business, and what is good for business, is what drove the first Republican paradigm and it has a strong presence in the current paradigm of today.

But a paradigm doesn't exist in a vacuum. The Republican Party paradigm, for one, was quite dynamic for the first 16 years of existence, changing rapidly and often due to the Civil War, (OK.

We are talking about Northerners now so we need to use a language they understand.), and events immediately after the War. The Republican paradigm may have begun in economics, but it was molded and forged in war and polished with the honesty, beliefs, doubts, and courage of President Lincoln. The oral traditions, rituals, and embedded political thought of the Party after the War were derived more from that War and the people that were affected by the war than the ideals of those whom formed it ten years earlier. The Civil War gave the Republican Party a history and a basis, besides personal economy, for foundation of their paradigm for the next thirty years. President Lincoln became the Party's founding icon and source of inspiration. Lincoln gave the Party social and moral legitimacy.

The actions of Lincoln in the War and his tragic death gave Lincoln an almost saint like persona in the Republican Party, if not the nation. His war time leadership and tragic death also imbued the Party's paradigm with the concept of a strong Executive Branch, centralized leadership, and a strong leader. Basically the chain of command you see in an army. (Which goes a long way to answering the liberals question of why Republicans always seem to work in lock step and group think. But enough Republican bashing for now.) Considering that many of the Party elders were former Jacksonian Democrats this is not unexpected. Considering also that many of the prominent leaders in the Party were former soldiers and officers in the War this should be expected.

The war also embedded the Republican Party with a deep sense of individual freedom. Brothers, sons, daughters, sisters, mothers, and fathers all died to free a people enslaved. So did Lincoln. Regardless of the initial position of the founders of the Republican Party, the immorality of the institution of slavery became a fabric of the Republican Party because of the War. Being forced to acquiesce to the demands of others with no consideration given for personal wants, needs or beliefs became abhorrent to members of the Party. This abhorrence translated into the freedom to do as you will and as you are able, to be self-reliant and only responsible for your own actions.

The War, and war time tactics, also imbued the Party with a notion of defending your position by making sure the opponent has no means of which to strike back. Many in the Party had suffered under the former makeup of Government whereby the South, by virtue of their numbers, dominated the chambers of Congress and the legislation passed within. Former slaves, wounded veterans, and ruined merchants blamed the South and the South's greed for the need to have a Civil War and they wanted retribution. They also wanted to make sure they didn't win the War to only lose everything they gained through future Congressional actions from another dominate "Old South" coalition. Once again, considering a lot of Republicans were taught at the foot of the Jacksonian paradigm of "to the winner go the spoils", this is not unexpected or untypical of the times.

But while the paradigm had undergone changes it had not coalesced yet into a recognizable set of rules, traditions or principles one could consider a norm. First of all the Party was still in infancy. What had happened had been a quick and violent birth. Also the father and spiritual leader of the Party had been killed before he could exert his influence on the final makeup of this new empowered organization. In essence the King was dead with no heir apparent and there were plenty of princes in waiting ready to claim the crown, including members of the so-called "Radical Republicans" and the self-described "conservative" Republicans. (Radical Republicans were a loose faction of strong willed, right wing, determined individual politicians who were convinced of the righteousness of their position. In this case the abolition of slavery and the punishment of the Southern people who rose against the Union. Think early TEA Party. There is nothing new under the sun.)

Remember also that Lincoln was elected in 1864 as a member of the National Union Party, partly because the Radical Republicans opposed the Republican nomination of Lincoln for president in 1864. In essence Lincoln wasn't really a designated Republican at his second inauguration or at his death. His Vice-President, and the new President at Lincoln's death, was also a National Union Party member and a former Democrat. Andrew Johnson was never a Republican. So a void was created in the leadership of the Party and remained that way until Grant's election in 1868. This void, and the inner turmoil within the Party, hindered the development of a fully accepted political paradigm for the Party. Grant's election and subsequent terms in office coalesced into a recognizable paradigm. But still the Republican Party and its defining paradigm vacillated under the pressures of differing views within the Party on reconstruction, civil rights, patronage and many other issues.

The prevailing Republican paradigm, advocated by Grant and instituted by the Radical Republicans of which he was a member, advocated and added a strong Executive Branch, centralized leadership, personal freedoms, and sanctioned retribution, to its foundation of equal competition for Main Street economics. This prevailing paradigm and the dominance of the Republican Party seemed tailor made for the economy that followed the War. Many would argue that Republican Party made the period after the Civil War, but lack of understanding about the foundation of national, state and local political institutions in the immediate years after the war would account for this ignorance. Let's face it. The United States was in ruins and its governing institutions were in shambles. Half of the United State's Congress wasn't even allowed to take their seats as the other half insisted that their citizens be "redeemed" first. (Whatever the heck "redeemed" actually meant.). Many institutions in the North and especially the South were physically destroyed and their leaders had died on the battlefields.

It was going to take time to put back into place fully functioning governments, but time wasn't waiting and neither were the people. Economic expansion and industrial might was waiting in the wings to grab its place and it was ready to consume the United States. While the Republican Party was busy solidifying the basis of its current hard fought paradigm, the overwhelming power of these two factors led to a recreation of the paradigm before it even matured.

With the issue of slavery, the lack of the right of state succession, and dominion of national government resolved through the blood of the nation's sons and fathers, the remaining citizens wanted to get to work making a living. The War had developed new inventions, ideas and means of commerce. Foreign countries, not at war, had moved economically and technologically forward and foreign investment was eager to reap the bounty of opportunities in the United States. Nature abhors a vacuum and by my experience I have found that power abhors a vacuum as well. In the absence of an overriding and strong political institution, business moved in and began to grow and direct government actions. Business also started re-writing prevailing political paradigms of the dominant Party. In this case, it was the Republican Party.

It all started with railroads. They had to be rebuilt after the war and railroads were the primary modes of transportation and making money in the 1860's to 1900's. Jay Gould, Cornelius Vanderbilt, and J. P. Morgan came of age during this time and made money financing railroads as well as building them. Prior to the Civil War the stock market usually just traded in government debt. After the Civil War it was used to finance railroads and get foreign investment. The investor culture and big business took root.

To ensure its dominance, business, and particularly the brand new phenomena called "big business", invested in government as well. In particular business invested in the Republican Party, as it was the Party in charge. It was also the Party with a base paradigm foundation of support for Main Street business, a natural fit. This influx of power and money solidified the Republican paradigms association with everything business.

It also added a few new principles to the Republican Party paradigm. The first principle is "smaller government". This wasn't a surprise. With a smaller government, big business was in charge. They called the shots and ensured they controlled the direction of the country. In other words business continued their dominate power that they had come to know in the "weak government" period following the Civil War. Also small government meant less regulations and the ability for unrestricted industrial growth. Let's face it business thrived after the Civil War. But then so did corruption, consolidation of income to a privileged few, poverty, pollution, exploitation of children and financial enslavement of workers. Just to name a few of the bad things that happen when business tries to run government.

The second principle was that government should be involved in national economic development. (Yes, for all you activists that think government shouldn't be involved in business, it was the Republicans who ushered government in. Albeit so they could use government power to increase their profits. It wasn't altruistic, folks.). The third principle was unrestrained economic expansion is good for the country. Finally the paradigm included an admiration of exorbitant personal wealth, or financial aristocracy, and the right of wealth to rule. Basically during this time the Republican paradigm took a strong turn and embraced all things business and economic.

But if there is one thing business likes more than power it is profits. (Profits allow business to buy more power. Sort of a chicken and egg thing.) This need for profits triggered a Republican association with the Progressive movement starting in 1890. With the election of Hayes as president in 1877 the "redeemer" period ended in the United States, and so did a lot of the issues of Radical Republicans. The paradigm dominated with Radical Republicanism had been fully replaced with the business paradigm. However, the national governing institutions were beginning to regain their footing and power. Stronger political leaders were beginning to influence national, state, and local policies. But the new government institutions were still based on pre-war structure which was highly inefficient, partisan, and corrupt. Business by this time had focused government's primary attention away from national security and social order to further their economic development. But the old pre-war governing structures were affecting profits. The overriding power of a few businesses and businessmen were beginning to draw resentment from rank and file Republicans. Progressivism offered a means to instill order, professionalism, and reign in business, while increasing business incomes. The Republican Party entered a new phase of paradigm development.

For the next thirty years the Republican Party business paradigm had an uneasy alliance with the Progressive movement, mostly instilled through the efforts of Theodore Roosevelt. It was not an easy alliance and many in the Party did not want to accept Progressive principles in the Party paradigm. Progressivism was a departure from a business paradigm and those adherents to the business paradigm fought to return the Party to that foundation. Leaders of the Progressive movement often were Main Street businesses and they fought back. They had lost ground to big business in the acceptance of the current party paradigm. They were looking for a little parity and a reassertion of the rights of the individual. The leader of the Party, Teddy Roosevelt, was a big supporter of Progressivism, even running as a Progressive on the Bull Moose Party ticket when the Republicans wouldn't re-nominate him to run for president in 1912. So the fight for the dominating paradigm of the party was intense. Eventually this infighting allowed a Democrat to become president. This forced the Republicans to choose a winning paradigm.

Progressives as we discussed earlier, (once again I'm not rehashing everything here for those who skip ahead.), believed in efficiency, scientific management and municipal administration. Progressivism embraced a professional bureaucracy, organized labor, and trust busting. None of those were issues high on the agenda of business and caused dissent in the Republican Party. Through Progressivism influences in the Republican Party, Republicans in the House and Senate did pass an amendment in 1919 giving the right to vote to women. However, shortly after granting women the right to vote, progressivism died out in the Republican Party. (It does make one want to draw an inference or at least a snide remark. But there is no real evidence of a link so I will let this one go as much as I don't want to.)

The exit of Teddy Roosevelt from the Republican Party in 1912 is considered by many to be the real end of the Progressive movement in the Party. William Howard Taft, his successor in the Presidency, was a supporter of Progressivism, but not on the scale as Roosevelt. As a result adherents to the old paradigm of business reasserted their dominance. It was one of the failures of a new political paradigm in overtaking and replacing an old paradigm. (I told you these paradigms just don't die after an election or death of their members. They fight back.) The old business paradigm did take on some newer principles. Education, professionalism and efficiencies in government, holdovers from the Progressive movement, were all included in a new emerging paradigm. A solid interest in Main Street remained as did a respect for individual freedoms. But for the most part the base principles of business, including smaller government and less government regulation, that had dominated the Party and helped it become the dominant political organization was the overriding paradigm for the Republican Party. In this background the roaring twenties took off after World War I and the county continued its fantastic economic expansion. Republicans and their policies took credit for this expansion and when it hit the wall they also ended up having to take responsibility for its fall. The Great Depression was here.

I still don't think current U. S. citizens understand the extent of the Great Depression and how it affected the United States. First and foremost it was triggered by all accounts by the selloff in the Stock Market. It rippled through the country and the world. Personal income, tax revenue, profits, prices, all dropped. International trade dropped more than 50% and U. S. unemployment rose to 25%. In some countries it rose to heights of 33%. One quarter of our workforce was out of work and couldn't find jobs. There was NO unemployment benefits and NO social security. This lasted over 10 YEARS and by all accounts only was ended by a World War. (And citizens are upset Obama can't resolve a Recession after 2 years on the job? Get real! It took years to get into this mess and it is gonna take more than 2 years to get out of it, just like it did during the Depression.)

The Great Depression essentially ended the reign of the Republican Party, and adherence to its business paradigm, for sixty years. The Party fought to regain prominence and position but its basic paradigm foundation and sixty years as an engine for business kept it as a bastion of big business for many of the years during the Depression, World War II and well into the 1960's. With most of the population looking towards the Democratic Party for solutions, the Republican Party aligned itself closer to business and Main Street. The dominating paradigm was the business paradigm, until the elections of 1968. Richard Nixon wanted to be President and the Solid South didn't want anything to do with the Civil Rights Bill and Great Society that Lyndon Johnson embraced. Enter the "southern strategy".

Now before we get too all righteous here, let's remind everyone that the South was primarily a Democratic bastion, slaves and all. The power center of the Democratic Party was often the South and it was so much a reliable Democratic power center after the Civil War it was called the Solid South. Andrew Jackson and Thomas Jefferson were both from the South, owned slaves, and were Democrats. In both instances, especially Jackson's they studiously avoided handling the slave issue directly which, to many minds at least, led to the Civil War. In other words, Democratic hands are not clean on this issue. Also it is also important to note that the first Civil Rights bill was not written by Democrats, but by Republicans in 1871. The first Civil Rights Act was written in order to ensure Southerners accepted that former slaves had civil rights and to do so by force if necessary. These facts are important because in 1964 Lyndon Johnson, a Texan and Southern Democrat, presented, worked to pass, passed and signed into law the Civil Rights Act of 1964 and the Voting Rights Act.

The passage of these Acts was a complete rejection of Southern Democrats and Southern Democratic principles of states' rights and segregation that the Party had complicity and sometimes openly accepted since its formation over 150 years earlier. It was the end of a group of actions begun with Franklin Roosevelt and nourished by Harry Truman, (A Missouri Democrat), to gain equality for blacks in the United States. It was in essence a repudiation of racism by the Democratic Party. It was a rejection of a set of beliefs that were so heinous that they subjugated a race of people to a status of lesser human beings for no other reason than the color of their skin. It was a refutation of policies that had led to a horrible internal conflict that divided the nation and cost hundreds of thousands of lives. It was an act to correct a terrible wrong and remove the Democratic Party from the bondage of racism. Democrats were laying a filthy stench on the ground and walking away. The Republican Party, in its Southern Strategy, picked it back up.

Yes, the Republican Party, the bastion of personal freedoms, the freer of slaves, the Party of Lincoln, Civil Rights and a reliable large black voting bloc, (Yes almost all blacks voted Republican then, if they were allowed to vote.), chose to adopt the platform of state's rights and segregation in order to win elections. It was a conscious choice by the leaders of the Republican Party, (Leaders meaning Richard Nixon and John Mitchell.), and accepted as a viable method to gain votes. In essence in 1964 the Republican Party and Democratic Party switched the internal makeup of their constituencies and, with the switch, some fundamental beliefs. Democrats became more integrated, diverse and, if possible, more liberal. Republicans became more segregated, white and, if possible, more conservative.

Kevin Phillips was the architect for this strategy. He did not name it, but he did invent it. It was a program to polarize ethnic voting. The strategy was based purely on the seemingly natural bigotry ethnicities had for each other and played upon this bigotry and hatred to garner votes for Republicans. The Republicans purposely used the Voting Rights Act as a tool to drive white southern voters to their party and to gain their votes. There was a conscious understanding in the Party that the more blacks that registered to vote, due to the Voting Rights Act, the more whites will quit the Democratic Party and become Republican. The Republican operatives knew and counted on the Democratic registering of black voters to ensure that white voters stayed in their party and voted Republican. The Southern Strategy was a major documentation of a Party using the polarization of voters to gain political advantage. It was a blatant, politically sanctioned act to use fear to polarize voters. It was done for no other purpose than to win elections. Republicans knew the largest group of voters during this timeframe was whites and gaining the white voters meant gaining wins. Unfortunately, it worked. Maybe not to the great expectations of many, but it did work.

This action obviously changed the paradigm of the Republican Party. The Nixon paradigm came of age. Main Street was still the bread and butter, but added to this mix was now a strong dose of small rural white individualism. Basically, the Republican Party placed a "Whites preferred" sign on their door. The beginning of rich and white as an icon of the Republican Party was formed. The paradigm of the Republican Party became one based on individual freedom, the right of association, Main Street businesses, big business, and state's rights. The Party that had gone to War to exert the rights of the nation over the rights of the states, had passed Constitutional Amendments and the first Civil Rights Act to secure those rights, now defended the rights of states over the federal government.

But as we have shown changing paradigms does happen easily. In this instance the group the endorsed the change, the Nixon campaign, still garnered 39% of the black vote in their 1968 campaign. It was a slow process, but by 1972 the southern strategy was ingrained into party politics. There were too many reported instances of political victory, and a number of prominent Democrats becoming Republicans, (include Strom Thurmond in this group), as a result of this strategy, that the strategy created enough adherents to make the Nixon paradigm, the Party paradigm.

While the Nixon paradigm was successful to a point, (it helped elect him twice), it only made inroads in the U. S. Congress. It wasn't until Ronald Reagan became president that a few new twists of the Republican paradigm were put into place and Republicans took both the Senate and the Presidency, in essence becoming the predominant political party. The first ingredient was the Moral Majority. Jimmy Carter's self-professed evangelical Christian religion hung about him like a cloak, but Jerry Falwell's

Moral Majority gave Reagan two-thirds of the white evangelical vote and forever tied white evangelicals to the Republican Party. With Republicans firmly entrenched in the South and especially white rural South, this was a perfect match and provided the fuel for the engine of the Republican Party and its new Reagan paradigm.

The moral majority was a conscious effort by the Reverend Jerry Falwell to go against the United States principles and his Baptist principles of separating church and state. It was an open effort by a church organization, an evangelical church organization, to influence and involve religion in politics. The Moral Majority organized political action committees of conservative Christians to campaign on and support candidates who backed the Moral Majority's conception of Christian moral law. The Republican Party in acceptance of the Moral Majority, also began to accept the dissolution of the separation of church and state as a foundation of its paradigm.

Reagan also instituted supply-side economics, which basically justified the emergence of financial aristocracy and the belief in always lower taxes to support the economic theory and the aristocracy. With the introduction of supply side economics Reagan tied the Party inexorably to the wealthy elite and support of the wealthy elite as an engine of the economy and job creation. This was a change in the paradigm because more than just supporting business or big business, supply-side economics supported the actual wealthy individuals.

Once again, the Republican's Nixon paradigm did not change without challenge. The Republican middle ground saw the alliance with the Moral Majority and with the financial elite as a step too far. Uncomfortable with the use of the southern strategy many saw the shift in the paradigm with these new additions as becoming too conservative, too right wing and too polarizing. Unable to change the course of the Party due to the Party successes in the elections, these "liberal Republicans", began to change party affiliations or even leave politics altogether.

The result was the establishment of the Reagan paradigm in the Republican Party. This paradigm embraces conservative religion in government, embraced individual wealth as a foundational principle, embraced state's rights, right to association, Main Street business and big business. It also fully embraced a fully armed, fully supplied, strong military even in peace time. The final principles were the continuation of smaller and smaller governments, even in the face of a growing population and world economy, and forever plugging for lower and lower taxes to support the new economic theory. Individual freedoms had remained but shrunk behind the rights of free association, or in other words, segregation of the races.

The Reagan paradigm remained even through the election of George H. W. Bush. However, the House remained in Democratic hands even during Reagan's years. In 1986, during the second term of Reagan, even the Senate moved back over to the Democratic column. The Democrats had regained the primacy of political parties again. The Reagan paradigm, however, was strong and embedded within the Republican Party due to the fervent beliefs of the activists it had adopted. But, these strong positions were being discredited outside and even inside the Party and resulting in pushback from the electorate. It wasn't until the election of 1994 and the "Contract with America" that the Republican paradigm was able to put it all together and post a significant win over the Democratic Party.

Now the Contract for America was not solely the brainchild and work of Newt Gingrich. (I know, I know. This is such a big shock to all you Gingrich haters. I'm talking to you, liberals.) It was in fact a written by Larry Hunter, a White House staffer under Reagan among many other conservative job appointments. He was, by all accounts, aided in the production by Newt Gingrich, Richard Armey, Tom Delay, (Yes, That Tom Delay), and our own John Boehner among others. The contract included 8 policy reforms for the United States House of Representatives and 10 bills that the Republicans promised would be voted on in the House.

What the Contract did or did not do in electing Republicans is someone else's debate. The contract was presented six weeks before the election and subsequent to its presentation, for the first time in 40 years; the House was in Republican control. In conjunction with the House elections, the Senate also returned to Republican control after 8 years. The scandals and problems that plagued the country could more properly be credited with the turn in fortunes for Republicans. But the Contract openly displayed the primary intent of a political party if it found itself in position of governmental prominence and this openness resonated with voters.

This contract also portrayed the Republican paradigm in open unambiguous form that all members of the Party could ascribe and independent minded voters could abide. Included in the act was a call to fiscal responsibility through passage of a balanced budget amendment. Reining in and reforming social programs, tough on crime, national security, small business, (read Main Street), incentives, and legal reforms were all part of the contract. Small government was a component and even included was a term-limit proposal for members of the U.S. Congress. (Now there is something I bet a few liberals wished would have passed.) In short the contract embraced important precepts of the Republican paradigm, but purposely left out those principles that catered to the more extreme beliefs of the Party. The contract sanitized the Republican Party paradigm, made it palatable to voters, and allowed the Party to return to prominence. But the contract did not change the paradigm.

Those that had been brought onboard the Republican Party through the Southern Strategy and the Moral Majority still held strong sway in the Republican paradigm. The new commercial version of the Party paradigm generated considerable popular support for the Party and all factions of the Republican paradigm took advantage to press their positions. But the commercial version regulated Christian values and states' rights to the background of the paradigm. Not a popular position with the Moral Majority and Southern strategy activists. Newt Gingrich, one of the initial authors and a primary beneficiary as Speaker of the House, supported the contract and its precepts. His support of the contract in effect continued to keep the predominance of the commercial version of the paradigm in the forefront and served as a barrier to the more extreme wings of the party. However Gingrich ran into more than one scandal and became a polarizing figure. Under pressure from other members of the House and his Party, he resigned his post and seat in November of 1998.

With his resignation the Christian factions and Southern Strategists found a new vocal supporter in Tom DeLay, a born again evangelical Christian from Texas. Newt Gingrich's departure vaulted Tom Delay, in spite of his controversial image, to the leadership of the Republican Party. With his ascension he brought along the Christian Conservative movement born of Ronald Reagan and the Southern strategy born of Richard Nixon. These two factions became prominent once again in the Republican paradigm and worked to elect George W. Bush President of the United States along with a Republican Senate and House in 2000.

George W. Bush benefited from the resurgence in prominence of the Christian Conservative movement in the Republican Party, but, on the whole Bush is a Methodist, not an evangelical Christian. (Bet that sets some in the Christian Conservative movement back a bit. I know a couple of liberals that are shocked.) However, Bush's faith and the religious leanings of Tom Delay helped propel Christian Conservatism to a leading role in the Republican paradigm. (To liberals we sum this time up as "Gays, Guns, and God".) Basically Bush didn't stand in the way of the Party more fully embracing Christian religion, and allowed others such as Tom Delay to make it a more functional part of the Party.

While Conservative religion regained prominence under Bush, the states' rights issues under the southern strategy did not receive the same distinction. In fact Bush actually gained support from blacks from 2000 until 2004. He was active in supporting "guest worker" programs for illegal immigrants, appointed the first African-American as Secretary of State and the first Hispanic as Attorney General. During his terms in office he actually increased regulatory actions of the Federal Government and imposed nationwide mandates such as "No Child Left Behind Act". That President Bush publically was perceived to actively support the southern strategy issues was more a product of his allegiance to the Republican Party and association with people of influence such as Tom Delay than in actual fact. George W. Bush actually spent a lot of his time enlarging the e powers of the executive and making that more of a mark of the Republican paradigm.

The resignation in disgrace of Tom Delay in 2006 reduced the influence of the Conservative Christian movement in the Republican Party. The falling poll numbers of George W. Bush further eroded their influence as other factions moved to readjust the Republican paradigm. But, as has been said frequently, paradigms die hard and those with prominence in the paradigms fight quite hard to continue their position. The resurgence of the Democratic Party in the 2006 elections and the election of Barack Obama as President provided a means for a significant shake up in the Republican Party. It didn't take long. As previously discussed, (Once again, don't skip ahead. This was discussed under the TEA Party section. I am so past reminding you.), even before Obama and family had lived in the White House thirty days, efforts had begun to attack the new administration. This effort in fact was an attempt to reposition the Republican paradigm, if not outright remake it.

A new emphasis was placed on states' rights and "right of association", (Can we call it re-segregation yet? I mean really, that is what it is. Don't you just hate "code-words"?). A dependence on Conservative Christian values was expected, but not pre-dominant. It was, in essence, a repositioning of the southern strategy to a place of prominence over the Christian Conservative movement. Not expecting or finding a ready audience within the Party structure itself and too eager to wait for old processes this new group formed its own organization. Using its active base it pushed from the outside to make changes on the inside of the Republican Party. Initial results indicate the method worked. However, subsequent moves by Party insiders have managed to blunt the effort and even hijack the movement for their own ends. Paradigms die hard.

With no capable dominant political leader, or group of leaders, it remains to be seen what will happen with the Republican Party paradigm. The elections in 2010 returned conservatives to the prominence in the House of Representatives, but not necessarily the Republican Party. As many as 60 new members of the Republican caucus have indicated they are TEA Party members. They use the Republican Party to gain votes, but they do not feel the need for Republican Party allegiance as other Republican representatives.

This indicates a still fermenting internal argument over the Republican Party paradigm. Main Street remains a foundation as it was in 1854. But the southern strategy is fading in many parts of the country as the author predicted it would in 1968. Conservative Christian movement has alienated a number of voters and created quite a pushback. John Boehner as one of the authors of the Contract with America, an associate of Tom Delay and having worked to oust Newt Gingrich as Speaker seems more aligned with older Reagan paradigms that are not quite responsive to current trends or voters. This position places him outside of the majority of Republican positions and in a weakened position to influence the paradigm.

Votes are what are needed to gain seats in Congress, State Houses, and gain the Presidency. Re-districting works well even against the will of the electorate. But eventually the Party has to represent a belief system, a set of oral traditions and principles. It will need a defining paradigm to exist. Who and what that defining paradigm will be will determine the success of the Republican Party in the next generation.

People are Inhaling Fear and Breathing Anger, Paradigms are Changing. So What?

Well yeah. So paradigms are changing. They've always changed. So what does that mean to me? Why should I care? Well don't care. But the last group of Democrats that didn't pay serious attention ended up creating their nemesis, the Republican Party, and plunging our nation into a War Against Northern Aggression, (I am back South now buddy.). Just saying.

Also when people are fearful and strike back in anger nation's fall. Just ask the Soviet Union. Just saying.

So maybe we better pay attention. The TEA Party is trying to influence the Republicans and the nation from outside the tent. They are trying to make predominant an old belief system that has seen its best days. In short they are the last breaths of the Southern Strategy and fighting hard to be relevant and remain a force well after they have passed on. But in my opinion, (and it is my book), the country is just so past worrying about skin color as a driving force in making national, state and international decisions. We just want to make decisions that move the whole country forward. The population of the U.S. is not looking to hold the country back, restrict options or regress to earlier times. We trust the decisions made in the prior centuries by our fathers and grandfathers were needed and we want to move past these issues. We do not want to fight old battles.

The same applies to Progressives in the Democratic Party. We just don't want, and as Americans, feel that a central government should or is required, to take care of every malady that strikes its citizens. We do believe in the power of the individual states and just because one state provides or denies service, does not mean the others must march in lockstep. The power of this nation is in its states and the power of the states lies in the Union. We are a nation of individuals, groups, races, organizations, communities and religions. We do not want to impose our beliefs on all the groups as we do not want all the groups to impose their beliefs on us. (Yes, I can hear Progressives out there huffing and declaring that it is the other side imposing, not us. Well, darlings, when you tell others we have to have a national health care program, national fight against poverty, and a national education program you are imposing your beliefs on others. No matter how noble, or even right, the programs may be.)

The point is that there is a fight in each party as to what paradigm it will adopt. Neither TEA Party in the Republican or Progressive in the Democratic Party has dominance and is accepted as the prevailing paradigm. Members in the respective Parties are fighting back against these groups and building their own coalitions supporting their own paradigms. In fact there are at least three if not four paradigms in each party right now fighting for position and prominence. Of these competing paradigms there is limited support for each of them, so the fight goes on. But, once again you ask; why should I care? At best I am an independent voter. How does it affect me?

Well history shows prior paradigms did fare better and evidence suggests this is a good thing for the country and world. So declaring a victor soon would help the Parties and country. The Roosevelt paradigm lasted sixty years in the Democratic Party, Jacksonian paradigm thirty years. The Jeffersonian paradigm lasted thirty years as well. The business paradigm lasted thirty years in the Republican Party, followed by almost forty years of the big business paradigm. The Nixon paradigm lasted only 12 years which was followed by the Reagan paradigm which lasted twenty. In these paradigms the country grew and prospered. It was successful.

In other words paradigms, particularly Roosevelt's, created stability in their Party and in doing so, the nation, creating a foundation for success. This stability creates loyalties, positions and less animosity between the parties than is experienced now. Congresses and their members, aware of each other's positions based on the accepted paradigms, work together on issues important to the country, not on partisan paradigm building. Stability, therefore, is a good thing as it is sought by those winning paradigms. Well, as long as the winning paradigm is your paradigm. This lack of a dominant paradigm creates the constant bickering, fear and anger within the Parties. It divides governments and raises its ugly head in national debates. It affects those outside the Parties, the nation and the world. At its worst it retards growth, success and leads to destruction of governments and countries.

One of the reasons a dominant paradigm can't be chosen easily is times are changing and what was true last decade, or last century, is not necessarily true this decade or century. It is also because of the size of the baby boomer generation, their experiences and the way boomers were taught. Also, it is because the generations that follow the boomer generation basically don't have the same experiences as the boomers and are frankly fed up with hearing about them. Basically no one can agree on what is important. At least a majority can't. Let's explain.

As talked about earlier, the current keepers of the paradigms in both parties are the elders. The elders in this instance should be the baby boomer generations. And I mean generations. There are at least three iterations of baby boomers. (The news media likes to only talk about the boomers as a group. It makes it so much easier, and as we know we have to make it easier for the media. Thinking would take too much effort on the part of the anchors and pundits, whether conservative or liberal media.) The three iterations of boomers I refer to as first boomers, second boomers and third boomers. First boomers were born immediately after the war and up to 1955, give a year or two. They really became aware as a group in 1965. The second boomers were born between 1955 and 1965, give or take a year or two, and became aware as a group in 1975. The third boomers were born between 1965 and 1975, give or take a year or two, and became aware as a group in 1985. The oldest of the first boomers is now 66 years old getting Social Security and Medicare. The youngest of this first boomer group is 56 years old.

But I say should be in charge. The reason the boomers should be in charge is frankly their father's generation died out and they overwhelmed them. But, their older siblings won't leave. You know the tweeners we spoke of earlier, those not World War II heroes but not really boomers, the ones born between 1935 and 1945. Health care success has caught up with us. Those that would have met their maker a generation ago are lingering around and refusing to leave the political stage. Let's face it Social Security was set up in 1940 to begin at age 62 because most everyone died by the time they were 65. Now the average age is well into the seventies with some putting it at 79. And this group is not only lingering they are quite active. Serving in business, board rooms, legislatures and Congress well after most of their ancestors would have toddled off and left the next generation to its own devices.

This has created serious conflict with the first boomers. They feel that the prominence promised them in their early days has been stolen. Yes, this group has had its moments, with Bill Clinton getting elected and George W. Bush, but all in all they have not had a free hand at redefining the Party paradigm. As example, one of the richest men in the U. S., with a great deal of influence, is Warren Buffett, age over 80, obviously not a boomer, first or any other kind.

This refusal to exit the stage has created a serious backlog of competing beliefs and principals in the Party all the while the world moves along. Think Prince Charles, immobile King in waiting, as his mother still sits the throne. Time's a wasting and we got better things to do than deal with our predecessor's issues! But wait we must, or kill the old geezers off. But that is quite frowned upon and civilized societies just don't do those things.

But why is there such a disagreement in beliefs, principals and oral traditions between the groups? Weren't the current elders the older siblings of the first boomers? Weren't they taught the same? Well, no. And the second and third boomers weren't taught the same as the first boomers. The time from the end of World War II until 1980 was very dynamic in society, technology and thought in the United States. More so than at any time in the United States and that is saying something. Educational theories changed almost every ten years and these new theories were instituted in the schools as quickly as they hatched. We went to the moon and computers became an everyday part of our lives. The Civil Rights Act, Voter Reform Act, and Great Society all came during this time. Kennedy, Luther, and Kennedy again were slain and Nixon lied. Vietnam soared and we fought the Cold War and nuclear arsenals. It was in a word, volatile. The generation before the boomers and each iteration of the boomer generation learned a new set of values and learned it in a new way.

To add to this volatility even the boomers, within their iterations, or tweeners within theirs, didn't learn or adhere to the same beliefs as a homogenous group. In the sixties we had first boomers marching against the Vietnam War, taking drugs, participating in free love, and worst of the worst the boys were growing long hair. Basically rebelling against everything they thought their fathers generation supported. But we also had a strong group of first boomer men and women that supported their fathers and mothers beliefs, didn't do drugs, didn't jump into bed at the drop of a hat, (any hat I might add), and supported the efforts in Vietnam. They actually volunteered to go fight the commies. Schizophrenic I believe is the word. A lot of this difference can be seen in the election of President of two seemingly opposites of the same coin, Bill Clinton and George W. Bush.

So instead of a generation basically growing up together experiencing the same issues, debating the same problems, we have a large generation with disturbingly different levels of experiences trying to relate to each other. And an older generation that has no clue what the other generations are talking about trying to lead, while the next generation is pushing them off the stage. In the wings we have younger generations just rolling their eyes at the futility of it all, because when we are gone they are going to change it all anyhow. Think of a traffic jam where everyone wants to get home but they all bunch up behind the large slow moving truck up front. All want to lead and all feel it is their turn, but they can't seem to get the guy up front to pull over to the side of the road. Which begs the question; what are these differences? Why can't they reconcile and what happens when one of them win the paradigm war?

Educational values are a good place to begin to answer these questions. For those of you not introduced to theology I can only apologize for taking this path. But it does have some relevance here so where the big words come in I will go slowly. (Hey, not for you, for me. I am not a theologian and these things can get hard!) That said, how students are taught is as important as what students are taught. In other words the theory behind the teaching is important. Public education in the United States has historically been a generally local and state issue. As such compulsory education really didn't become nationally accepted until 1918. (Yes, an accepted national compulsory education ideology, education that says you have to have at least an elementary education, was a product of the just last century. It isn't even 100 years old yet!)

Since education was a local issue, what was taught and how it was taught was a local issue as well. The nationwide acceptance of the idea of compulsory education was a product of the Progressive Era, 1890-1920's. During this time Frederick Taylor introduced scientific management and Ford introduced the production line. Cars were overtaking horses. What was new and progressive was what was important. Into this stepped a theory called positivism that espoused that the only authentic knowledge is that which, by experiment, can be positively proven. That there is a single truth and with patience and effort this single truth can be found and understood. In this theory what can be observed by the human senses, what is in other words, empirically evident, is authentic. Just believing something is out of the question. You must prove it empirically. Rationality raised its authorative head.

Sounds good doesn't it. No more belief in the supernatural. A plus B equals C. No equivocation. We have created boundaries that we all agree upon. If you can't prove it, it ain't so. This theory was adopted by the public educational institutions across the United States and was a staple in them until about 1960. Oddly enough just about the time the second boomers entered first grade and the first boomers were leaving elementary school. So the tweeners and first boomers were taught in the positivistic vein, but the second boomers and third boomers weren't. The second boomers and third boomers were taught post-positivism or post-modernism theories.

Post-modernism said well, it depends. There is no one truth. Truth depends on your point of view. For example, if you have two football teams competing, when the game ends one wins and one loses. If you are the winner, the Truth is the outcome of the game is good. But to the loser, the Truth is the outcome is bad. So Truth depends on your point of view. (To you golfers the analogy would be; "Every golf shot makes someone happy."). This adaption of post-modernism in education created a situation where we have two groups from the same generation taught in essence two opposing theories that espouse opposite viewpoints.

The tweeners and boomers begin the process of not understanding each other's position because we basically haven't the same learning foundation. We just don't understand how the other can think what they do.   The first boomers and tweeners expect a rational, definitive answer. One Truth all can see and agree upon. The second and third boomers accept that there may be and is more than one answer for the same question. There is no one rational answer. There is no one Truth. It is always relative and depends on who is answering the question. If the groups are not even accepting each other's basic premise how can we expect them to agree on anything! (OK group, right here is where we blame our moms and dads. It all their fault because they let us go to these crazy schools.)

Education wasn't the only major difference. The way tweeners and the iterations of the boomer generation interacted with each other and received their information was vastly different. How they perceived that information was also different. Tweeners were newspapers and radio. First boomers added television. Tweeners and first boomers saw the first televised Presidential debate. Walter Cronkite, Huntley and Brinkley, and the very heavy hand of Broadcast Standards and Practices were the staples on television.

These announcers and the perceived protection of Standards and Practices created a trust in the content provided by television. While television was a novelty for their parents, TV was a major source of information for tweeners and first boomers. Compiled with the teachings standards that emphasized empirical results, what can be observed is true, tweeners and first boomers believed television and more importantly television news. First boomers and tweeners continue this trust and belief to this day. (Which on many levels explains FOX News, I'm just saying.) Historical associations permeated by their parents also created a strong attachment to newspapers and radio as a source of information. This attachment is evidenced by the continued existence of newspapers companies through their sale to older generations. It is also evidenced in the growth of talk radio.

Second boomers looked behind the curtain. Taught to look at issues from many perspectives, second and third boomers, don't trust any single answer.   If it was presented as Truth on television, their first response was "prove it". Drove everybody mad. Television was a fantasy for second boomers. It was a primary source of information, but one that should be questioned. No longer impressed with the "magic" of television, second boomers took TV as a utility, a source of entertainment. They were aware that shows were depictions and often false depictions. Still TV became omnipresent in the household and secured a place in the main living room. The day wasn't done until the TV was turned off.

Third boomers were even more attached to the constant noise of television, but at the same time distant from its content. Television to them had turned into more of an entertainment source that an information source. Monday Night Football, the World Series, and MASH were the programs that third boomers watched. Third boomers saw the introduction of computers and cell phones. They also began watching cable television. Their news sources became much more varied and plentiful. Like the second boomers before them, they realized Truth was relative. But they had more sources of information that proved the concept.

Events were very much a source of differences to the tweeners and boomers. Tweeners were heavily pressured by their fathers and mothers that won the "Great War". Under their parents guidance the United States had gone from a regional power into a world power. Its industrial might was unquestioned in the world. In the four decades that followed World War II the United States became and was the most powerful, rich and influential nation in the world. The tweeners and boomers grew up in a time of prosperity and wealth. The boomers particularly never knew a time when they weren't number one in the world. The boomers knew the "American Dream" and fully expected it to be given them.

But the tweeners and boomers were also isolations in a sense. Aware of the world, but yet mired by a policy that looked inward toward success. Tweeners and boomers looked to be a success in the good ole USA market. Competition was within the country. Who was the biggest U.S. company? Who won the World Series? Even though only teams in the United States competed in the World Series. The United States was defined by its internal assets, it wealth, not what its standing was as compared to the world's countries. After all, why should they? They were basically the only ones left standing at the end of World War II.

But the tweeners had a war of their own, the forgotten war, Korea. Boomers had Vietnam. Neither ranked in the pantheons of success as World War II did for their fathers. Korea was a tie, Vietnam, by many accounts, a loss. Instead of cheers and ticker tape parades, (Ticker tape. Now there is another difference between the generations. Ticker tape wasn't even around when these boys came home.), Korean veterans just marshaled out and went to work.

Vietnam veterans were often spit upon, called names, and went into drug rehab.

First boomers saw a president assassinated, Sputnik soar, and a space race started. First boomers rebelled against the oppression of their fathers and mothers beliefs. First boomers also fought each other over the righteousness of those beliefs. Folk music, rock and roll, the Beatles, sit ins, love ins and the draft were all a part of first boomers environment. The interstate highway system was built, making the individual and the family mobile. The Boeing 707, commercial jet aviation, and the "jet set" had their influence on the first boomers. The women's movement to reclaim rights their mothers and grandmothers had grew side by side with the Playboy Club.

Second boomer watched their brother and sisters in the first boomer iteration fight each other and their parents over the war. The second boomers saw fights in the streets over black's civil rights, the assassination of Bobby Kennedy and Martin Luther King. The idea of two opinions, more than one truth, was burned into their minds through these confrontations. Second boomers also saw Nixon resign in disgrace, Pentagon papers and knew the government did and does lie. Second boomers also saw Gemini, Apollo, Armstrong, and the landing on the moon. Second boomers lived through the Cold War, possible nuclear annihilation, school busing and the country turning 200 years old.

Third boomers survived busing and watched Iran tell the greatest country in the world to take a hike. Third boomers saw personal computers take the stage and video games begin to take our attention. Third boomers witnessed oil become a commodity for war and gas shortages. They saw the malaise of recession and the ascendency of a movie star to president. Third boomers were the first iteration of boomers to know that the country could fail. They witnessed the loss of jobs and the invasion of Asian economic giants. Third boomers understood that the virtue of their birth did not guarantee they would be the biggest, best and brightest. In short third boomers were witness to the end of the golden age of prosperity in the United States and its guarantee of the American Dream.

These backgrounds, environments, learning and historical differences all contribute to a generation of people that really don't know what the other is talking about. One group demands a simple, rational solution developed in a logical manner between choices. This group seeks a truth. The other group looks bewildered and wonders what planet did this idiot come from? There is no Truth. There are choices. Since they can't communicate, where do we go from here?

The answer is not simple. The natural response, most prominently with tweeners and boomers, is to beat into submission those that don't understand, refuse to accept the stated position, or just basically don't do what they are told. But compliance by brute force is not acceptance. To establish a lasting paradigm you need adherents. Adherents can only be won by persuasion and evidence. So what do the individual paradigms have to offer? Why should we accept one and not the other? Nice question. Let's look into it.

So Why Not Have a Tweener and First Boomer Paradigm?

Are you kidding? Have me tell my older sister she was right? Seriously that is not going to happen. Besides the sibling issue there are other reasons. First in the tweener and boomer iterations, as in all other iterations, there are conservative and liberal paradigms and a flurry of those in between. So we have to look at what the liberal and conservative paradigms have to offer.

Whether an individual, and in extension an organization, can accept a paradigm, whether the paradigm can attract adherents, is directly related to the environment an individual experiences and how they were taught. Therefore, the events, parental influences, peer influences, teachers, and socio-economic environment all have an impact on what an individual will accept in their lives as guiding principles, traditions and rules. Of these influences, it cannot be overstated how important the influence of positivistic theory, (the theory that there was only one truth), was on tweener's and first boomer's educational background. Positivistic theory also had a direct impact on the analyzation and evaluation processes of these individuals.

And why shouldn't positivistic theory have an impact? Using this theory the United States went from a regional power to a world power. Our scientific management and resources produced an abundance of ammunitions, planes, ships and other products that overwhelmed the enemy and won a war. Sounds like a winner and any paradigm built upon it would wear well. But there are issues. First and foremost is that positivistic theory believes in only one truth and a truth that can be empirically proven. Positivistic theory also believes that everything, even human nature, can be categorized, manipulated, and pigeonholed. (Sound familiar, liberals. I know. Conservatives have no idea that this is an issue. We'll go on.) Positivism believes that experiments can be performed on human society and nature in the same vein as we would experiment on any chemical, material or gas. In other words, humans are just cogs in the machinery.

Conservative boomers and tweeners embraced this logic. It was so clean and sanitized. Conservative affirmative attitudes towards positivism can be expected as positivism had a contemporary in economic principles also embraced by conservatives, classical liberalism. Classical liberalism combined with positivism had controllable rationalities for the organization of humans and human behavior, a great benefit for those that must be in charge. Classical liberalism as we have discussed earlier made four basic assumptions about human nature: 1) People are motivated solely by pain or pleasure. 2) People make decisions to minimize pain or maximize pleasure. 3). If no opportunity to increase pain or reduce pleasure, they sit. 4) Society is no greater than the sum of its members. In simpler terms humans can be easily manipulated. Well that is if you are from a lower economic and intellectual structure. The elites are so far above manipulation.

You place the classical liberalism and the positivistic theory together you have a very rational belief system in the structure of society and the interactions of human beings. Measurements can be done. Standards can be created. There becomes an emphasis on tangibles. Money, cars, homes, have value and are marks of success. The bigger the homes, the bigger the car, the larger bank account, all have value. Poor are poor because they want to be. Interpersonal relationships, because they can't be seen, can't be measured, have no value. Money becomes the only standard by which value is judged. It becomes a very materialistic belief system.

This is the values environment that conservative tweeners and first boomers grew up in. You see this in a lot of the organizations in which they take part. (TEA Party and Dixiecrats comes to mind.) Simple solutions for direct questions, a belief if you aren't working it is because your lazy, money is the only motivator, and success is in proportion to your wealth, are all inherent beliefs.

It is not unusual to connect the wealth of an individual to his intelligence and status. The more wealth an individual has the more intelligent they must be and the more status they must have. All of these values are based in tangible measurements, rationalistic teachings, and belief in the idea of one simple truth.

But if it looks like I'm just picking on conservatives, I'm not. Tweener and first boomer liberals were taught in the same schools. They were also taught by their parents and peers. They weren't taught differently, they just learned different lessons. Remember Roosevelt and New Dealism? Well liberals were strong on the belief that government, primarily the federal government, had a duty to support the people. Welfare, Social Security, Medicare, and a host of other programs were ushered in by the parents of tweeners and first boomers. Like conservatives there was a belief in the one truth. Unlike conservative first boomers and tweeners, liberal tweeners and first boomers believed truth was based in social liberalism, the belief in the well being of the whole community. They believed that you have to remove poverty, ignorance, and disease. Once freed from those problems, individuals become productive members of the community.

Wealth was not a measurement of success for liberal first boomers and tweeners. It was a sign of potential corruption, a belief in the materials of life, not the quality of life. If you were rich you were greedy and didn't care about society. The measure of success for liberals was the reduction of poverty and want, the production of public schools and the availability of hospitals. Each, as in a positivistic manner, was given a measure. Poverty was measured as part of the whole country. The number of hospitals were counted, the number of hospital beds and doctors were counted. Schools were counted, as were the number of teachers. Wage standards were created. Companies and governments were judged by these standards. As with the conservative first boomers and tweeners all of these values were based in tangible measurements, rationalistic teachings and belief in the idea of one simple truth.

The tweeners and first boomers are all pragmatic and practical. Fix this, it will repair that, simple straight forward solutions to difficult problems. We just have to find that one truth that will solve the puzzle. And like positivistic theory problem solving teaches, just because we didn't get it right the first time doesn't negate the solution. We just have to adjust and tweak the experiment a little more to get it right the second time, or third, or even more tries. A little more money, a little more understanding, a little of this and a little of that and you will finally get it right. (How many times have I heard that from tweeners and first boomers? It is so frustrating because they are NEVER wrong. It just wasn't done quite right! Dude, you were WRONG!)

This positivistic theory and learning pervades first boomers and tweeners on both sides of the aisle. When Bill Clinton came to office and had a majority of his party in the U. S. House and Senate his first priority was to solve health care. Didn't succeed, but there was a large effort expended, even putting the most effective member of his staff, Hillary Clinton, in charge of the process. Under Clinton attention was paid to the alleviation of pain and suffering and measured in the percentages of unemployed or poor.

When George W. Bush came into office he brought with him social scientists and policy makers that favored a more conservative positivist mode of thinking. Rational thinking was King under Bush and public programs that wanted political support had to provide measurable, quantifiable results based on conservative measuring principals. Social programs as well as health programs were evaluated based on whether they could provide these empirical results. As in positivistic theory, if there was no means for empirical results, then the program had no value and was rejected.

The adherence to these values continues unto this day. They are embedded in the tweeners and first boomers regardless of the events that have happened since their groups became aware all of those years ago. Recent emails have been sent out by Progressive liberals that express seven basic tenants that will resolve our issues with Congress. Each of the tenants has social basis and express thoughts of making the Congress more like the common man that they govern. By making the Congress more of the community, the community will be healthier and have better laws. Quantifiable actions, empirical results, one simple truth, these are the elements of positivistic theory.

But conservative tweeners and first boomers are no less adherents in this day. The recent efforts to expand standardized testing for students are no more than a need for quantifiable results. A need for an empirical justification of the education programs we have. (As if to say over 200 years of success in public education is not enough justification. I'm just saying.) A reliance on the stock market, a specific stock market average, the Dow Jones average, to gauge the wellness of the country is also a product of positivistic thinking. A continued search for one truth, quantifiable and empirical is part of the rational conservative belief system.

And both groups, liberal and conservative first boomers and tweeners, belief systems are all based on theories over 100 years old and haven't been used to teach any generational members for over fifty years. In essence to use positivistic theory, social liberalism, and classic liberalism in this day and age is to discount all the research and progress made in theory and practice for the last 100 years. It is to assume that what was created once is forever filed in the Book of Eternal Truths and never to be debated again. This is why so many first boomers and tweeners always want to go backward and recapture the past. They want to recapture a time when the U.S., its industry and the country was world renowned as number one. It is what they know, lived and learned. Tweeners and first boomers are concentrating so hard on what they feel they lost. They are not paying attention to what we have gained. The antiquity of their belief system, the emphasis on their past, the antagonism towards events unfolding, the refusal to accept any alterations to their positions, and the imposition of the unquestioned belief in one truth is what makes tweeners and first boomers paradigms unacceptable to the majority.

Yet the first boomers and tweeners staying power, due to the enhanced longevity of age in the United States, makes this very paradigm and it variations between conservatives and liberals a constant ignition point for political debate. Tweeners and first boomers wish to embed this logic and their beliefs into the fabric of their respective parties, and thus the United States governing bodies, as their legacy to this country and its people. As if their belief systems are the only correct possible choice for their heirs. They are afraid and angry that their younger brothers and sisters won't accept their guidance. They are after all just doing what is best for us, our children and our country.

But at best the argument is futile. Second boomers particularly, (There is just no way we are going to do what our older brothers and sisters think is right.), third boomers and those that follow will not accept this paradigm. It is too steeped in disputed theory, it looks inward instead of outward and it looks to the past instead of the future. First boomer and tweener paradigms have persuasive points, single truth and measurable results, but even those are fabrications against reality.

Why not accept first boomer and tweener paradigms? What is wrong with them? Basically because they aren't based upon the experiences and learning theories of those that follow. Their arguments are exposed as flawed and what remains is not persuasive enough to make them foundational. As soon as enough first boomers and tweeners leave the stage, the other competing paradigms will dismiss this legacy. It is only a matter of time. Simply put, those that follow think the tweeners and first boomers and their paradigm, are old fashioned and irrelevant. But until that time when this group literally dies off the fight rages on between the conservative, liberals, second boomers, third boomers and those that follow them.

So What is So Great About Second Boomer Paradigms?

Well since I consider myself more of an older second boomer than a younger first boomer, everything is greater about second boomer paradigms. Duh! First of all second boomers were raised in postmodernism theory. This theory as stated earlier believes everything is relative. There is no one single truth. Truth depends on your point of view. You can have multiple points of view and all of them are right. Subjective is the term for it. We even accept as truths things that cannot be empirically proven. (I can hear you. Spirits, ghosts, UFO's. Yep, the loony's are in town.) As a consequence material things are not the only things of value and monetary value is not the only measure.

If this doesn't put us at odds with our older siblings, nothing will! But a result of having an infinite number of truths is we do not have just one to hold onto. This can be a drawback when trying to establish a set of beliefs and principles. We often find ourselves questioning the decisions that we made. Second boomers are very situational. In other words, what you choose depends on the situation. The truth is of the moment and the time. To many this doesn't present a defined path and a defined set of values. To our older brothers and sisters who depend on knowing which direction to be traveled this is idiocy.

Positivism, as we have said, was the dominant theoretical perspective, and gained total commitment from the first boomers and tweeners after WW II due to the great success of the United States economy. The United States economy and wealth grew exponentially during the time after the war, proof positive in most of the tweeners and first boomer's minds that this was the one true path. But it can be strongly argued that the growth of the country and economy was due more to a devastated world economy than any influence of classical liberalism and positivism. After WW II the European economy for all intents and purposes didn't exist. It took the Marshall plan to get it moving. Japan had literally been reduced to embers after the fire and atomic bombings on its country by the Allies. The devastation Japan had visited upon China and its other neighbors during the war left those countries in ruins as well. The United States remained as the primary, if not sole nation, with facilities capable of creating needed materials worldwide. The United States was the sole source provider for a world that had a ready and desperate need for manufactured goods. Basically anything we made got bought.

The economic good times, under positivism, lasted for about thirty years after the war. But the good times did end. For those of you boomers and tweeners old enough, remember the first gas crisis in the early seventies, or even the spiraling interest rates in the late seventies early eighties? What was happening was the countries that were destroyed were rebuilding. By the 1980's Japan was often referred to as Japan, Inc. as it made huge strides buying up United States properties and businesses and selling Japanese goods to U. S. citizens. In essence our victory in WW II gave us the ability to become big and it also placed the U. S. in the lead of a new global economy. However, positivistic theory and classic liberalism don't work as well in a global model. Positivism and classic liberalism were more internal structures meant for individual corporate structures or isolated governments, places and areas that could be controlled. People and cultures around the world can't be controlled, especially from one centralized source, so positivism started to fail. A United States Truth is not necessarily, if not ever, a foreign country's Truth. A new structure was needed to cope with a new environment and postmodernism stepped into the need.

Postmodernism said let's share. Let's learn about each other and each other's needs. Let's try to understand what you need and give you what you want instead of telling you what you need. Postmodernism believed if you took the time to find out what someone wanted, what their Truth was, and worked to give it to them, you would increase your success and their productivity.

Everyone didn't want money as a reward. Respect, security and dignity were just as important as cash. Understanding what individuals needed globally created success globally. This is the values system second boomers, third boomers and those that followed grew up in and were taught. The values system works well in a global environment as it has been found each culture has different values and requirements often completely devoid from the requirements of other civilizations. In essence globally there is more than one Truth.

Postmodernism met the needs of the emerging global environment the United States economy and political environment were enmeshed. Where positivism required, nay demanded, structure and control, postmodernism embraced organic functions and improvisations. Positivism couldn't work in the new environment that that the destruction of WW II and rebuilding of the global market created. Positivism, its cohorts scientific management and classic liberalism, looked at employees and people as cogs in the structure, interchangeable and dispensable. Positivism believed that everyone, but those at the top were inherently lazy, worked as little as possible, and were only concerned with their well being.

Postmodernism recognized the dignity and inherent work ethics of men and women. They were not interchangeable parts in machinery. Postmodernism believed that people had a self interest in the betterment of themselves and their country. Postmodernism realized and accepted the multiple cultures and beliefs. These were not obstacles to be overcome but assets to be embraced. Postmodernism spoke to inclusion, positivism spoke to control. (Sounds a bit new ager and touchy feely don't it? Conservatives, especially conservative guys, are saying no way! Not us! But actually, way, dude!)

Learning theory wasn't the only driver of second boomer paradigms. Second boomers were also, in essence, the middle child. The one forgotten until they did something great and then everybody takes credit for teaching them so well, which goes to the point. Second boomers formed opinions from observation of what was happening around them. They were in the invisible kid in the background while mom and dad were struggling over what to do with older brother and sister. Second boomers were watched their older brothers and sisters. They heard their music, looked through the keyhole why they participated in free love, watched them march off to war and not return, and picked at the remains of the last drug fest. Second boomers were the kids bused away from their friends and schools so blacks could be accepted. They watched the moon landings and saw U. S. soldiers leave Vietnam on a chopper. Second boomers learned about endless war and government betrayal.

In other words the lessons learned by second boomers were not the lessons of an infallible United States standing as guardian for all that is good and wonderful as impressed upon tweeners and first boomers. Second boomers learned the United States and its government, especially its politicians, can be and often are corruptible. They learned that there are hidden conspiracies designed to use the United States for the furtherance of personal agendas. Second boomers are inherently suspicious of their government and their politicians. They do not believe that every action the United States makes is right for those affected, especially in international affairs.

Second boomers also find it odd that so much emphasis is placed on politicians "flip-flopping". Actually many find it amusing and distracting to the issues at hand. To second boomers, not having a second or even third opinion is incredible and a sign of ignorance and lack of experience. The sign of intelligence, to a second boomer, is recognizing that not all the facts were available when the first decision was made. Making a second decision, based on new evidence, is preferable in an individual. Second boomers can accept that their decisions were WRONG. (As opposed to first boomers and tweeners.) This leads many first boomers and tweeners to the erroneous belief that this second boomers need to be led because they obviously can't make a decision. This belief cause's continuous turmoil between the two groups as one frequently tries to get the decision right and the other keeps trying to direct them to an obvious choice.

The paradigms created by second boomers as a result of postmodernism, lessons learned in silence, and understanding of fallibility, stood in stark contrast to the required simplistic view of positivism.   Where tweeners and first boomers looked for one answer, second boomers saw more than one answer. Where tweeners and first boomers repeatedly tweaked solutions to make them work, second boomers discarded failure and tried something new. Where tweeners and first boomers believed in the American

Dream and United States infallibility, second boomers accepted that the United States' decisions were often wrong and the American Dream had to be remade.

Second boomer liberals never gave up the idea that education and an end to poverty would, in the end, create freedom and allow individuals to succeed and grow. How they succeeded and how they grew became different ideas. What measure, if any, you used to determine success was up to the individual to decide. While national measures were still a part of the focus, more local and individual measures were embraced. For second boomers liberals it was more a right of choice than a requirement to succeed or move out of poverty. The primary factor was that if you chose to move, there were no barriers to your progress. In second boomers minds government needed to provide help where needed, but more importantly it needed to ensure it wasn't the problem.

Liberal second boomers are suspicious of the private sector, politicians and government programs. They feel strongly that they have reason to be. They can accept that the national government literally cannot afford many of the large national programs embraced by first boomer liberals. They also know that these programs often are corrupted, burdensome and intrusive and no amount of tweaking will ever get it right. But even in their suspicions and pragmatism, they realize that government, national government, can serve as a means to prohibit other state and local governments from inhibiting the choice of individuals to move out of poverty and create their own success. This is where they get into arguments with conservative second boomers.

Conservative second boomers paradigms reacted to the emerging world market in a more positive way than tweeners and first boomers. Drawing upon their postmodernism teaching they embraced and worked with the various markets and their needs rather than trying to control them. Knowing the fallibility and corruptions of governments and government programs, conservative second boomers began working hard to decentralize governmental controls and place government programs into the hands of private business. Neoliberalism theories that stressed private enterprise, liberalized trade and open markets in creating and implementing public policy and public programs emerged. This followed closely with their postmodern teachings that stressed more than one solution, or Truth, for any problem.

This is an obvious contradiction from liberal second boomers who still believe in the necessity of a strong hand of government to control corrupt private enterprise. Conservative second boomers looked at government as corrupt and liberal second boomers looked at private businessmen that took advantage of governments as corrupt. While second boomer liberals are looking for more balance between government and the individuals they govern, second boomer conservatives are trying to shift government functions to the private sector and increase private sector power.

This works well with conservative second boomers perception of the emerging world markets. Governments are perceived to be archaic. While enabling processes such as defense, infrastructure and identity, governments also stand in the way of a freer market between countries. Many conservative second boomers perceive themselves as citizens of the world than actual citizens of a country. Their identity lies more with their company and/or party than the country they claim citizenship. This is quite a departure from the solid identity and positivistic learning of tweeners and first boomers and it may not be wrong.

The increase in speed, world trade, markets and information is breaking down the boundaries of countries and opening many venues of trade. Looking at the world as one large potential market instead of individualized governments makes the interpersonal relationships of individuals across the globe possible. Recognizing that often business, or the possibility of business, led the way to progress across the globe is acknowledgement of fact. Seeing yourself as a citizen of the world first allows you to view international solutions to poverty, hunger and fear. Continuing to view governments as a needed fixture precludes the possibility of the evolution of the human condition. It also prolongs the probability of continued global armed conflict.

But unilateral abolition of a strong government also places the country in jeopardy of being overrun by those less enlightened. Establishment of corporate controlled armed forces creates the probability of feudal warlords that work for the highest bidder. Privately run prisons, fire departments, and sheriff's offices lead toward services and justice only for those that can afford them. While the world has changed and men and women have definitely evolved, greed is still an overriding desire of individuals. When given the power to command and control over others, humans still succumb to the desire. These factors leave the conservative second boomers in a constant conflict with liberal second boomers and those that follow. Their abandonment of positivistic established tweener and first boomer paradigms also leaves them in conflict with their own conservatives.

As a consequence of these conflicts within their own ideologies it is hard to ascertain the direction that second boomer paradigms will eventually embrace. The first real recognized second boomer political leader of either Party is Barack Obama. While supported mostly by Democrats, you will often see first boomer liberals and tweeners expressing disappointment at the direction his presidency has take. His signature legislations seem to embrace both Main Street and social liberalism. He wants to raise the level of education and support for the poor while maintaining the ability to make money off the result. He does not fully embrace first boomer social programs that require full implementation by the government. But he does not abandon the need for government oversight, regulation and requirements of the programs. Final analysis will have to be done after he leaves office and/or after another second boomer liberal replaces him in a leadership role to define the actual direction second boomer liberals may be heading.

With the pressure of third boomers, those behind them and the backlog of first boomers and tweeners refusing to leave the stage, depending on the outcome of the election, Obama may be the only second boomer to claim the presidency. This would leave us to derive the direction of second boomer conservatives from multiple venues of leadership. (As a liberal I would not find this lamentable.) But this possibility does leave a strong reason for the vocal vitriolic of the second boomer conservatives. If something doesn't happen soon, they and their ideas may be left behind before they even have a chance to be heard.

The creation of party political paradigms will not be done by second boomers, much to my chagrin. The evidence lies in the loud voices of the second boomer conservatives. There is precious little time to be heard let alone create a paradigm that can attract enough adherents to build a lasting paradigm. We are the middle child and we were born too close to our brothers and sisters. In addition the siren cry of business that the second boomer conservatives would have us hear and heed to resolve all our woes had too many known flaws.

First and foremost is the previously stated axiom that business is not in business to encourage competition, it is in business to eliminate competition. It goes against the very nature of the beast to allow competition of any sort to live and thrive while it can be eliminated. This very nature prohibits the use of business to guide and/or even be government as those second boomer conservatives and others that adhere to tenants of neo-liberalism present. Business cannot be a neutral arbiter that encourages the creation of new and better businesses. Business does not encourage democracy, even within its own shell. Shareholders have votes, but one shareholder can have more votes than all other votes combine. In business this often happens, thus negating any free exchange or vestige of democracy.

Secondly business isn't in business to make things better for everyone. It is in business to make things better for itself and its owners. Business has a huge self interest and is not designed to be altruistic. Business, as in its nature, will always work for the betterment of itself over others. These natural instincts of business are the reasons running government like a business is not in the best interests of a country, especially a country on the edge of working in a global economy.

Government, whether history judges it so or not, is supposed to be a neutral arbiter of what is best for the people. Government, especially democratic government, is supposed to encourage competition, work for the future of everyone and ensure all voices are heard regardless of wealth, position, or the number of shares you own. Votes are to representative of the people, under the principle of one vote for one person, not base upon the percentage of ownership. We move in a direction, because the majority of individuals chose to move in that direction, not because the majority of shares chose to take us there.

Justice, in government, is blind because she is not supposed to be influenced by position, power or wealth. Justice is supposed to weigh what is just, not what the majority, position or power wants, but what is just and rule in favor of those principles. Too often an understanding of democratic principles of majority rules, gets in the way of understanding justice. Justice doesn't rule in favor of the public majority. It is justice's job, the courts job, to protect the rights of the few from the will of the many, too rule on what is just, not expedient. Justice, or the courts provided by government, is designed to protect the least of us from mob rule. These principles are in constant conflict with the nature of business. This conflict will prohibit and impede any progress second boomer conservatives have on creating a dominant paradigm.

But second boomer liberals have the issues of their own with creating an acceptable paradigm. They do not believe as their parents and many first boomers and tweeners believe that large government programs are the solution to future problems. The advent of the Health Care Act, if it survives, may be the last large government program initiative implemented. Second boomer liberals saw the corruption in many welfare and medical programs of the Great Society. They realize that at the current rate of expansion that 60% of the federal government's budget will be set aside for social programs. The government is becoming one big social service agency. Like the business paradigm suggested by conservatives, this is not the role of government.

Second boomers have seen the required "neutrality biases" imposed by government programs and departments. Too often the needs, emotional and otherwise, of those that are intended to be helped are ignored in favor ensuring the governments neutrality in the interaction. One individual or family's needs cannot be measured by another's. Yet government in an everlasting mission to be fair, attempts to do just that. Government issues food stamps with formulas, places children in foster care based on ratings criteria, and advances medical care on based on ratings.

Large government programs have been corrupted and abused. They are expensive, even when the citizens pay directly for the support themselves through payroll tax deductions. The evidence of liberal second boomer's reluctance to impose these large massive programs lies in the health care debate itself. Democrats controlled both houses of government and the presidency. Yet, a Democrat favored program, could not generate enough Democratic votes to ensure its passage until it looked as though it would be dead forever. Many blamed President Obama for lack of leadership. Others blamed the politics of the Senate that required a super majority.

Yet Congress provided the votes and created the law. But the Democratic Congress couldn't agree. Liberal second boomer reservations came into play. The compromises accepted by President Obama are evidenced of this. Placing more emphasis on the states to implement health care and creating health exchanges instead of single payer programs were items acceptable to many second boomer liberals. This created more choices, placed the burdens more on individuals, states and companies and in essence embraced the logic of more than one solution.

These stances will not bring adherents to second boomer paradigms. Trying to allow a solution for every instance is not good government, but leans towards anarchy. Second boomer liberalism paradigms rely too much on consensus and not enough on direct action. There is a fallacy in consensus building that it will lead to the best solution for all, but often consensus leads to the lowest level of agreed upon solution, creating a weak, useless decision and weaker government. Consensus building and trying to allow for multiple solutions disallows the dynamic leader that makes hard decisions. Consensus inhibits and disdains those that would lead by decree. But it is often those that take the hard course and are willing to jeopardize their own position that move the rest of us forward. Leaders are needed.

Unacceptable parameters will not allow second boomer's paradigms to flourish. But even more than parameters time will stand in the way. There was not a president born after 1924 until Bill Clinton and he was born in 1946. Basically President Clinton was a first boomer; the tweeners really haven't seen a member of their class in a leadership position. Presidents Clinton and George H. W. Bush were both first boomers, but were followed by President Obama who is definitely a second boomer. There is every probability that after the 2012 elections the next president will be a third boomer.

The elders at the top, the tweeners, will be, if alive, well into their seventies by then. They are arriving at the point where even advanced medical care can't forestall the inevitable. Inside of five years they will be leaving the stage whether they wish to go or not. But what would be a moment for first boomers and second boomers will be shortened by the backup created by those in front. If anyone has been in a traffic jam behind some lumbering big rig, as soon as a new lane opens up the flow starts to pick up and move freely. But there is inevitably that group of young, speedier, and more aggressive drivers that jump past you to gain the front and move beyond your line of vision. This group is, for our analogy, the third boomers and those that follow. Seniority, or being the elder, doesn't matter in the creation of the paradigms at this juncture. This third boomer group has been waiting and watching for too many of the wrong reasons and doesn't want to listen to any more. Second boomers will not be heeded by third boomers or their older first boomers. But this doesn't mean that second boomers won't try. They too have been denied there allotted time in the sun.

The next obvious section of this book should be about third boomers. It seems that is what we are leading up to. I mean there is some thirty plus years of births since the second boomers became aware in 1975. You would expect a detailed dissection of their emerging paradigms if they are going to be so important. Also some detailed discussion of those that follow third boomers, would be an interesting piece. But, truth is third boomers are still new to the stage and becoming aware of their importance. While third boomer ideas are emerging, paradigm development is not shaping up. Mostly third boomers are just tired of the bickering between tweeners, first boomers, and second boomers and just want it to end. They know they will do it their own way anyhow, so why listen to a bunch of old timers? Let's just get going.

Third boomers became aware as a group in 1985. This means the youngest was ten years old in 1985 and the oldest was twenty. In 2012 it will have been only 27 years since this group became aware. The oldest will be 47 years old and the youngest 37. Acquisition of power, money and prestige,(Bill Gates, Steve Jobs and a few exceptional others exempted.) historically begins in the mid forties and culminates in the late fifties of an individual's life. Mid forties is when most individuals develop enough contacts and experience to begin considering their opinions valid. Mid to late fifties is when most people are able to capitalize on their contacts and experience to turn these assets into wealth and power. Under these historical markers, third boomers are just now beginning to have an impact and opinion on the development of paradigms. The reason their paradigm is not dissected at this stage is they haven't really developed one. But in five years, by 2017, or the beginning of another presidential term, they should be ready to fight for the acceptance of one of their making.

Basically, third boomer paradigms in the making, make the next few years critical in their development. The events and environments that they will encounter will have significant affect, along with their prior learning experiences, in the development of the next paradigm. The ability of this group to engage in longevity in politics greater than tweeners, first boomers, and second boomers, will make their emerging paradigms of great significance to the world and the country. The reason for the possible longevity of their paradigm is in the ability to benefit from the pile up of the tweeners, first and second boomer paradigms. To continue the traffic analogy, third boomer will view from a distant vantage point the wreck created by those they follow and choose another course to implement their paradigm. They will bypass all the old traffic tie ups that have consumed those that have gone before.

Those that follow the third boomers quite frankly are just too young. The next group that became aware were not boomers at all. Their experiences and environment, just because they will be the first not labeled boomers, will be interesting to observe. They will be guided by a more global experience than any of the boomer generations could have imagined. But the oldest of this group is 37, unless they are a new Bill Gates, Steve Jobs or other person with exceptional history or talent, their experiences and contacts will not be developed enough to affect paradigms for at least 15 years.

So Where Does This Leave Us? What Now?

Since discussion of third boomer paradigms and paradigms for those that follow would be premature or irrelevant, attention then must be paid to what has been learned. I began this trip to discern why the political rhetoric has been so volatile. Why are people so afraid and so angry? Are TEA Parties evil cottontops or are they concerned patriots? Are Republicans the source of all our partisanship or are Democrats to blame? As usual I wanted simple answers and, as in life, nothing is simple.

One of the first things learned is everyone's resistance to nature's inevitable mood, change. As commented frequently those that prescribe a paradigm often want their ideas to be enshrined in the Book of Everlasting Truths. Men and women are not allowed to write in that book. This inability frustrates them and they use threats, pale arguments and false logic to convince many that they have, in fact, writ in the Book. But nature will have her way, (Yes, nature is a woman. It has to be. It is so changeable.), and she ignores these vain attempts. Time eventually draws back the veil and shows them false.

But why do individuals keep presenting ideas as fact that has no validity. Why do individuals that are seemingly intelligent, well read and with the best intentions present ideas and thoughts that have no basis in fact? And then these same individuals expect that this information must be writ in the Book of Everlasting Truths. Let's face it we all wonder why people keep pushing an idea or belief, that well, just doesn't hold water. Evidence, when allowed to be presented, shows clearly that what is thought was true, wasn't. Why do individuals present these arguments if they just don't know? Why do we have to tell them that if they don't know, just say so? Well a group of businessmen wanted to know as well. Why did their employees hide information or perpetuate a course of action that was, with little effort, shown false? Chris Argyris decided to find out and did a study to answer this question.

Argyris believed, and with evidence showed, that individuals, all individuals tweeners, first boomers, second boomers, everyone, create mental models. These mental models are the experiences, stories of themselves, their families and others and the assumptions they have developed over time based on those stories and experiences. Basically it is the empirical evidence of their lives. For first boomers and tweeners their teachings in positivistic theory make these experiences all the more valid. But, these mental models are largely untested, unexamined and therefore, often wrong. In other words we witness something or heard something from someone we trust and give it immediate validity. It becomes part of our mental model and we base our arguments we present to others on this mental model. The argument holds up well in our mind based on our internal information sources. But is it? Let's give an analogy.

I saw a wonderful magic show that had a lady impaled upon a pole. (No, the show wasn't wonderful because the lady was impaled. Pay better attention please.) Now obviously she wouldn't have survived if she was really impaled. But there she was, clearly showing a spike through her back, extending through her stomach and the spike continued to a few feet above her body. She flailed around and tried to remove herself from the impaling. But only with the help of the illusionist was she able to remove herself. No ambulance was called. No doctors need provide assistance. In fact she appeared shortly after the illusion, with no apparent injury, and taking a bow with the illusionist.

Now I knew it was a show, a farce put on for my amusement and wonder. So I made little of the experience save the entertainment value it provided. But, if I had not known it was an entertainment. If no stage was apparent, no audience, and I had seen this illusion in its raw, in a field, I could ascertain that women could have a stake driven through their back with no apparent injury. Empirical evidence would support that conclusion. I saw what I saw; therefore, my conclusions are correct.

As far as Argyris is concerned, this is a poor example of single loop learning. You witness something, someone of authority or trust tells you something and you believe it. You do not put what you have seen to the test. You don't ask simple questions that would cast doubt on the observation or information. People do this often. In my experience everyone does it. This false observation becomes a part of your mental model.

In everyday life someone on a plane witnesses an immigrant coming to the United States to have a child. A casual conversation with a seatmate reveals a little known fact, if the child is born in the United States the child will be a citizen of the United States with all rights and privileges. Once off the plane this conversation and incident is repeated to another, then another and then another. Just like the old "telephone game" played in elementary school the tale gets told, then twisted and distorted. But suddenly we have an epidemic of women sneaking over the border to have their children born United States citizens.

This becomes a true statement in the minds of many. It was witnessed by a man all trust. He saw it himself on a plane as he was traveling, empirical evidence that has never been tested. No one spoke to the immigrant. She may have been traveling to have her child born in the country of her husband who is a U. S. citizen. Her unborn child may have been in grave danger and she was coming to the only country that could save her baby. The fact the child would be a U. S. citizen is only a minor convenience in this woman's mind. In fact the mere assumption U. S. citizenship is all that is desired is another sign of extreme arrogance of U. S. citizens. There are plenty of individuals born in other countries that feel blessed to be citizens of that country and bear no will to be a part of the United States.

Worse than not understanding the plight of the woman, the empirical evidence derived alleging an epidemic of women sneaking into the United States isn't even tested. No surveys are done. No numbers are given. No proof is offered save the blanket statements derived from the trusted sources that passed on the information. This reflection, this testing, this questioning is a poor example of what Argyris calls double loop learning. To really learn, to understand, you must participate in double loop learning. You must test the empirical evidence given. But the mere participation calls into question your mental models, which challenges your experiences and belief systems. So people don't.

What they do instead is argue, entrench and dispute. When confronted with evidence contrary to their beliefs, or mental models, most people feel threatened. Basically those challenged get angry and blame the messenger. Individuals challenged attempt to maintain a sense of control over themselves and others. They try to force, through personal association, peer pressure, or more inaccurate data an adherence to the erroneous belief. Having a group maintaining the belief, however erroneous, gives security. In many parlances they are embarrassed at having been wrong and attempt to save face.

So since individuals won't participate in double loop learning and question what is presented, seemingly intelligent, well-read people adopt erroneous ideas as fact. They continue to support them for personal validation of their mental models. It is the nature of the human condition. But it is also the nature of the human condition to challenge and ask questions. Therefore, when presented a supposedly irrefutable fact, test it, challenge it. For just fun and general orneriness ask those supposed superior intellects to validate their assumptions. The resulting fireworks will be better than the fourth of July. At least the bluster while they attempt to regain control will be entertaining.

But it would be foolish to stop here, to believe that just the nature of the human condition is the sole reason for all the high volatility in the current political climate. It is a contributing factor. It has to be. We are all humans. But this condition has been with us in the early days of the political climate. It was with us in Vietnam, Watergate, Reagan, and September 11, 2001. It requires more analysis to understand why we are where we are.

Guiding Economic Theory. The Argument Over How Our Money is Spent.

One of the biggest bones of contention in the political climate is how the taxes we do collect are spent. Which, leads us to the current economic climate and supply side economics. Currently the dominant theory is supply side economics. Particularly the supply side economics as presented by President Reagan. There are variations of this theory and they have key differences. Prior to supply side economic we used Keynesian economic theory. The economic theory postulated by John Maynard Keynes. The country did well under Keynesian economics. True, it had a serious hiccup and liberals groan at the memory because Reagan Republicans used that hiccup to burden us with Jude Wanniski's supply side economics. But Keynesian economics moved us from a depression, through World War II, Vietnam, the moon shot and Watergate into becoming the greatest industrial power in the world. So despite the hiccup it did well. Keynesian economics was focused on the masses. Basically believing if the masses had enough discretionary income to spend, they would. And they did.

Yet despite this history and the basic facts of the benefits of Keynesian economics we have moved to supply side economics. Now lest we all be misled, supply-side economics has been studied and supported by much more learned men than Jude Wanniski and Ronald Reagan. Supply side economics has a long and distinguished history. Jean-Baptist Say, a French economist in the 1800's supported a supply side economy. The "Say's Law" attributed to him was a guiding economic principle until the Great Depression.

Even the Chicago School, a group of influential economists from the University of Chicago, argued against Keynesian theory. Supply side theory and components of this theory did guide us, and helped propel the U.S. economy up to the Great Depression. So despite many misgivings from the liberal side of the aisle the theory does have the weight of a successful history to support its use.

Despite the successful history, liberals will not agree with the current supply side economic theory as envisioned by Jude Wanniski, adopted by Ronald Reagan and subsequent Republicans. To liberals it is an economic policy that rewards concentrating the majority of funds into a select few and depriving the masses of the ability to contribute significantly to the growth of the economy. Now supply side isn't supposed to do this, it is supposed to generate great economic impact just like Keynesian theory did. But liberals insist the inherent nature of the current theory manifests itself in the creation of a funded class and eliminates the middle class. Now why do liberals claim such a terrible thing?

As we have said before, supply side theory postulates that if you create a product, you will be most anxious to sell it or the product will lose its value as it sits on the shelf. The producer of the product will want to sell their product as soon as possible before the product loses its value. It is also postulated that the products produced will only be products that are needed by the population because you can't sell what isn't needed. In supply side economics you therefore need to create more goods in order to stimulate the economy. The creation of consumers is irrelevant, because consumers are only a result of having products to sell in supply side economics. Once you create more products, these products will be bought and the economy will rebound. (Sounds good. You make products that people want and they buy them. Simple. So what is the problem?)

Well in many people's view the problem is in its basest beginning form. Supply side must have a person create a product. Not a bad thing in itself. The mere creation of the product, in the instant of its creation, generates other values as raw materials are purchased and labor is engaged to create the product. This process generates more needs for more products and the economy grows. Sounds good, but even in this primordial event, to create this product they must have the means to do so. To have the means they need the idea, the raw materials, and the ability to pay someone to put the product all together. In other words, in the modern current world, they need money. This, according to liberals, is where it all falls apart.

In current supply side economics, as practiced by conservatives, the only ones that can create products are those that already have money, basically the rich. To "prime the economic pump" so to speak, we need the rich to create products. But they currently aren't creating enough products. Now the conservative response to this lack of creation is that we need to entice the rich to make more products by giving them more money to create more products. Liberals logic at this point would ask, "Why not give money to those without money so they can create product, or better yet buy a product? Then we would have more suppliers, more products, and more buyers of products."

Ah, but here's the rub. If you don't have money, in our society, you don't get money. You must prove yourself capable of using money by already having money. If you don't have money, it follows that you don't know how to handle money. Therefore, those without money don't get money. Only those that have money get money. Got It? No? Well reread the paragraph and try understanding again.

Conservatives retort to this logic is they really are giving money to those that already have it because this group already knows how to make products. In actual fact conservatives don't believe they are giving the money to only the rich at all, but they are giving money to people that currently own businesses, business owners. Considering conservatives are associated with the Republican Party and Republicans are the party of Main Street and business, this is not so far out of line with their paradigms. But while their inclinations lean towards business, conservatives will point out rightfully that just because you own a business doesn't mean you are rich. And this is true. There are many micro businesses and small businesses that barely make any money at all. They make enough to pay the owners a salary, and that is about it.

Conservatives believe giving money to business owners is the safest bet, most logical approach, and the quickest way to get the economy moving if you support supply side economics. (And conservatives do.) The business owners are geared for this. They have the factories, people, materials and everything needed to make products. We just have to get them motivated. They need to get the supply side moving.

But liberals claim this process is flawed. First of all the tax breaks and other incentives geared to business by the government are not set up to benefit small and micro businesses. This portion of the supply side theory is a fallacy. A supplement in taxes of a few thousand dollars for hiring one unemployed person is not going to incentivize a small business to hire additional people. Nor is it going goad them into creating more products. Obviously this action only has a benefit to an employer that can hire multiple employees. In reality supply side economics only helps medium and large businesses, or in effect, the policy favors the rich or their companies.

Another concern liberals also have with this policy is it reduces greatly the number of suppliers that can participate in reviving the economy. Medium and large businesses employ a lot of people, but the majority of businesses in the United States by far are small and micro-businesses. Making policy that favors medium and large business takes good players out of the game and puts all of our recovery eggs into a much smaller basket. In other words instead of relying on the skills and abilities of over 300 million people, we are relying on only 3 million. The odds of success are reduced substantially.

To the minds of liberals another side effect of supply side economics as currently practiced is the inherent preferential treatment creates a financial aristocracy and concentrates power into the hands of a few. It is Thomas Jefferson versus Alexander Hamilton all over again and the conservatives are in the Hamilton camp. Conservatives would retort that supply side economic theory doesn't support this concept. That as business expands more people become employed, successful and rich. It is the nature of the theory. True a few medium and large businesses will have an initial benefit due to their position and our need to begin the process, according to conservatives, but that initial advantage will be overcome as the economy expands.

The liberals response to this is "famous last words" and they are incredulous at the conservatives seemingly ignorance of human nature. They point out that, as one would expect, once someone has position they work to keep that position. People are not going to voluntarily engage in any practice which in and of itself will diminish their power, position or finances. Theoretical support or not, rich work to remain rich. If given the opportunity to expand their businesses and/or others they will do so only if they exert control over the businesses they help expand. Business, once again, is not in the business to compete, it is in the business to eliminate competition.

Liberals point out that this process is with precedent in our country. The Gilded Age between 1870 and 1900 created super-rich industrialists and financiers of the likes of John Rockefeller, Andrew Carnegie, and the Astor family. Not so coincidentally this was also a time when supply side economic theory was still dominant. It was also a time of a very small middle class, large poverty class and extreme poverty in the cities. Children worked in factories and the work week was seventy two hours six days a week. Not exactly the hallmark of democracy we hold dear today and citizens do not, as a whole, wish to return to these dark times.

Other issues liberals have with supply side theory is the claim that if a product is made it will sell. "Balderdash", they claim. A look at the landscape of built, but unsold houses dashes that assumption. Creating products doesn't mean it will be sold at any price if the potential buyer has no discretionary income to buy. (Discretionary income is that money you have left over after food, housing and toilet paper.) Giving money to the rich, or job creators, (Job creators are the conservative's term for the businessmen, or rich people that get government support, sort of in line with the whole supply side theory thing.), doesn't even guarantee that the money will be spent to drive the economy. There are no guarantees at all from the job creators. We are just giving them the money and being hopeful their altruistic nature takes hold. What if the job creators get the money and just hoard it instead of creating jobs?

"Balderdash, right back at ya." Say the conservatives. It would be against the best interest of the job creators not to create jobs if given this money. They would deny themselves the ability to make even more money. Business is in the business to make money not hoard it. But at this point liberals point out a caveat. What if hoarding the money, makes more money than spending it? Job creators have found out that there is less risk and more money in investment than job creation. So they don't use the money to create jobs. They hoard it.

This is one of the flaws of supply side economics. Now to be fair, the theory was first created when barter was more of a means of exchange than money. Trading your timber for a cow and then holding onto the cow would not in and of itself increase your wealth. In fact the feed you need to maintain it and barn you would need to build to contain it would be far more expensive than bartering it for the saw you need from the tinkerer. Holding product, or in this case animals, does not gain the additional value money does when it is placed in an interest bearing account. Money can actually make money sitting in a bank because banks pay you to put it there. Good for banks, bad for products. This process actually has money making money without ever putting it into product development. Sorta like selling and reselling derivatives in an ever expanding game of hot potato. Whoever has the potato when the music stops loses everything. (Hey weren't the taxpayers the ones holding the potato when the music stopped last time?)

Anyhow, besides having the theory developed during a time of barter it was also used in a time when large mega corporations were few, if any. Stock exchanges were not used to finance companies. Mostly they just dealt in government finance. So we are dealing with a theory that did not include dollars in the initial basis of its theoretical analysis, or account for interest bearing accounts, large mega corporations, or the use of stock exchange for buying and selling corporations. Doesn't sound like a theory that should be used in modern economics. And that is the liberal's point. Supply side economics sounds like another attempt to return to some halcyon days that really never existed. Once again, to liberals, conservatives are looking backward instead of toward the future.

So to liberals, creating supplies doesn't create need or purchase. It does concentrate the discretionary income in the hands of about three million people. But these few cannot generate sufficient need or purchase to restore our economy. To liberals concentrating all the funds in the hands of a few is akin to the "funnel theory". The funnel theory, to anyone that doesn't know, is when you pour everything at once into a funnel. The funnel can only pass so much through its narrow stem. No matter how much you pour into its mouth only so much will flow out the neck and only so fast. Ask any cook what happens when you pour too much milk into a funnel. The milk spills onto the counter and is useless. To liberals the same applies to supply side economics pouring more and more money into the job creators funnel. These job creators, even if they were inclined, can only do so much. The rest of the money just goes to waste.

To make use of that money instead of wasting it we need to include more funnels, or in this case more people. To liberals, demand is what drove our economy for the last eighty years and demand is what will restore it. There is no way 3 million people can match the ability of 300 million for that capacity. So per Keynesian economies, as opposed to supply side economics, we have to concentrate on getting money to the masses to revitalize our great country. We need to get the masses the money and in turn, when they spend it, and they will because they need to, the job creators will also benefit. The job creators will benefit because they will have market for products and will actually make more money producing instead of hoarding. As the job creators, (read rich), create product, the masses will get jobs, have more resources to buy, and the job creators will in turn generate greater profits.

It sounds good. So what do conservatives hate so much about Keynesian economic theory? Well to begin with it allows government interference in economic policy. It actually encourages it. It also encourages use of the public sector through the Federal Reserve to monitor monetary policy like interest rates. Keynesian economics also believes in government deficit spending in recessions and raising taxes in boom times. In other words Keynesian economics tells us that government, rather than being a passive participant, needs to put their hands in our back pockets and have some control over how we spend our money. Not exactly an ideal to embrace in a country based upon self-determination and independent actions. Conservatives don't want anyone having a hand in their financial affairs, especially the government. They want to spend their hard earned money how they want to, when they want to, and on what they want to spend it on. In its most abhorrent version conservatives see Keynesian economics as redistributing wealth, most particularly their wealth.

The reason Keynesian economic theory believes government needs to be involved in the economy is simple. It believes that individual business decisions are made for the self-interest of the business, to increase its profits and position. Remember business is in the business to eliminate competition. While that may be good for the business, it does not mean the decision is good for the country. In fact Keynesian economics doesn't believe that all the individual business decisions made by all the businesses in total each day and each year are necessarily good for the country. Even if they tend to be beneficial the total decisions are inherently inefficient leading to frequent economic crisis like recessions, boom periods, bust periods, and depressions. Which, under supply side economic theory this happened quite frequently, destabilizing governments and creating and destroying fortunes in its wake for decades. Keynesian economic theory thought there was a better way.

This belief is in stark contrast to supply side theory which believes, over time, economies tend to reach a balance that is good for all and will work to maintain this balance. Liberals and Keynesians will point out rather emphatically that long supply side history disputes this argument entirely. In fact in recent supply side economics this theory has lead to two of the worst economic crisis in the nation's history, the Great Recession and the Great Depression. But conservatives and supply side theorists will counter that their theory has also created two of the greatest economic expansions, the Gilded Age and economic booms of the 1980's and 2000's. Conservatives also point out that Keynesian economics lead to the Great Stagflation of the late 1970's. To put it simply Keynesian economics is not the panacea that liberals paint it.

Conservatives and Republicans will point out that under Keynesian economics record interest rates were created as well as inflation, the Great Stagflation, and an unwieldy extremely expensive government funded social support system. Conservatives will point out that Keynesian economics exploded our government spending when the government became involved in fiscal policy. The social support system not only saddled the government with an ever growing, out of control, budgetary obligation, it didn't require anyone to work to receive the money. In fact it encouraged people to remain poor. In many circles this is a much more cruel use of government support. It created a large inescapable poverty class. These are valid criticisms and they are right.

Conservatives will also point out that they tried using the Keynesian theory of creating more demand and it didn't work. Bush the 2nd gave money directly to the people to ramp up the economy. They people used it to pay bills not buy products. Liberals will counter that when Bush gave all the taxpayers the money they were only giving them a rebate of up to $600 per person on their own taxes. Liberals would point out that $600 per person of their own tax money was hardly the same as giving billions to banks and states in the bailouts of 2008 as the Republican administration did. If each individual was given $6000 you might have seen the effects that were hoped. In fact the bailout worked to prove liberal's point. When given the billions in dollars, banks and states were supposed to funnel that money to the general population. But in fact, the banks hoarded it, paid dividends and bonuses and fortified their companies. States used the bailouts to keep from cutting budgets so legislators wouldn't lose their offices. Money, as it was supposed to do, did not make it to the general population.

The strongest liberal argument against Reagan's supply side economics is, well, it just hasn't worked. We have been burdened with the Great Recession, only 80 years since the Great Depression and only thirty years since the re-establishment of the supply side theory. We have record deficits and an even larger government all under the auspices of the conservative movement and supply side economics. Now positivistic theory, as learned by tweeners and first boomers, would insist that the supply side theory is correct, it just needs more tweaking. But liberals and the rest of us just want the conservatives to admit it failed so we can move on to something new. In fact a lot of us, liberals, conservatives and others would like to see any new economic theory. Both of the current theories are more than 80 years old. Supply side theory is over a century old. None of them take into account a global economy that we face. It is about time to look to new theories.

But self-determination is a strong embedded trait in United States citizens and a brand of honor with conservatives. Any economic theory that impedes on the right to control their own funds will face stiff opposition from conservatives. Most are sure that Keynesian economics is just the majority trying to get the minority to pay to them to sit on their butts. Liberals argue that dogma such as that ignores the fact that the majority pay taxes also and all the money governments get isn't from the minority. Liberals won't support any economic theory that abandons the safety nets the government has created and works to place all the funds into the hands of a privileged few. Liberals just don't trust them to be altruistic and they have good historical cause for the concern.

The debate over economic theory is a strong argument for the cause of the current political climate. Combined with the argument over the nature of the human condition both would lead to a general understanding of the heated animosity between both sides. After all one of the strongest areas of disagreement between any two individuals is the argument over how money will be spent. But to stop here would be to ignore an even more passionate argument in government circles, taxes, or how money is to be raised. Taxes are part and parcel of any economic theory as they are a determining factor in how that system is to be implemented. But regardless of the economic theory used, everyone is paying too much and the other guy isn't paying enough. How does the current system add to this animosity?

Graduated Taxes and the Laffer Curve

First of all I am for a much simpler tax code. Liberal or conservative, what we have is way too complicated and needs fixing. No, to the detriment to a few, (believe it or not), liberal friends I am not in favor of a flat tax. That system ignores too many pragmatic issues. But I am for something I don't have to worry about or file every April 15th. We are way beyond having to do taxes once a year. Our technology is just too advanced. That said let's look at what we got.

Historically the first personal income tax in the United States was created in 1861 to help pay for the Civil War. (Yes, boys and girls, we went almost 85 years as a country without an income tax and did pretty well to, thank you very much.) In 1895 the U. S. Supreme Court ruled that, while income could be taxed, property had to be apportioned to be taxed. Since deciding what income came from property as opposed to individual wages was impractical in 1895, (We were an agrarian society then, basically farmers to you and me.), this effectively ended the income tax until 1913. In 1913 Congress had the 16th amendment to the Constitution approved by the required number of states and the income tax was reborn. (Yes, ladies and gentlemen, the U.S. Supreme Court has ruled it was ratified correctly. The U.S. does have the power to levy income taxes.)

Now early on, even during the first taxation in 1861, Congress always had an exemption for the less fortunate. In 1861 you didn't have to worry about an income tax or income tax rate if you didn't make at least $800 a year. (Now folks, back then that was a lot of money, about $20,000 in 2008 money.) So exemptions for low income were always a hallmark of taxation and exemptions are embedded in our taxation systems. But what most people don't know is that we have a graduated tax system in the U. S. and those that do know don't really know what that means. Let's explain.

Everybody get's taxed by the federal government. Let's understand that from the beginning. As opposed to the original income tax in 1861 there is no exemption for lower income. So whether you make $1.00 or $100,000,000,000, (We're thinking of you, Bill Gates.), you have to pay taxes. Now how much taxes you have to pay depends on the amount of money you make, or your income. Everybody paid at least 10% of their income to the federal income tax in 2010. That is the law. But they only pay a 10% tax on the income they made up to a total income of $16,750.00. If you made $16,750.00 or less 10% was your top tax rate. That rate is your average and real tax rate.

Wait a minute, wait a minute, I hear your say. What's all this racket about one percenters and ninety-nine percenters, and flat taxes if everyone already pays 10% of their income to income taxes? What kind of wool are you pulling over our eyes?

Well if I was pulling the wool over your eyes, it would be the finest kind, but I'm not pulling any wool over your eyes. The tax rate on everyone for the first $16,750 you make is 10% in 2010. Go look it up, it's in the federal tax code and it isn't any secret. (Go ahead. Look it up. I'll wait. This is a book.) But the point is the tax rate is 10% on income up to $16,750, if you make over $16,750 then the tax rate changes. But not on the first $16, 750, it still is 10%. It will always be 10%. The tax rate changes for any income you make over $16,750. In other words if you make $33,500 (or $16,750 multiplied by 2) the first $16,750 would be taxed at 10% but the next $16,750 would be taxed at a new rate of 15%. You would owe $1,675.00 in taxes on the first $16, 750 and $2,512.50 in taxes on the next $16,750. Add the two amounts together and you get $4,187.50. Your total tax owed the federal government would be $4,187.50.

This is what a graduated tax rate is. You have a base tax rate that everybody pays on a base amount of money. Then those lucky enough to make more than the base amount of money get a higher tax rate on the additional money above the base tax rate. But they pay the higher tax rate only on the amount of the money they make over the base amount. What gets more confusing though is the federal government doesn't have just two levels of taxes, the 10% and the 15%, it has six levels. And every time you cross the threshold into a new level of income you have to pay a higher tax. But you only pay the higher tax rate on the additional amount of money you make over the threshold, not the amount below the threshold. That tax remains as it was. As we said it is confusing to most, so everybody seeks a simple explanation, a simple idea of what our tax rates are. Thus income tax detractors seeking to advance their agendas come up with a figure called the "average tax rate".

The average United States tax rate is 24%. It sounds terrible. If everyone had to pay 24% of their total income to the federal government in taxes it would be a travesty. But that statement is inherently true and untrue. The average tax rate is 24% but you get that figure by adding up all the tax rates in the tax code and dividing by six. Simple, but it ignores income, the second base measurement. Truth is the median household income in the United States in 2010 as determined by the U. S. Census Bureau is only $49,455. This wouldn't even take income out of the first two tax brackets. If you used this more accurate figure the average tax rate would be the two income rates that affect the majority of citizens based on income and divide by two. That puts the average income tax rate for the majority of citizens at 12.5%, roughly half of what fear mongers want to shout about and not nearly so scary.

So basically we could claim we already have a flat tax rate of 12.5%, after all the majority of citizens pay no more than that rate. So why are we yelling and screaming about not enough money and too high of taxes? Well, in a word, exemptions, which is one of the reasons a flat tax, even the 12.5% flat tax, as seductive as the math is, is impractical. Everyone has to pay the initial 10% on the first $16,750, but only on what is defined as income. But what is the definition of income? This is where it gets really tricky and opportunists seek to gain an advantage. Individuals, businessmen and the aforementioned opportunists all work to define income and seek exemptions from the income definition for their own purposes. In practical terms, if we can't define what income is, then how can we tax it and make sure everyone is taxed equally as in a flat tax? How can we know what the real tax rate in the United States is since the tax rate is dependent on both income and the tax rate classification?

Because there are exemptions on everything, defining income defies a single designation. For example, just because you exist in the United States and are a taxpayer you get an immediate exemption of $5,700. Now it is called a standard deduction, but it is an exemption. Even if you don't own anything, go to school or if you live in the woods you get an exemption, or deduction, on your income of $5,700. This means that if you made the base amount of $16,750 you would immediately subtract $5,700 from that total. So your income now would be $11,050 instead of $16,750 for tax purposes. You would be taxed only on $11,050. Your tax burden would be $1,105, instead $1,675 just because you exist.

Tax exemptions are what make the tax code so hard to understand. Every lobbyist worth their salt is looking for the next tax exemption for their clients. We have over 1,500 pages of tax code doing nothing but trying to define what income really means. And there are significant questions. Does someone who doesn't take home a paycheck make an income? Well he made over $10,000,000 in stock dividends last year, but it wasn't a paycheck. He lived off of it. He paid his house payment, beach house payment and hired help off of the dividends, but he didn't in fact get a paycheck. So should he be taxed on the dividends or the fact he had no paycheck? If he isn't taxed on dividends, then the guy that only made $16,750 is going to pay much more than the guy getting dividends of $10,000,000 even though he has no house on the beach. This doesn't sound fair to most liberals and more than a few conservatives.

Thus our income, as defined by exemptions from income, actually tells each individual one of us our tax rate. Since everyone qualifies for their own set of exemptions and the number of exemptions is covered in 1,500 pages of tax code it is just impractical to be able to ascertain an "average tax rate". Even the flat tax rate of 12.5% I alluded to earlier is just a best guess based on my own calculations and probably just as good as any other definition. What is known is that exemptions significantly lower the actual tax income that the federal government could have expected to receive based on the tax rate classifications in place. As a result, this is one of the reasons the federal government, even with its current tax rate structure, doesn't have enough money and runs a deficit.

Because it runs a deficit, those in the government who want to balance the budget, want to reduce the cost of government, or raise the taxes, in order to get rid of the deficit. Those that want to raise taxes are castigated because the current rates are too high. Those castigated wonder how tax rates can be too high when so many exemptions significantly reduce the approved tax rate classifications. This set of disagreements is one of the reasons there is so much yelling and screaming about tax rates. Another reason is how tax rates affect the economy and how the economy is affected by tax rates.

Which, brings us back to Reagan supply side economics and the Laffer curve. In 1980 Keynesian economics created a severe case of stagflation. This is when the cost of goods and services rise even as unemployment rises. There was no demand for products, but the price of products kept going up like there was a demand. This isn't supposed to happen. Supply and demand were totally out of sync. To offset this and create a solution President Reagan reintroduced supply side economics, but with a twist. He also included the Laffer curve.

The Laffer curve is an illustration of how much money the government gets as it raises the tax rate. The curve basically looks like the first hill of a rollercoaster ride. The term was coined by Jude Wanniski in recognition of the work of Arthur Laffer. Laffer himself did not originate the concept and never said he did, but politics is as it is. We will continue to use the same reference originally designated by Wanniski so we don't confuse the subject.

The Laffer curve is built upon a graph of X and Y axis. (Yes, this has to do with math. You should have paid better attention in your high school math class.) The X axis, or the line that runs along the bottom, is the tax rate. The Y axis, or the line that goes from the bottom to the top, is the amount of money the government gets. The Laffer curve assumes the higher the tax rate the more taxes a government receives. But the Laffer curve also claims that there is a maximum of taxation. Once the maximum rate is reached there is a pushback by the governed. At this point, no matter how high the government raises taxes, it will actually get in less money because the governed will have less reason to work and will produce less to tax.

Going back to the roller coaster idea, once we get to the very top, or the maximum rate in this case, we start to go down again.

Laffer also believes that if the government does not tax at all, as in the tax rate is at zero, the government will get no tax revenues. I believe we can all agree with the proposition that if the government doesn't have an income tax the tax rate is zero and it

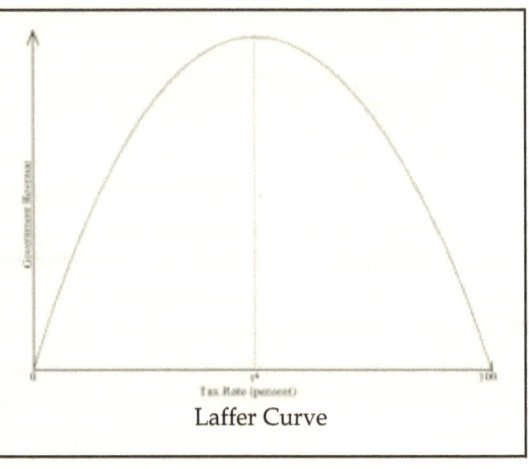

Laffer Curve

gets zero revenue from an income tax. But here we part company.

Laffer claims, and it is shown on the graph, that if the government taxes at 100% the governed will have no reason to work because they keep nothing of what they make. Thus no tax revenues will be collected and the tax income will be at zero. There is however a point, the equilibrium point or point at the very top where everything is balanced, (You know the point right before the roller coaster starts going downhill, that point where you briefly sit at the top and can see everything and anticipate the fall.), that the population will continue to produce and the government will get the maximum tax revenues. This whole process is represented by a curve on a graph, or simply the Laffer curve. (See Figure)

Now as seductive as this logic is, (And it is quite seductive. Reagan and a whole group or past and present Republicans as well as confirmed conservatives swear by it), it makes a whole lot of assumptions that have been proven wrong time and again. Also, because of this curve, there are a lot of conservatives and Republicans that think reducing taxes will increase revenues. It doesn't.

One of the main reasons this curve is wrong is because the tax rates to be represented on the graph are distinctly one of your choosing. There is no standard incremental division of the X axis which represents the "average tax rate". In other words it is up to you to put a tax rate of 10%, 30%, 50% or even 70% at any point, even the equilibrium point. Whatever floats your boat and makes your case. There are only two required points on the X axis, 0%

and 100%, everything else is up to the maker of the graph.

When we make graphs in high school, (or for the younger crowd, in elementary school), the teacher always tells us to divide the line along the bottom in nice neat sections called units of measurement. Each section represents a fixed set of numbers. If we are going to use 0 and 100 as the starting and ending points on the line, we would probably divide the line into sections of 10. So the first section on the line would be 10 followed by 20 and then 30 until we reached 100. Each of these numbers and sections would be represented by a point or mark on the line and labeled as 10, 20, 30, and so on.

When doing this you would expect the middle number, or unit of measure, on the line to be at 50. In a perfectly drawn graph that is as symmetrical as the Laffer curve is supposed to be, you would then expect the equilibrium point to be at 50. This is where you could draw a line from the point representing the number 50 to the very top of the curve and the line would be perfectly perpendicular, (This means the line is straight up and down with nary a deviation right or left.), and match up exactly with the equilibrium point. As perfect as this would be there is no such required relational standard measurement associated with the Laffer curve. The unit of measure on the X axis that matches up to the equilibrium point does not have to be at 50 or any other prescribed place on the X axis. Basically you can just put any number at the middle unit of measurement, your choice. You can also divide the line into sections on either side of the point of equilibrium point as you choose. In essence you can game the system, just like a shell game on a street corner.

Of course, when you are arguing for reducing taxes from 30% to 20% or even lower, you don't want your opponents pointing out that the equilibrium point for taxes on your own graph is 50%. That would severely defeat your purpose. So using the Laffer curve's embedded convenience, conservatives place the tax rate unit of measurements along the X axis anywhere that clearly makes their immediate argument. As a result the equilibrium point on the graph can be 60%, 20%, 30%, or any other number. Under this ruse, if you did reduce the tax rate to say the 30% you were informed was the equilibrium point, the conservatives could come back and insist the equilibrium point was actually 20% and you needed to reduce taxes even further. This becomes a never ending, circular argument, that you must reduce taxes to stimulate the economy. Now that argument sounds distinctly familiar.

This fallacy of measurement standards is also the reason conservatives and Republican advocates insist that reducing taxes increases revenues. This belief, for the lack of a better term, is called the right-hand curve theory. When looking at the Laffer curve you will note that it is supposed to be symmetrical. This means it is a well-proportioned and doesn't bulge out at odd places. In a symmetrical curve a straight line can be drawn from the equilibrium point at the top of the curve straight down to the X axis. This essentially divides the graph into equal right hand and left hand sides, or right-hand and left hand sides of the curve. If Joe or Joan Citizen looked at the graph they would understand that on the right side there is a terminal point, or point where the curve ends. The number associated with this point is 100%. At this point the Y axis, or the line on the left of the graph, going up and down, has a value of zero and means no money is coming into the government. The 100% on the X axis represents a tax rate of 100%. Therefore, on the right hand side of the curve you have a tax rate of 100% that by the curve's definition does not bring in any tax money.

Which, goes to explaining the Y axis to those of you not quite up to date on graphs. The Y axis is the line that goes up and down and it is located at the extreme left of the graph. It, like the X axis, has a 0 point. On the Laffer graph the Y zero point is at the exact same point as the X zero point, or in mathematical terms, they intersect. Like the X axis the Y axis is supposed to have its line divided up into equal sections. The Y axis line on the Laffer graph, like the X axis line does not have any standard designated measurements, so like the X axis, you can just make them up. (I mean isn't this graph so convenient! You can make any argument with it. So cool.)

The Y axis on the Laffer graph indicates the amount of money you receive for each increase in tax revenue. So, for instance we can decide, (because we can!) that the first mark up, after 0, is $100. The next mark we put at $200, the next at $300, the next $400 and so on until we decide to end. (The Laffer graph has no end point on the Y axis. We get to decide that also. I told you it was convenient.)

By using these two lines, the Y axis and the X axis, or the amounts of revenue and the tax rate, we are supposed to get a measure of the amounts of income we will receive for the tax rate that is imposed. This means, using the numbers I created, by increasing the tax rate say from 0 to the first unit of measurement on the X axis which is 10% we can get $100. How do I know this? Well because by

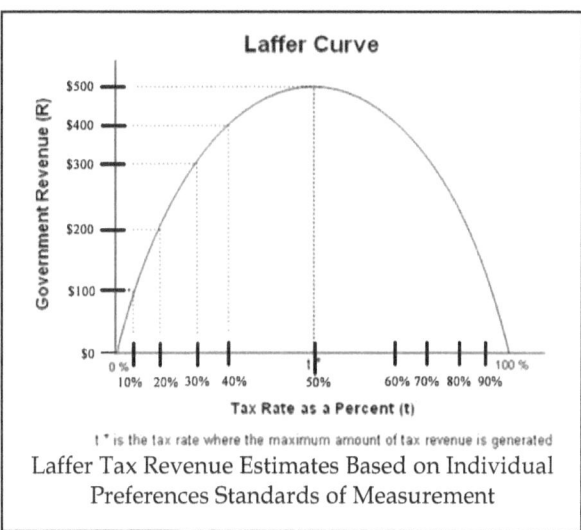

Laffer Curve

t * is the tax rate where the maximum amount of tax revenue is generated

Laffer Tax Revenue Estimates Based on Individual Preferences Standards of Measurement

drawing a line up from the 10% tax rate to the Laffer curve itself I intersect the line with the curve. At this intersection point of the line and the curve I would draw a straight line left to the Y axis, or the amounts of revenue. This line would intersect with the $100 unit of measurement on the Y axis.

If I drew a line for every unit of tax measurement on the X axis to the Laffer curve a corresponding amount would intersect with that line's point on the Laffer curve. So according to my made up numbers, if I went from 10% to 20% in taxes I would get $200 in revenue. If I went from a 20% to 30% tax rate I would get $300 in tax revenue. Tax revenue would increase every time I raised the tax rate until it reached the equilibrium point. This is where the right hand curve theory comes into play.

If we use the numbers I created out of thin air at the top of the Laffer curve or the equilibrium point is a tax rate of 50%. At this point we would receive $500 in income tax revenue. Now being the greedy liberal I am I would want more money and increasing the tax rates have worked for me so far, so the next move would be to increase the tax rate to 60%. But, according to the Laffer curve, I didn't increase my tax revenue, I actually lost money. According to the Laffer graph, by increasing from 50% to 60% I will only get $400, the exact same amount as if I only taxed 40%. Why?

Well, according to Laffer and many conservatives, we have passed over the equilibrium point and are starting down on the graph. We are on the down slope of the roller coaster. We in essence have taxed so much that the governed are resisting the taxes and refusing to create income to be taxed. Therefore, even though the tax rate is higher there is less available to tax so there is less income. It is represented on the graph just as before. A line is drawn up from the 60% unit of measurement on the X axis to the Laffer curve and a line is

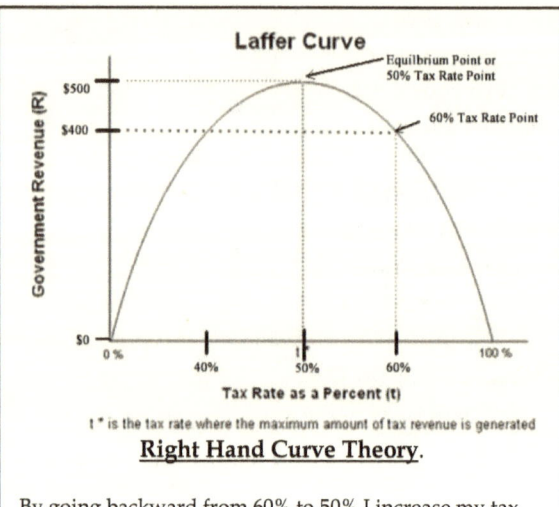

Laffer Curve

Equilibrium Point or 50% Tax Rate Point

60% Tax Rate Point

Government Revenue (R)

$500

$400

$0

0 %   40%   50%   60%   100 %

Tax Rate as a Percent (t)

t * is the tax rate where the maximum amount of tax revenue is generated

Right Hand Curve Theory.

By going backward from 60% to 50% I increase my tax revenues from $400 to $500. In other words by going backward I go up the right hand side of the curve to make more money.

drawn from this intersection on the Laffer curve to the Y axis. The amount of money represented is the aforementioned $400. Tax increases from this point onward actually reduce tax revenues until the government will get nothing at 100% in taxes.

But a strange thing is pointed out by conservatives and Laffer curve acolytes. If we continue to use the same graph I created and the same numbers, by moving from 60% in taxes back to the equilibrium point of 50% we actually will get $500 in taxes. We increase our tax income by, drum roll please, reducing our tax rate! How is this miracle possible?

Well, the graph never lies and we are using my own figures. At 50% tax rate on my graph I get $500, at 60% I got $400. So it goes to show if I want more income I need to go backwards to 50%. This is shown on the graph by drawing a line from the 50% and 60% tax rate units of measurements up to the Laffer curve and then drawing a line from these intersection points to the amounts of revenue on the Y axis. Indeed, it does show that 60% tax rate only brings in $400 and a 50% tax rate brings in $500.

Now this only works on the right hand side of the Laffer curve, which gives us the moniker "right-hand curve theory" as practiced by conservatives. It doesn't work on the left hand side, which is pretty much one of the points of the detractors of this theory and the Laffer curve in general. Conservative have no problem highlighting the right hand curve theory when making a point, but studiously avoid the left hand side, which totally repudiates the argument. On the left hand side, increasing taxes increases revenues. The only real point of contention on the Laffer curve is where you place the units of measurements. Conservatives want to place the equilibrium point at a unit of measure of 30% or lower. Liberals, if they were ever inclined to use such a questionable and fraudulent measure, would place the equilibrium point at 80% or higher. Both measures would be just as valid as the other, which measure you choose depends on your position.

Some would argue that even if you used liberal positioning that reducing taxes from 90% to 80% would still increase tax revenues. Therefore the Laffer curve is still valid. It is just a matter of creating an agreed upon standard set of measurements. Good point but the issues with the Laffer curve go beyond the lack of standard measurements. Laffer uses the average tax rate, a rate as we have discussed, that can't be calculated. Laffer also claims that at 100% the government will not receive any revenue from an income tax because of push back from the governed. This assumption, and it is an assumption, is wrong on its face simply because of the definition of income, which has, in the United States, not ever been definitively defined. There are just too many exemptions. As example of how tax rate doesn't affect tax revenue as a result of exemptions and other issues, in World War II the upper tax rate went to 90% and the country produced more than ever. The upper tax rate has often been above 70% and still we have produced. Not only did we produce, but we grew into the strongest country in the world. The lesson here is not to confuse the government's highest tax bracket with the country's tax rate. They are not the same thing and the vast majority of the country's residents don't have to worry about the higher tax bracket anyhow.

The reality is our government income and tax rate cannot be graphed on a simple curve, so the Laffer curve or any curve for that matter, can't be used. It is just an invalid unit of measure. Since a curve can't be used you can't raise income by reducing taxes. Income in relation to tax rate is more of a trend line, a linear regression analysis, than a curve. There are many more variables to include than just income and tax rates. How much people produce depends on much more than the cash they receive for their labor after taxes. What they get for their taxes is just as important as what they pay in taxes.   To some, (mostly liberals), if the government takes care of all basic necessities, food, water, shelter, health care, for all as required by need, the taxes they pay are justified in the services they receive. These people will produce just as much if not more because they do not have to worry about survival. That issue is already provided. Taking risks, exploring new boundaries and advancing knowledge become necessities and requirements, not day to day living. (All hail Star Trek!)

To other's (mostly conservatives) this perceived utopia is hogwash. If given the means to survive most people will, in fact, just survive and the government will end up paying for them to sit on their ass. This, in turn, means that since conservatives are perceived to have the bulk of income, they will be paying for someone to sit while they work.   Truth is the history of human nature is on the conservative's side on this issue more often than not.

In either instance, conservative or liberal, the perception of what is received for the taxes paid is what generates production and income not the actual rate itself. At best this perception measurement can only be graphically illustrated by opinion polls measuring the confidence of the people. Confident, secure citizens expecting a better future are more likely to produce more and pay more in taxes than citizens concerned with their safety, security, and ability to provide a living for themselves or their family. Even in this graph, however, there will not be a single curve illustrating when and how taxes, tax rates, and income rates should be adjusted. This graph would also resemble a linear regression analysis and trend line more than a curve.

The whole issue with the Laffer curve and the graduated income tax is the parts they play in the much larger argument about the economic theories that drive this nation, its economy and by extension its government. These issues draw the most visible fire, so they must be addressed in any discussion about national economic theory development.   Excepting they are only individual battles in the struggle for economic theory dominance.

The supply siders need the Laffer curve to work because it drives the current version of Reagan supply side economics and justifies reducing taxes regardless of the economic times we face. The matter of reducing taxes creates more money for the "job creators". More money for job creators means more investment, more jobs, a growing economy, and in the end more income tax revenue. If it all works, then supply side economics works. Republicans and most conservatives, married to the issues of Main Street, could then justify and extend their supply side economic solution. The success of supply side economics would be justification for their viewpoints and as they believe, lead to continued success of the United States economy and world leadership. It is a matter, to Republicans and conservatives, of personal security, national security, and economic superiority. In its basic essence, supply side economics, and currently Reagan supply side economics, is a core argument of their ideology, a reason for the Party's existence, and will be strongly defended.

Keynesians, or liberals, on the other hand shake their head in disbelief at the illogical devotion to the Laffer curve and supply side economics, particularly the Laffer curve. It simply does not represent economic theory as related to taxes and even if it did by any remote chance the curve itself is flawed at design. Liberals also point out one of the side effects of using the Laffer curve even under Reagan supply side economic theory, the curve creates deficits. Not only deficits, but use of the curve in economic theory creates large deficits. This seems counter to the whole idea expressed by supply side supporters of having a balanced budget and eliminating deficits.

Supply siders acknowledge that deficits are created, but only when tax cuts are instituted to generate an economic stimulus. The initial tax cut always results in immediate loss of income to the government, but over the long term more revenue will be created to offset the income loss from the tax cut plus more revenue. In other words the deficit is temporary and will be eventually eliminated due to new revenues. It has never happened, but as people brought up on positivistic theory, supply siders keep trying. (Now you know why we had the Bush tax cuts, supply siders trying to re-establish supply side economics after Clinton. Bet you thought they were just giving your money back.)

The whole deficit idea does go to a Keynesian point. Deficits are a governmental means to control the economy. Even in supply side economics deficits are required. This is one of the reasons why a balanced budget amendment is anathema to many supply siders as well as Keynesians. Such an amendment would prohibit the successful use of either of these economic theories. Keynesian theory insists deficits are a legitimate governmental tool in hard economic times to revitalize the economy. Supply siders need the deficit to support immediate tax breaks without cutting what they consider vital government programs such as defense. Of course many supply side supporters feel that budget cuts of current government programs can offset any deficit thereby negating any need for any deficits. However, the government programs they target happen to be the domestic programs Keynesian economics support.

The balanced budget amendment many are trying to pass goes to the core of Keynesian economics and is a reason why it has such strong opposition. Many conservatives and even liberals want to know why the government just doesn't buy what we can afford. Need a new army? Raise taxes, so to speak. However, practicality as well as economic theory gets in the way. It is easy to say we will raise taxes, it is much harder to do so, even when there is a general agreement that it needs to be done. The current flocks of wealthy individuals insisting they are willing to accept a tax increase, but having the Republican house refuse to even consider it, is one practical example.

But Keynesian economics as favored by liberals insists that taxes, monetary policy and deficits are legitimate tools of the government to influence national economics. To pass a balanced budget amendment would mean an end to much of Keynesian economic policy. Government would be wedded to supply side economics. Government would no longer be able to intercede in economic affairs. It would have to adopt a laissez faire attitude, which means private business would be free from all government intervention, including regulations. A business utopia sought by those that believe fervently in supply side economics. In essence a balanced budget amendment is more an attack at the core values of Keynesian economics than an effort to save the country. It is a blow to win the war between these two economic theories. As such it is a strike against the core values of Keynesian economics and will be defended against fiercely by those seeking to restore Keynesian theory.

The support and defense of these economic theories go to the core of our current animosities. They provoke antagonistic debate and determined acts by each contender to the crown to eliminate their opponents. The debate is fierce because the stakes are high. How the United States moves forward in the coming years depends on the results of these actions. We could lose everything we and our ancestors fought to gain by being ignorant and small in the face of large challenges. The economic theory opponents know the risks and challenges. They believe in the righteousness of their causes. They know their beliefs are under attack, they risk everything, including their vision of their country, and so the fighting is wicked, the weapons brutal.

The economic fight is the basis of the great force that is polarizing our country, creating fear and breathing anger. It is the reason for the creation of the TEA Party, the continued resistance of the Dixiecrats and the bitter struggle between Republicans and Democrats, liberals and conservatives. It will define our country and our country's future and future place in the world. The fight, and the subsequent victor, will tell us whether we lead the world with our ideals, or regulate ourselves to the once great United States. The wrong choice, a choice that looks backwards instead of embracing the future, will condemn us to another second or third world country, our ideals quaint and our ideas funny. We cannot look back and try to relive past glories. The world has changed and we no longer can suffer the isolation we coveted behind great oceans. We are in a new evolution of our country and the world. The Internet, multi-national companies, out sourcing and a million other new inventions and means of communication have made us a world partner with those literally a half a world away, now our neighbors.

The third boomers and those that follow won't allow a return to the old systems anyhow. It is theirs to define and ours to prepare. We have to embrace the world and take the leadership position we won. The winning paradigm and economic theory will be the foundations for how we exist in the next incarnation of the United States. And frankly I don't give a damn for any of the current offerings. They fall woefully short. They are too weak and too parochial for a global economy. They are old ideals and theories made in bygone days and times during events that no longer have significance. We need new theories and ideals built greater and stronger on the foundations of those that went before, but forged in the global events of today. These new ideals and theories need to be ones that the whole country can get behind. Ideals and theories the whole world embraces. Then and only then can we rid ourselves of the fear and forget the anger.

The Sum of All Events.

It has become evident that historical events and the current world environment have conspired to create the polarization and animosity plaguing our county. For if events foreshadow certain ends, then those actions that have gone before have certainly defined the challenges we now face.   The economic theory we as a country will embrace is at the core of our anger and fear. Why should it not be? As we handle our wallets, we take offense at others directing our discretions. Yet we are even further angered that those we encounter do not take the same prudence we engender in our financial transactions. Those that live within their means and pay cash for all products and services have no tolerance for those that rely on credit. But it is those that use credit that created the economic giant that is the United States. Without credit purchases we limit ourselves to the means at hand and in doing so limit our willingness to risk. It is this willingness to be greater than ourselves that drives the dreams of this country.

It is not without precedent that money should be at the core of this anger and fear. Indeed the very founding of our country was based on the monetary issue of "taxation without representation". As we have seen, even Thomas Jefferson created the Democratic-Republican Party to offset the fear created by Alexander Hamilton of an aristocracy being reborn and controlling the wealth.

It is equally noted that the Republican Party was created for the purpose of advancing Main Street issues that would allow freer exchange of goods and services and end the competition created by slavery. But these issues have been contested before. It is the global environment makes these issues so much greater an argument.

Our current arguments are based on parochial teachings and paradigms. We were a country in and of ourselves, in the beginning primarily agrarian. The majority of newly minted citizens did not venture far outside their local hamlet let alone work to sell product much beyond its confines. When industrialization did come to the United States it was to better the local economy. Ford did not make the motor car to be sold around the world. He made it to be sold here, in America to his fellow citizens. U. S. Steel created metal for our cars, our ships, and our skyscrapers. We were a domestic dynamo. This was the way of the majority of the world. As a result the economic theories, the way we were expected to make and spend our money, were developed using a single entity where all the elements were available for measure and manipulation. It was for theorists a mental laboratory separate from the contaminations of outside influences.

And these theories for the most part worked. But the theories were products of their times. Supply side economics is a product of the agrarian barter period. Does it have validity still? Yes, to a point. But it was never created with the understanding of the use of stock markets for private business financing, or money as a major form of transactions, or monetary policies in general. Additions, corrections, and alterations have been added to include these processes, but the basis of supply side economics has a foundation of over 180 years past. Keynesian economics is more inclusive of current economic models, but it too was conceived over 80 years ago. Think what has happened in the last 20 years with online stock trading worldwide at your home computer. Nowhere was this microeconomic event considered in the macroeconomic theoretical expression. Nor could it be. The idea was at the time inconceivable outside science fiction. (All hail Isaac Asimov.)

But these theories helped, directly or indirectly, make the United States as strong as it is. So competing political parties bought into them to differentiate themselves from each other and bolster their belief in how our moneys should be spent. To justify their positions on how much the government should regulate, or as many would say, interfere, in business transactions. The Democrats born to protect the "average man" against the dominance of an aristocracy, financial or otherwise, gravitated to an economic policy that would allow them influence in monetary affairs. The Republicans born of Main Street and business, gravitated to a economic theory that released them to do business as they may without any interference and lowest taxes.

Time and success, political, financial, and nationally, embedded each of these theories into the very souls of the political entities. Adherents, garnered in each paradigms periods of success and prosperity, became elders and remembered the great success that bore them to adopt that position. These elders created the rules commanding each political entity and worked, when out of public favor, to regain their fortunes and return the country and their party to the land of prosperity they perceived they had once lived. This learning and teaching created a calcified tribal mentality within each Party where winning to dominate became the primary goal.

But a strange thing happened on the way to the market. We as a country became the single greatest power in the world. We actually won all our immediate battles and vanquished all our foes. It was unexpected and unprecedented and placed us atop the leadership post. We had not prepared for this and faltered in our approach. The new responsibilities literally placed fear in the hearts of citizens and they sought more familiar ground. Thus TEA Parties came about and Dixiecrats reasserted themselves as more and more people sought to return to the isolation and introspective models that secured them before.

However, the world will not allow it. In the domestic attacks from foreign nationals to the dizzying attentions paid to our current economic condition by markets around the world we are in a new global economy and global leadership position. We fought for it. We won it and they are waiting for what we intend to do. In the absence of our leadership, they will seek to fill the void themselves. Forcing us to adapt to their methods and return to the third level obscurity our county enjoyed prior to the World Wars. We are a man on the mark. If we seek to build our country, secure our future, pass on our dreams, we cannot falter now. We must take the leadership role we won and use it to guide ourselves and the global economy.

We are not without the tools to lead. We did not win solely on military might. The U.S. economy is the biggest in the world by far. Let's get this clear to isolationists and hometown patriots. What happens in the United States affects the world, whether we like it or not. This is a world economy now and those that work on a balanced budget amendment, supply side economics, and even

Keynesian theory, all parochial self –centered ideology, are of small minds and limited vision when it comes to the duties and responsibilities of their position in the country and the world. Much more is required of them. We need to be the world leader we ascribe to be.

This importance in the world is what scares us, many of us anyhow. As much as we like to brag and point out our national superiority we have only been in this position for about 22 years. Just recently we have been able to declare with some assurance that the President of the United States is the "most powerful position in the world". While nationally popular, its side effect has been to elevate a position equal in the Constitution to Congress and the Supreme Court, to a public level never before seen. This position has always had the bully pulpit as its finest weapon. But the bully pulpit is now heard around the world. This newfound prominence makes this position a prize to be sought above all others for no other reason than a mark of personal success. Not to seek this position is virtually impossible for men and women of great egos and vanity.

If the position of President takes on new importance we must consider what global prominence has done to those of position inside political parties, the keepers of the paradigms. Many, if not all, Party Charters and bylaws have not been re-written for decades, maybe even centuries. These rules and regulations are the means by which elders hold onto their power and determine the success or even failure of those aspiring to political prominence. Global requirements at their most basic shake the foundations of the prescribed and embedded paradigms that were based on the single country ideal. Outright challenges to positions as well as the paradigms are taking place. Demands for new rules and directions are being made that more reflect current times. Yet, defenders of the faith are fighting back, trying to retain what they feel is essential, trying to retain what they know. Defending what brought the great success whose fruits we now enjoy.

In this group of defenders lie the first boomers and tweeners. They know how they won the cold war. They remember well how there dad's and brother's won the World War. They know how they built the economy to become the powerhouse it has become. This group advises against change. It demands we stay the course. Yet the second boomers, third boomers, and younger, see them as anachronistic. This second boomer group has only lived with our success, our position as a great power. They don't see the need to treat the world as "us" and "them". They prefer the term "we". Second boomers and the rest are not ignorant or naive. They have had their brothers and sisters die in wars and have seen the attack of the World Trade Centers. They are aware of the risks involved in trust. But they refuse to live in past glories, ideologies, and a world they didn't really know.

The second boomers, third boomers and others have lived with modern communication. When you have friends you speak with daily in countries as far away as Malaysia, India, and Egypt it is impossible to consider the whole country enemies. "Us" versus "them" doesn't work here. It is "we" versus "him" or "her". This generation sees the individuals involved in the great acts of destruction.   They know that one individual or a group of individuals do not speak for the citizens as a whole. The Arab spring is a reflection of this new group of individuals. Not satisfied with the dictator at the top they removed him. They didn't change their country, their beliefs or their way of life. They removed the one individual that was causing all the problems.

Second boomers, and those younger, are already building the new world in which they want to live. They know they will win this war of paradigms for one reason only. The first boomers and tweeners will eventually die off.   Impatient they add to the din of those wanting to change the paradigms and old political frameworks. In their view one of the drawbacks to recent medical successes is those that would have passed on in earlier generations are hanging around. So first boomers, and tweeners, are living longer, healthier, and refusing to leave the stage. But second boomers are confident in their eventual victory.   They just wish the older generation would take the retirement they so richly deserve and quit trying to relive the past.

But changing paradigms and generations have not in and of themselves married the basic differences between conservatives and liberals. We are not going hand and hand into the great flowery future full of unicorns and rainbows. (Not that I have anything against unicorns. Never met one. I was told they never existed. But a young lady of recent acquaintance insisted they did. Having no proof otherwise I defer judgment.) Conservatives and liberals regardless of changing paradigms have and will have foundational ideological differences. These fundamental differences add to the din and the rhetoric that are shaping the current vitriolic animosity. These will be part of the discussion, and the dominating ideology will be a part of any resolution. Gaining some understanding of these differences leads to an understanding of current anger and future arguments.

Currency is one of those foundational issues, at least as perceived by liberals. To conservatives, from a liberal point of view, currency is money. For many conservatives United States greenbacks are the preferable currency of choice. Yet to liberals there are many types of currency. Information, social status, political status, poverty, lack of poverty, all are currency. An exchange of needed information carries just as much risk, potential gain, and success as any monetary transaction. It is the difference between tangible and intangible. Liberals accept intangibles as currency. Conservative want a measurable element as a proof of currency. The importance of this disagreement is in the perception of what should and should not be funded in governmental programs.

Governments create and maintain parks and roadways. It is a function of their duties. However, in a conservative view, if public money, your taxes, is going to be spent to beautify a highway or build a park a measurable monetary benefit must accrue. The park, according to conservatives, must have a means to recoup some of the cost. Can the facility be rented? Are we able to hold sports events and generate some income? The idea of merely having a piece of ground that lies still for occasional use of its citizens is a waste of taxpayer's money and should not be accommodated. Yet, to a liberal, the currency in such a scenario is the peace of mind citizens attain not being crowded out by commercial interests. To liberals, governments can and are supposed to invest in programs that return little if any currency to city coffers. To many conservatives this is just a colossal waste of taxpayer's, in other word, their money.

Employee and business perceptions will always divide liberals and conservatives. Liberals see a business as a collection of people engaged in an ongoing activity. Conservatives see business as an entity in itself. This is a unique distinction engages the economic theory that each supports. If one looks at a company as an entity into itself, it maintains an inherent need to exist. It will operate and act in its own best interest. This is a basis of belief behind deregulation and the removal of government from economic intervention, which are precepts of supply side theory. The understanding here is that a company will not engage in activities which will harm or injure its customers, or the general public, because such harm is detrimental to the company and it will cease to exist. A sound theory for deregulation that was supported by none other than Alan Greenspan, the Federal Reserve Chairman under Presidents, Bush 1, Clinton and Bush 2.

But even Alan Greenspan admitted in October of 2008 that he was in error after the financial crisis in the derivatives market. In essence individuals within various companies placed pressure on other individuals in other companies to produce "paper" in order to increase short term profits, to the detriment of both companies. This pressure resulted in the collapse of the financial markets worldwide. Which is the point that liberals like to emphasize. Companies are not entities, they are groups of people and people are self serving. They will not work in the best interests of the company. They will work in their own best interests, even more so now that owners of companies are just collections of faceless and nameless investors.

There is little employee loyalty to companies anymore. The current large mega corporation has achieved the same perceived indistinctness previously reserved for government departments. A failed company is not news, it is a common occurrence. The only difference is the managers still seem to walk away with billions. Meanwhile the company reorganizes or gets bought for a largely discounted price and the same products are made with a new label. The only individuals getting injured in the process are the middle, lower level employees, and minor investors. If there is no possibility or perceived possibility of shared loss and risk, why would companies expect employees to invest in the best interests of the company over their own? Business is no longer perceived as in business to make things better for everyone or even the company. Business is apparently in business to make things better for the select upper management and large stockholders. In this sense, as business becomes a greater device for personalized needs and wants of a privileged few, business itself has a developed a greater self-interest.

The images of Enron employees forcing rolling blackouts over the west and southwest, taking savings from vulnerable individuals for their personal gain, will not be removed from public memory. The bilking of thousands of people in a $50 billion dollar ponzi scheme will not be forgotten. Enforcement of government oversights could have prevented these abuses, which is a hallmark of Keynesian economic theory. But most of all it highlights to many liberals that businesses are just a collection of individuals, they are not and do not act as an entity and should not be given the same considerations or rights.

Another foundational difference is the workers themselves. Born out of a need to understand economies and build on economic theory, the working man and their incentive to produce, work, and purchase goods was theorized. However, these theories were initially created over two hundred years ago. Yet their explanations generated or supported by works of such revered men as John Locke and Adam Smith continue to elicit devotion to the content. It is if no new, greater theories have ever been produced. It is believed that these seminal works are, once again, inscribed in the Book of Everlasting Truths.

But as most writings of historical content, the quotations and inspired thoughts are what most integrate into their knowledgebase. Few if any ever actually read the books and theories. Let's face it economics is not light reading and does take a modicum amount of understanding. Most of the population does not get past the checkout stand periodicals. Therefore, sayings such as "people are poor because they want to be poor" and "you can always find a job if you need one" are embedded into our modern business mythology and supported by evidence attributed to these theologians. Also embedded is an understanding that everyone is motivated by more income and that everyone works to achieve a greater success.

These mythologies in and of themselves would be a great disservice to a lot of people, but they also lead many conservatives to a general paradigm which blames the poor for their state. It creates characteristics that, if they exist, exist on such a minor scale, as to be insignificant to the whole. Thus no workable solutions can be created. As liberals would point out, work is not guaranteed even for those that want to work. This recent Great Recession would prove that out even if the last Great Depression didn't do so before. Liberals would also point out that individuals work for more than just monetary gain, success is not only measured by a greater position, more sales, or higher salary. More recent studies, much more recent theological studies, have proven this time and again. But the stereotype persists and the mythology endures.

But as liberals condemn conservatives for their stereotypes and mythologies the same condemnation should be leveled at liberals. All corporations, all multi-nationals are not distant giants concerned only for the welfare of a privileged few. Even if they do work for the welfare of the privileged few, this does not mean the privileged few are in and of themselves self centered and uncaring. These are the mythologies conceived and embedded by liberals. Liberals, including myself, have to remember and understand it is these same corporate giants we condemn that have made our country great and handed us the standard of living we have become accustomed. It is the small company that grew into the corporation that made us wealthy as a nation and individuals. It is the people that made the company, which made the corporation, which made the country.

This point goes to the issues that are creating the din. We have to look beyond the stereotypes and the mythologies that have been embedded in our paradigms. We have to engage in double loop learning within our own archetype and question, really question, those who would off handedly make a stereotypical comment as if it were fact. It is not enough to challenge those we are opposed, but the challenges must be made within. We automatically suspect our opponents. We would consider the comments of our friends.

We are finding this is happening more and more, particularly in the third boomer generation. Individuals are being held accountable, not whole organizations. Once again the evidence is in the Arab Spring, but also in the Exxon Gulf Oil Spill. The majority of the country did not blame the company as a whole. We demanded to know who in the company was responsible. When the president of the company was disrespectful we demanded his removal and it was done. While liberals are looking at a company as a collection of people, conservatives are looking at it as an entity with individuals with individual responsibilities.

These are small distinctions, but necessary in the development of global economics. We cannot hold a whole country responsible for the actions of a few. Nor can we hold a whole company irresponsible, when a few act irresponsibly. Yet, we are aware that embedded cultures, company as well as country, can make a whole entity act to the detriment of all. These entity's cultures must be changed and when they as a group act irresponsibly, held to account. But we know change begins with the individual. We are, more than ever, trying to hold individuals responsible for the mistakes as well as the successes. It is no longer acceptable to look at an entity, whether country or company, as responsible for all actions good or bad. This attitude is in opposition to tweeners and first boomers understanding of evil empires and whole countries as "the enemy". Their times were born of the U.S.S.R. and Vietnam. Third boomers experiences are Al Qaeda and domestic terrorists. To third boomers a well placed bullet is better than an atom bomb.

These foundational and fundamental differences, and others not mentioned here, between liberals and conservatives will remain. It is a never-ending argument that plays out in the theater of life daily. Who is successful at the time depends on the time and those people involved. The foundational differences are however mortar in the building of the new paradigms and must be considered as arguments arise so an understanding can be reached. Understanding will not in and of itself create a solution, but understanding may reduce the vitriol to a level that will allow discussions to compromise. This is the country we have, through our teachings, come to expect. One that strongly defends their positions yet expects compromise. We do not expect our country, or our representatives, to have polarizing intractable positions. We know that all the answers do not lie with one position or another. We seek the best of both.

I started this journey trying to find out why the rhetoric is so vile, why the anger is so loud. I observed that while we have always had political arguments, the polarization was greater than it had ever been. I, as a liberal, would love to blame the conservatives, but felt compelled to get some real answers not the convenient ones. What I found was a nation at battle, not just conservative against liberal, but a generational battle. Leaders to be are working to embed their beliefs and logic over those tried and true. However, the older generation is fighting back. And why shouldn't they.

The older generation became the final super power. The older generation guided this country to the largest economic power on earth. The older generation won so why shouldn't they expect their ideals to be written in the Book of Eternal Truths and followed faithfully by their progeny?   Besides, the war is not over. The final battle is not won, the clean up goes on. The older generation is not only out for self preservation, but to finally win the idealistic war, deal the death blow to their domestic opponents in a battle that has raged at least since the early sixties.   This is the country and a citizenry that never gives up. This trait is born into us. It is in our DNA. We will fight to the last man or woman to defend our freedom and our beliefs.

This old war shows in the old generation's choice of battles. Past issues such as welfare, abortion, gay rights, and civil rights keep rearing their ugly heads. Neither side is satisfied with the solution. Theirs was not a complete victory. They have measured their time and feel there is only a few minutes left on the clock to win the game. So gloves are off and a vicious final battle is at hand to declare their supremacy. Old dogma is reborn as if new. Tattered flags are waved and new recruits sought and placed into battle. But in their effort for final victory, they have failed to note that not everyone is cheering their side. The stands are emptying out as the younger crowd seeks a more relevant battle.

Rather than allow them to move on, this generation stands at the gates, rails against the desertion and tries to force the deserters back into their game. The irony is thick. It is the same generation that defined the "generation gap". This is the generation that pointed out how out of touch their father's and mother's generation was with theirs. Yet, here they are, years later, themselves demanding that their children fight their old battles with the same fervor that their parents demanded of them. Generational battles, ideological battles within generations, unfinished business and a dramatically new and changing world, it would be a surprise if the rhetoric and polarization didn't exist.

Why are we yelling and screaming? Why is the din so much louder than before? Because, we, as a country, are evolving. It is as dramatic as the industrial revolution a hundred years ago. Those that want to hold onto the past, the comfort of known success, are desperately fighting to retain their time, their place. The new comers, the ones coming up are excited and ready for the future. It is as terrifying and exciting time as it was when replacing the horse with the car.

The younger generation, liberal or conservative, knows oil is not the future and dependence on it risks their security. The younger generation, liberal or conservative, really doesn't care about your sexuality, just don't interfere with theirs. To the younger generation, liberal or conservative, color of skin is not a valid measure of a person's worth. The younger generation is proud their national boundaries, but know these boundaries are political, not hard lines drawn on a map. Their playground is the world. Through the Internet they can as easily have friends, do business, and speak with understanding in multiple languages. They communicate at the speed of light in social networks that the older generation has no understanding. The new generation coming knows it will need to be a leader in the world and the world demands it of them. The changes are already happening. Grinding resistance from generational fighting and new framework constructions are adding to the din.

So what do we expect? What is happening? This book was never intended as a "How To?" It was conceived as a why and what. No offers of solutions will be offered. But observations and suppositions are acceptable, (It is my book. I set the rules.). First and foremost, the world waits for no man. If the United States doesn't step up and fill the void as World Leader, someone else will. Nature abhors a vacuum, so if we want to have a say in what we won we best get moving.

Second, and most important, we are evolving into a global economy. Not just trade between countries or an exchange of services and parts between multi-national corporations, but a real global economy. Consider the United States as encompassing the whole world, (Got a few local rednecks to perk up their ears at that comment.). This is what we are speaking. As in the United States there are regions of manufacture, science, industry, medicine, raw materials, white majorities, white minorities, different levels of education and learning. We as a nation, when we developed our resources, developed these resources for the benefits each region provided. We made lumber from the forests of the Northwest because that was where lumber was. Gold was in California so we did our gold mining there. Oil in Texas, maple syrup in Maine we make and produce our products in the locations that they exist.

In the global economy we would do the same. Many worry about the loss of manufacturing. But why would we manufacture here in this geographic region when we could do it cheaper, better and close to needed resources in another geographic region? It has nothing to do with just cheap labor. It has everything to do with cost, quality and resources. The same as was required when we were an isolated country. Now we look at it through global vision.

The resources, availability of qualified labor, and cost of production favors other regions. Why would we as a country wish to compete at this disadvantage? We need to work from our strengths. Many would ask if this means the end of U.S. manufacturing. The answer would be no. But it will be different. The age of the Mega Corporation is ending. There will be large worldwide companies. They won't all cease to exist, (I'm so sure Wal-Mart was worried.).

However, it would seem there will be a return to mid-size and smaller companies. It is just too hard to be all things to all people. Large corporations are shedding distractions and concentrating on what they know. It is also easier to keep track of upper management and garner more company loyalty when the company leadership is no longer a nameless entity. You are also witnessing the advent of the one man, (or woman) international company. It is quite easy with the internet to buy, sell and transact all sorts of business internationally. Need 1000 flash drives to sell your latest software? Contact the manufacturer in Taiwan or China for a direct purchase.

Does this bode ill for the blue collar worker in the United States? Will manufacturing jobs pay substantially less? I really wish pundits would stop demeaning the blue collar worker of the United States. They are not as dumb and ignorant as stereotypes would have us believe. We have a well educated, highly skilled blue collar work force. Can they compete globally pay wise with menial line jobs? Well, no. But they don't have to. Smaller companies mean more reaction and rapid turnaround times. Smaller companies and the Internet mean more business worldwide. This means better educated and highly trained workers, U. S. workers are just the type of workers that these companies will need. The pay will reflect this need. We won't have the large mega workforce we have seen in the past in GM, Ford or Chrysler, but there will be a lot of smaller companies needing a lot of skilled workers.

The primary products the United States will produce will be the envy of the world if we take the lead we won. Information, research and finance will be our leading exports. With acknowledgments to Isaac Asimov, the country with the knowledge, knowhow, and money is the leader of any society regardless of their natural wealth. We have this in abundance. Our universities, schools and technical centers are unsurpassed. Our financial centers, even after the fall, are well equipped to handle international transactions. We are prepped. We are prepared. So how do we get there?

As I said, this is not a "How To" book. I do know that we have to get past the rhetoric that is dominating the political landscape right now. This rhetoric, whether admitted or not, is mostly created from fear, in my view fear of the unknown. We also have to get past the self centeredness surrounding the "boomer" generation. These people, including myself, have been so venerated over the term of their life many really think the sun rises and sets on them. It doesn't.   We have to know that our better days are ahead of us, not behind us. The 1950's were 60 years ago. The majority of us has no idea what you are talking about and feels any relevance to "better times" is in your mind.

We also have to quit bashing our public schools and start building them up again. Public schools and public school graduates created this great nation. Education and the knowledge it creates is the lifeblood of our next great evolution and economy. There has been nothing as responsive and forward looking as public education has been in the United States, for all its flaws. Nothing responds as quickly to new information, new teaching methods and current events as public education. It has to.   The public and the legislatures of the public demand it. For all their hype and privilege private education facilities seem mired in tradition and the past. They are slow to change and even slower to adopt new ideas. In actuality private education thrives on emphasizing tradition and stability. There is a place for private education, but it is not as the primary source of public education. Education, above all, for our future, has to have a responsiveness and relevance to the environment our children will live. Public education provides these requirements.

We have to understand that business has a place in our country and in our politics, but that business shouldn't run the country or its politics.   There is a fine line and more often than not, for the benefit of the individuals within the business, this line is crossed. Government, particularly this government, is created by the people, for the people. It was not created by business, for business, no matter what revisionist historians wish to impart. Thomas Jefferson formed the Democrat-Republican party to stand in the way of the reformation of an aristocracy he perceived was being created by Alexander Hamilton through the banking business. This battle to prevent the dominance of business by a Financial Aristocracy has been raging ever since. The balance is difficult, but should be measured on the side of the people if we are to keep our founding values.

These are exciting times. I know that the polarization, vitriol, and stubbornness are taking their toll on the national population. But this too will pass. I know it will because history says it will. I also know it will because the United States citizens will go to the polls and change the debate. There is little the people of the United States will not put up with, one of them is stagnation. Those perceived to be blocking progress will have to go. So go they will and progress will move anew. Our evolution as a nation is coming and like any new life it will come with a lot of kicking and screaming. It just can't be helped.

The evolution to a global economy and global paradigms will be difficult, but nothing worth having is easy. Ideology will want to lead the way. However, ideology is fine and ought to be a guiding principle, but a guide is all it should be. Pragmatism must preside when decisions are made. We cannot eat ideology. Ideology does not cover our heads or prepare our meals. Ideology used may even be flawed. After all man and women are flawed why would we expect ideology to be perfect?

The country will evolve. How it does so is up to us. We can stand in the way and rail against it, but at best it will only deviate the course it will not stop the progression. These are times that measure a country and its people. The faint of heart place their planes in the hangar and wait for the storm to pass. But like the ship in the harbor, that is not what planes are for. They are meant to fly. The bold among us will jump in the plane, outrun the storm and courageously go forward to conquer new worlds. These bold flyers know all too well that our country will never move forward if all we do is sit in the hangar and protect the past.

I have found that the rhetoric is different this time. It is louder and more forceful. It is not born solely out of the TEA Party movement, or resurgence of Dixiecrats, or an abundance of carpetbaggers taking advantage of ignorant souls to press their advantage. My belief, drawn through my research, is the rhetoric is based upon a fear of the future. A future this country, through its skill, resources, and success, created. We as a nation are moving inexorably to a global community and business framework. We are the remaining super power, and for now, the ability to be the global leader is up to us. We are decried by many to "preserve" our freedoms and return to the parochial environments we knew, to give up this opportunity and seek refuge within ourselves. But there are those among us that know to preserve your freedoms you have to earn your freedoms every day. Retreat to a safe terminal is only eventual surrender. If we wish to earn our freedoms for now and the future we do have to embrace the future we have created and take the leadership generations before us have won.

The rhetoric is loud and the anger real. We have to stop inhaling the fear, change the paradigms, and breathe calmly through the next evolution. How we do that? I do not propose. But maybe, just maybe understanding the problem, the history of the problem, and the reasons we arrived at this juncture might lead someone, in a better position than I, to a solution.

www.ingramcontent.com/pod-product-compliance
Lightning Source LLC
Chambersburg PA
CBHW030309290526
45785CB00001B/270